In Sight
of Sever

In Sight of Sever

Essays from Harvard

DAVID McCORD

In contrast with the general confusion,
a circle of old men and warriors sat in the
midst, smoking in profound indifference
and tranquillity.   *The Oregon Trail*

Harvard University Press

Cambridge, Massachusetts

1 9 6 3

For permission to include "The Termite," a quatrain by Ogden Nash,
I have to thank his publishers, Little, Brown & Co.; for the use of
"Going to Extremes," a quatrain by Richard Armour, I thank
McGraw-Hill Book Co., Inc.; and for the four lines from a poem by
John Hall Wheelock, I thank Charles Scribner's Sons.

Library of Congress Catalog Card Number 63–19143

Printed in the United States of America

To My Classmates of Harvard College 1921

The past, as one winnows it, is spare and tidy. Pleasant images flit through the mind: E. K. Rand, beloved toast-master-general — *Gratulor quod eum, quem necesse erat diligere.* . . . Or Al Smith, one scalding Commencement day, cigar in his mouth, sweat on the brow, a pen in his hand, autographing the starched flare cuffs of the waitresses at the dignitaries' tent while Ambassadors Sir Ronald Lindsay and Paul Claudel watched with undisguised astonishment. Or Copey, seated on the steps of Hollis of a mild June evening, the stain of misery on his face as a student asks him if he doesn't consider Donald Ogden Stewart — whose writing the Sage admired and had often read aloud — a greater man than Dickens. Or Professor Julian Coolidge, first Master of Lowell House, breezing into Billings & Stover on a winter evening in a red-lined opera cape and saying in all honesty to a strange young alumnus who had greeted him by name: "How did you know who I am?"

CONTENTS

CONTENTS

Luminary

Ancillary

Monetary

Preface

THE writing in this book covers the span of about forty years — roughly 1923–1963. Like a numbered house, each item bears the visible date of first publication; but this date does not necessarily imply the date of composition. All but a few of the pieces are directly concerned with Harvard; and one of these exceptions (*An Acre for Education*) concerns Radcliffe College, which, as almost any Harvard critic will gladly tell you, amounts to the same thing, or more so. Certain essays were written in time of depression (my own or my country's) and several in time of war. The editorial on the great Democrat was composed by a Republican who feels uninclined to alter even a word of the text after nineteen years.

Mr. Churchill's remarks of 1943 (he was not yet Sir Winston when he made them) are not included here, though it is difficult for me to separate the man from his words. I have, however, preserved a long footnote which attempts to resolve the many variants in the printed versions of the text. The *Harvard Alumni Bulletin* of 18 September 1943 gave the speaker's words precisely as he spoke them. Few Harvard events have equalled Sir Winston's appearance in Sanders Theater and in the Yard. It will be a dark day when we lose sight of what he said to us.

Notes on the Harvard Tercentenary (1936) was commissioned by James Bryant Conant, then President of Harvard, and sponsored by the officers of the Harvard Alumni Association, the Associated Harvard Clubs, and the Harvard Fund Council. It was written between Thanksgiving and mid-December, and published by the University as a keepsake, with appropriate photographs. I am glad now to recapture it; but in the course of reviewing it, I have followed my publisher's suggestion of shortening the principal addresses as well as the long prayer. I cannot return it to print, however, without acknowledging my debt to the late Jerome D. Greene '96, LL.D. '37, friend of so many Harvard men, and the true genius of that now famous celebration.

In preparing *Notes on the Charity of Edward Hopkins: 1657–1957*, my private delight was the exquisite nonsense provided by no fewer than twenty-seven changes in the Charity's name, twenty-one of them authorized since 1743. *I beg the reader: see pages 122–124.*

An Acre for Education was written in 1938 at the request of the Trustees of Radcliffe College, and I now thank President Emerita Ada Louise Comstock (Mrs. Wallace Notestein) for gracious tutelage in that (to me) rewarding enterprise. The two revisions of *An Acre* (1954 and 1958) owe much to the help and kindness of another Radcliffe friend, Dean Mildred P. Sherman, who died in 1961. Finally, I would thank President Mary I. Bunting of Radcliffe for permitting me to reprint *An Acre* and for making possible a brief postscript covering the years 1958–1962. Robert T. Gabriel, Director of The Radcliffe Fund, gave generous assistance with figures; and Mrs. Edwin C. Lord, Director of the News Office, made the factual usable and the user sympathetic. To keep it all in balance, I have tried to point up the earlier part of the story, as one would an old brick wall.

It was Ralph Lowell '12 who suggested a brief study of the Lowell Fund; the Harvard Club of Boston which asked for some verses in honor of President A. Whitney Griswold of Yale; the Harvard Fund Council which encouraged my experiment with such as "The Alewives Are Running"; the American Alumni Council that first listened (in Hanover, New Hampshire) to "The Language of Request"; and the AAC's incomparable director, the late Ernest T. Stewart, a graduate of Princeton, who generously put together and issued (1961) with the help of *Time-Life* Educational Department a little collection of my Harvard Fund pieces under the above title. In shallow water it was always my friend Robert H. Haynes, Harvard's librarian-pilot, who took over.

PREFACE

For permission to include other essays in this book, I have to thank two editors of the *Harvard Alumni Bulletin*: William Bentinck-Smith '37, and his successor Norman A. Hall '22, and the *Bulletin* president, Walter D. Edmonds '26; the *Harvard Graduates' Magazine* (now extinct); *Editorial Projects for Education* which in 1962 commissioned "Alembic in Limbo"; Edward A. Weeks '22, editor of *The Atlantic*; and Walter M. Whitehill '26, editor of publications of the Colonial Society of Massachusetts. And I am not forgetting three older friends and employers, now dead, who gave a young writer latitude and encouragement: H. T. Parker '90, drama and music critic of the *Boston Evening Transcript*; John D. Merrill '89, A.M. Hon. '34, editor of the *Harvard Alumni Bulletin*; Joseph R. Hamlen '04, A.M. Hon. '33, first chairman of the Harvard Fund Council and for twenty-five years the *Bulletin's* president.

But my greatest debt is one unpaid: to Marion L. Anderson, for 31 years until her death in 1957, devoted Executive Assistant of the Harvard Fund Council. It was she who typed and proofread the majority of these contributions, beginning in 1926; it was she who often relieved me of other work so that I might write them. I am grateful in the same spirit to Mrs. Sylvia L. Reynolds, Mrs. Eva Avadanian, and Mrs. Dennis Rawlins for assistance in preparing the book manuscript; and to my learned classmate, James N. White, for helping with the proof. Lastly, my special thanks to the Harvard University Press for careful readings of the tentative text; for insight as much as editorial advice on what to cut, reject, or alter. I suppose (and suppose the Press supposes) that this is first of all a Harvard book. But I also think (and think the Press thinks) the scattered clauses here and there may interest others concerned with certain aspects and problems of education and with colleges and universities wherever.

Wadsworth House   D. T. W. McC.
14 April 1963

Solitary

The true Harvard is the invisible Harvard in the souls of her more truth-seeking and independent and often very solitary sons. . . . The university most worthy of rational admiration is that one in which your lonely thinker can feel himself least lonely, most positively furthered, and most richly fed.

William James

What makes a college good, in short, is its magic power, perennially renewed, to widen experience, and in so doing to work those transformations, even exaltations, in young minds and hearts, indeed in all of us, drawing us into fuller and deeper life and engendering in us processes of learning which, when sustained, enable us later in less favorable circumstances still to care when the bloom of fresh excitement shall have passed.

Nathan M. Pusey

Copey at Walpole

ONE of the privileges to which the students and friends of Charles Townsend Copeland attach an increasing importance is that of visiting him in the vacation months. But the greatest privilege of all was to visit him at Walpole, above the Connecticut river, where he used to retire in modest aestivation during all the 18 years from 1916 to 1934. I suppose that any New England town he might have selected for the purpose would have seemed to his summer callers more honorable in houses and hidden under a loftier growth of elms because he happened to be living in it. But even without him, there was something in the structure of Walpole which proclaimed it at once the likely habitation of a person of note. You felt that if any one spent a night at its green New Hampshire heart, which was really very old, or walked a few hours in the green New Hampshire streets, he would certainly find out his name.

Copey went to Walpole for the first time on a sudden impulse which I suspect he had thought out with ceremonial care. Copley Amory, Jr., a pupil out of the class of Harvard 1912, had recommended it as an ideal village in which to recuperate from teaching in the Harvard Summer School. Mr. Amory came from there and spoke with authority, and Copey was always quick to tell you of his gratitude for the advice. He went directly to the Inn, and although his friends, the Amorys, of whom he saw much, invited him to stay at their house, it is characteristic of the Boylston professor of rhetoric and oratory that he remained where he was.

It seems to me now that Copey belongs much more to the Wal-

3

pole Inn than Dr. Johnson ever did to the Mitre or the rarer Ben to the Mermaid Tavern. After that first qualitative passage in which he met the incomparable J. F. Wilson, the proprietor, who henceforth registered each guest with a more distinguished one in mind, it was as natural to look for Copey at the Inn as to climb those stairs of the more immortal Hollis. It rapidly became his second home. The Inn, like all genuine New England, made no pretense at being different from any other. In fact it was not. It was simple, regular, homely, adjacent to the village green, and, what was more important in this particular association, diametrically handy to the only barber shop in town. Its one physical distinction, perhaps, was the generous number and quality of its public rooms. If I speak of it thus in the past tense, it is only because Copey spends his summers now in Cambridge and Mr. Wilson, great innkeeper and great gentleman, is no longer behind the front cross-corner desk. The Inn and the town are otherwise much as they were.[1]

But yet not quite. They have both lost, at least temporarily, the subject which made them our unique objective. In the hot summer months it was cheerful to us all to feel that Copey had escaped from Cambridge and was up there somewhere in New Hampshire, perhaps as hot — for Walpole is insulated from the wind and river by its trees — but in country air, with freedom to walk and read, command and retire, and the magic of a journey involved when any of us were invited to come for a little visit. He liked to exercise a kind of remote control, and an invitation had the undertone of army service orders. "The Bishop was here looking for me several days before I came. He is now in the offing and so are several other people including the charming Mrs. X and . . . When are you coming?" Not, my dear friend, half soon enough.

My first sight of Walpole (in 1926) is confused with my first sight of Vermont and the upper Connecticut valley. The view of these from the Keene-to-Walpole road, though not remarkable as

---

[1] The town exists; the Inn no longer does.

samples of either, will rouse a normal stranger to suitable comment. I was surprised when Copey said it was "good enough"; but I did not realize then that any country to him was always measured on the St. Croix scale. Did I not notice that down east there was a *strangeness* mixed with beauty? But Walpole seemed more than good enough to me, and when I had driven past white fronts and colonial dignity, and felt the shade of ancient, mighty trees, and turned the corner beyond the stores and postoffice to the Inn itself, there he was sitting on the veranda: the small, familiar figure, alert and upright, looking abnormally respectable and of the city, and harmlessly approximate to the only tennis court in sight.

Of the number of times thereafter that I arrived in the same way, it was always with the same feeling of veneration at the first sight of the sleepy town, and a little nervous over the first stop before the Inn inanimate, lest I disturb its gracious withdrawal from a world I sadly appeared to represent. Inside the door I can still remember standing speechless and inappropriate. I doubt if Copey was aware of that. He always welcomed his visitor in a strong voice, taking personal care to see that someone carried bag and coat to a pre-arranged corner room. He would then look at you with that remarkable fixity, and offer certain admonishing remarks about the hour of breakfast and the likelihood of his breakfasting alone. I find in some notes which I kept of such a visit on 30 September 1931 that I was thereupon led into the dining room and shown the drawing room through tightly locked glass doors: "Like Moses," he said, "being shown the Promised Land but not allowed to enter."

Mr. Copeland himself lived in elegant seclusion behind the dangerous door of a large second-floor room in the very center of the Inn. It was always full of trunks and books, but very neat with the faint and reminiscent glamour of Hollis.[2] The light came in

---

[2] Glamour self-conscious with a "u". It was at Walpole in 1932 that the *Boston Evening Transcript* telephoned me for a front-page story on Professor Copeland who was soon to move forever from 15 Hollis to Number 5 Garden Street in Cambridge. I sat up half the night putting words together, and the next afternoon I dispatched

through windows, front and rear; and "a great jut of room" out back toward the Green, as he used to explain it, gave the appearance of two rooms made into one. But his visitors never had more than a glimpse of all this; and the talk and business of the social day was carried on below stairs, out in Walpole fields, and under Walpole sky. At such times he seemed more than ever the indefatigable walker. He once told me in valetudinarian voice that he was good for only a turn just out of the town. But in city clothes and with bowler hat carefully under his arm (as though he had just crossed into Brattle Street) he walked me two or three miles across the country with the steadiness of a mountaineer bred to leather. It was on that occasion that we paused for a minute somewhere above the town to peer into a little brook that trickled down between some boulders much too big. We looked at it in silence, and my thoughts ran to the possibility of fish.

"There are no trout in it," I said.

"There's music in it," said Copey.

On other occasions we drove out of Walpole; once, I remember, to Cornish and St. Gaudens', looking toward Ascutney; once to the less known Grafton in Vermont, and once to Keene, where we ordered from the massive four-chutney bill-of-fare of the now departed Cheshire House. But the drives were never quite so good as the walks, and it was even better when we simply sat and talked. His gift of graphic phrase and apposite quotation ascended with the barometer. It was at Walpole on sunny days and firefly evenings that I heard a good many things I shan't forget in this life. Trying to recall something, he told me, his mother used to say: "Wait till I sink the bucket" . . . I found him reading Strachey's *Portraits in Miniature,* and he spoke of Gibbon's influence as apparent in "the cool cucumber innuendo" . . . My notes bear fragments of

them over the private wire in Freyburg, Maine, where astronomers and reporters tensely awaited a total eclipse of the sun. But not so dark a one for me, I remember thinking, as the total eclipse of Hollis.

such observation. Now and then, as elsewhere, his talk returned to Calais and St. Croix. "An island," he explained, "has enough romance of its own." I do not know why I told him that Mayor Quinn of Cambridge was dead. "Eddie," he recollected, who had appointed him to serve on a committee to determine whether the Longfellow bust in the Hall of Fame should be a replica of the bust in the Abbey or a new one. "Eddie! I once shook his great fist and I thought that man could never die" . . . And at meals — particularly at lunch — there were gathered in front of him strange, fearful dishes, pots, and casseroles far off the charted menu: "David, you'll forgive my Persian apparatus."

Most of his visitors (I one of them) regret that they did not hear him read in Walpole. That is, read in public. He fell to doing this each year in churches, halls, even ex-cathedrally at Keene, and all for the benefit of the local library; so that Walpole has today a large capital sum known as the Copeland Library Fund, the income of which is used for the annual purchase of books. But perhaps it was well to have missed the public side. I only regret missing the audience. It was a private Copeland that we sought; the reexamination of an influence beyond the circle of book and classroom. Sought as ever — as he well knows — for his visitors never stop visiting. But no longer in the golden age of Walpole, and that to the sorrow of many.

1936

And Gladly Taught

IT is curious that none of the excellent editorial birthday tributes to Bliss Perry on 25 November made use of his brother Carroll's unforgettable phrase describing their father as "a professor of life." For surely the man who made us see beyond Emerson was also a professor of life; and what his generations of students carried away from the classroom reached beyond books to the men behind the books, and beyond the teacher's words to the man who was the teacher. One of the reasons why Professor Perry's autobiography, *And Gladly Teach*, attained the rank of a best-seller was because of the humanity that is in it, and because it is a man and not a pedagogue who is talking. Phrases from that talk stir in the memory still: "The words of a poem are stepping-stones across a brook. If you linger on one of them too long, you will get your feet wet." Or that quoted observation of a friend at the moment when B.P. had made up his mind to leave Williams for Princeton: . . . "She thought it good for the human plant to be repotted from time to time."

The human plant was to be repotted twice thereafter — first in the editor's sanctum of the *Atlantic*, and last at Harvard. Eighty years is a long span; and we are grateful that thirty-four of them are ours. If there be Scholars who, in an equal stretch, have known more of books than Bliss, there are surely few — if any — who have known so much of the relation of books to life. Tall men of his breed were never common in the classroom. The more lamentable that they are growing less common in our colleges and universities today; and more lamentable still, we need them now as never before.

8

AND GLADLY TAUGHT

Bliss Perry is eighty. A paragraph of his own from his own best book will certify the right to *emeritus*.

There is always a magic about one's summer home, yet it cannot quite be the old magic of arriving at night at the 'Bend' after a two-days' railroad journey from Princeton, and driving in a mountain wagon up the three-mile hill through the [Vermont] woods, while the sleepy children try to count the fireflies or listen to the whippoorwills; nor is it the magic of wet-fly fishing along the then solitary Lamoille with friends like "Jack" Hibben and Chester Loomis the painter. But the lake and the mountains and the sunsets are unchanged, and if the links are too crowded for comfort on August afternoons, I can sit under the pine trees which I planted thirty years ago and read a book, with half an eye open for the humming-birds hovering around the last tall blue spikes of delphinium.

1940

A Complete Man

WHEN the news of the death of Thomas W. Lamont reached London, John Masefield, the Poet Laureate, wrote a letter to the London *Times* in which he said among other things that "No American of the last half century has shown more fully the wonderful power America has of making a complete man." Of the many tributes paid to the memory of Mr. Lamont, each of them in various ways said or suggested something approximate to what his poet friend set down so simply as the essence of the truth. How complete a man was Mr. Lamont would be clear to a person who never heard of him, if that person happened to read his will. Written into it were the wisdom, vision, understanding, and appreciation that only spiritual greatness and humility can supply.

Mr. Lamont was a product of the best that is America. He made his own way in life from the beginning, and he grew into greatness as naturally as a boy grows into manhood. As the New York *Times* said in its editorial: His "driving force was an unremitting search for the good, the full and the gracious life. It was a search that was to carry him to all corners of the world, into innumerable activities, national, civic and private, having nothing to do with finance, and to account for the vast number and the imaginative character of his public benefactions."

His school and college never had an alumnus quite his equal. He was a member and president of the board of trustees of Phillips Exeter Academy for the long span of years when Lewis Perry was principal and Exeter was emerging as a national institution. To the Academy he gave from the heart as well as out of his wealth. "I have often said," wrote Mr. Lamont in one of the unforgettable pages of *My Boyhood in a Parsonage*, "that if it had been permitted me to attend only Exeter or Harvard, I should have chosen Exeter every time. And that is said in no derogation of college, which so broadened my outlook, gave me such an unconscious training in tolerance, such an introduction to life, to letters, and to loyal friendship." The tribute in the *Exonian* — which we suspect was written by Lewis Perry himself — vividly summarized the affectionate relationship between the man and his school: "To us at Exeter he was a generous older brother — simple, wise, devoted, solicitous, watchful [surely Dr. Perry's word!], dependable, with a smiling, genuine gratitude for the little things we could do for him, completely forgetting the great things he was doing for us."

But it would be difficult for anyone to draw a distinction between his loyalties. As a graduate [1] of Harvard, which honored him with an LL.D. in 1931, he honored her all his active life. He served two terms as an Overseer, was a member of the original Harvard Fund Council, President of the Harvard Alumni Association, the Associated Harvard Clubs, and the Harvard Club of New York; and his countless tangible gifts to the University exceed those of any other alumnus.

Harvard will remember him as a wise and friendly counsellor as well as a great benefactor. She too came to look upon him as an older brother, and in her he had abounding faith. His modesty was such that only those of the inner circle likely ever knew the full range of his interests in education. If his only outward monument were the Lamont Library for undergraduates,[2] it would be sufficient for the perpetual renewal of his ideals as future generations come to benefit from the ingenious service which that library will provide. But his monuments are many, and they need no plaque.

[1] Class of 1892, Harvard College.
[2] See "Beyond the Dewey Decimals."

IN SIGHT OF SEVER

In the days of a world dichotomy it is good to realize that a democracy such as ours can produce a man equally at home in international affairs and on the kinetic frontier of his own country. It gives new luster to an old truth: that there is nothing in the human scale of much value except character. Now and then we lose sight of that fact until we see it suddenly in the round. In last week's *Saturday Review of Literature* — which owes its birthright to Mr. Lamont — Henry Seidel Canby's editorial suggested that the banker might easily have made his name in letters had he elected to follow his first bent first. Thus is the man of character always respected in every province that he touches. Thomas W. Lamont also left a name in the humanities, and Harvard is proud to add it to the company of her elect.

1948

Mr. Lowell

LOOKING backward from the world's chaos, we see clearly that Mr. Lowell was a man born into his time.[1] An aristocrat, he had vision, and the strength to realize his vision. He was in no way "suckled in a creed outworn." He was happy. His life fitted into each day as the hand fits into the glove. Indeed, the intimations of that vigorous mind — even to the end amid loneliness and deafness — exhibited surprising ability to adjust to the new symbolic prescriptions of quantity and speed. His athletic body, to which Bliss Perry so wisely alludes, never ceased to suggest that the Scythesman himself was a handicap starter in the long race.

He inherited much, but he gave away even more. He chose to be rich by making his wants few, as Emerson said of Thoreau. His approach to everything was direct; and his decisions were unconditional. If he believed in a man — Professor Chafee of the Law School, for example — he would back him to the limit. He could, on occasion, be brusque almost to the point of rudeness, but he could also be generous to the point of anonymity. We may not know for a long time the full extent of his benefactions to the University to which he dedicated his life. It began perhaps with the rumored gift of the New Lecture Hall [2] in 1902, but the ending will never be reasonably defined. From the modified Elective System which he engineered, to the Society of Fellows which he founded, his influence on scholarship was enormous, though it was not until the mid-point of his career that Harvard undergraduate honors and

[1] A. Lawrence Lowell, 1856–1943, A.B. 1877, was the twenty-second President of Harvard University, 1909–1933.
[2] Renamed Lowell Hall in 1959.

13

social respectability were remarried after a long period of divorce.

The classics he stoutly defended; mathematics (in which he had taken highest honors) he recommended for discipline; the science of government he understood intuitively. He did not care much for art and less for music, yet he vaunted the new Glee Club under Dr. Davison. It is probably true that he nurtured the humanities primarily because the physical and biological sciences appeared increasingly able to fend for themselves. But it is wrong to think that he lacked an interest in science. An extreme sympathy toward men like the late Professor Lawrence J. Henderson, a biochemist; devoted service to the Medical School and various museums; his aid in the vast expansion of Harvard's many laboratories are an intimate part of Mr. Lowell's "sole and self-commanded works." He had his own way of making fun of the Ph.D., but character and ability were the twin criteria by which he chose the new men for his powerful Faculty. Most important of all, he fought consistently and openly for academic freedom.

There was no occasion, public or private, which he did not, merely by his presence, appear to dominate . . . Few will forget the marvelous simplicity in his reading of the Scriptures. When he spoke among others after dinner, shaking his distinguished head vertically to emphasize a point, his were the first words one carried away. . . And of all the quoted speeches in *Notes on the Harvard Tercentenary* no paragraph can match (I think) the rhythm and the richness of Mr. Lowell's opening in his charge to the alumni.

1943

A Poet in Science

Man appears as only an infinitesimal fragment of a stupendous whole, governed by precise, mathematical laws. With this realization, we feel intuitively that we as human beings are subject also to deep-lying spiritual laws according to which we must live or else finally perish; for this, it was written, "To fear the Lord is the beginning of wisdom." The second lesson is that of the unutterable power of the symbolic word which expresses some final truth, as suggested in our text (John 1.1–5) of this morning. The mathematical or logical proof of such a truth induces a kind of intellectual conversion which may be as essential as spiritual conversion.

Mathematics and Religion: A College Chapel Talk, 1943, by George D. Birkhoff.

Mathematics and poetry are not synonymous in the sense that the man on the street is apt to confuse them in his mind. Mr. Citizen expresses gratitude if he can add, subtract, and multiply correctly — give or take a few digits — and he probably reads little of Wordsworth or Wilbur and even less of the less intelligible moderns. For him there is no connection between the two: one process is mysterious and alien; the other, mystical and difficult. But in the range and realm of pure creation, mathematics not only is poetry, but poetry of celestial order. Few will understand this but the creative mathematicians. The poets can sense it, especially those gifted in the baffling search for form. The men of mathematics themselves make no boast of kinship, yet only they can touch that Newtonian

index of a mind forever
Voyaging through strange seas of thought, alone.

15

IN SIGHT OF SEVER

George David Birkhoff, Perkins Professor of Mathematics, whose sudden death a fortnight ago shocked the community and the scientific world at large, was such a poet. Just to look at him, one knew that he had genius. His mind and vision, like the keenness of his eye, focused on things beyond our ken. Yet he was also the true humanitarian, and students and colleagues welcomed every chance to talk or meet with him. His life-long contributions to the profession were original and disturbing; his equal gift in friendship lighted many candles for many people. He bore his international honors modestly, but proudly in the name of mathematics. He was indeed a creator, he was original; and he was simple and good. He was all that our great universities stand for; and his life was the old, unchallenged reason why they shall endure.

1944

Mr. Standfast

MANY will remember the alumni exercises in the afternoon of Commencement, 1938, when a markedly small, rather frail-looking man dressed in unAmerican morning clothes of astonishing covert-cloth grey, arose and stood like a soldier to deliver a response at once notable for profound dignity, sincerity, intelligence, and Scottish wit. A response so brief as to be worthy for that rare virtue alone, it was in addition so much the utterance of an educated and thoughtful man that it deserves reprinting that other men's memories may retain it. The words, incidentally, were spoken and not read.

But it was not merely John Buchan, LL.D. '38, who spoke them — who sat on the platform that warm afternoon with a world-figure in the Hollywood person of Walt Disney, as he had sat with him under similar circumstances the day before at Yale. It was equally Baron Tweedsmuir, late Governor-General of Canada. "A typical Scot of the Border breed," as he once explained himself to a newspaper man, he had alluded in his Yale address to this typical border raid on what turned out to be *two* American universities. Few men have ever crossed from one trusted country to another with such astonishing credentials of honor and respect.

"A British man of letters, eminent in three careers; novelist, biographer, and public servant, thrice welcome in this College," said President Conant, bestowing the degree. Soldier, lawyer, publisher, poet, historian, churchman, University chancellor, Member of Parliament — the list might justly have continued. But to us, at least on his part, he came as "the representative of the British

17

Sovereign in the great and friendly country which lies between you and the North Pole."

It was not the first address of importance which Lord Tweedsmuir of Elsfield had delivered in the United States. Some astute and gallant gentleman (unfortunately not a Harvard man) reminded the New York *Herald Tribune* on February 13 that in 1924 John Buchan had given the War memorial address at Milton Academy. In the course of it, the future Governor-General paid tribute to Abraham Lincoln — "To me Lincoln seems one of the two or three greatest men ever born of our [common] blood." It is no lip service to history to quote the final paragraph, for it deserves to run through the linotypes of the nation:

> There is no such bond between peoples as that each should enter into the sacred places of the other; and, in the noble merchantry of civilization, let us remember that, if we of England have given Shakespeare to America, you have paid us back with Lincoln.

And it is a curious fact, as the *Tribune's* correspondent suggests, that Lord Tweedsmuir's death "lacked not a very few hours of coinciding with Lincoln's birthday."

In the noble merchantry of civilization it is well to remember that John Buchan was first of all an illustrious example of the man of letters in the service of his country. Other men have been the same, as Woodrow Wilson in the United States. But with the author of *The Thirty-Nine Steps*, writing claimed a major interest in his life to the absolute end, for only recently he delivered into his American publisher's hands the manuscript of his autobiography. "I regard business as my profession, writing as my amusement, and it looks as if some kind of politics was going to be my duty," he said long before his ennoblement. But writing was obviously more to him than amusement. As an undergraduate at Oxford he won literary prizes, and was published. In his life he wrote more than fifty books in fewer years, and became perhaps the most popular romantic novelist in Britain since Stevenson. On the other hand, his

Montrose, Cromwell, and Scott, informed with scholarship and creative thinking, stand him even higher in biography. Thus he served letters, and letters served him. And it was the revanche of letters, surely, that carried him to positions of solemn trust and great importance, the last of which drew him happily within the Harvard circle. Where in his shadow do some of us range who say we have no time to write?

1940

Master and Scholar

PRESIDENT Lowell's Baccalaureate Sermon to the Class of 1918 was notable even in the field in which his thought and writing were particularly distinguished. A quotation from that Sermon is appropriate here. "Many men never see how much they have really achieved . . . although they have done much and brought the end nearer for others to attain." One may doubt if David Mason Little [1] saw but a fraction of how much he had achieved before he died. In one of his own Class Reports he quoted something from George Herbert Palmer which he might equally have said for and of himself: "Why should Harvard University pay me for doing what I would gladly pay to be allowed to do?"

That was in daily evidence his living philosophy. Few men have ever made and held so many friends for this University — a University which these very friends did not always clearly understand. He made and held such friendships through a long period of peace and war. He patrolled a good part of the world without leaving Cambridge; and his address was usually that of one or more of three college buildings which antidate the American Revolution.

He served Harvard under two Presidents, and had begun to extend that service under a third. He was a diplomat, endowed with certain qualities of tolerance, kindness, and consideration denied to others. As Secretary for the University, he made the distinguished visitor and the casual transient equally aware of the genius of the place — which was Saintsbury's word for Oxford; but he also, quite simply, made them feel at home. He sent hundreds of Faculty

---

[1] Class of 1918, Harvard College.

20

members to hundreds of Harvard meetings across the continent; and to hundreds of other meetings he went himself. In a curious and private way he alone was able to take the Yard along with him. As Master of Adams House, he continued to develop a spirit and loyalty as congruous as the incongruity of its Colonial-Byzantine interior. His popularity with the generations of undergraduates who lived in that House was deservedly great, and will just as deservedly become a legend.

A teacher and scholar apprenticed under Copeland, Greenough, and Lowes, his early Curatorship of the Theater Collection (then in Widener) was quietly extended to the endless and difficult task of collecting and editing the letters of David Garrick — whose dramatic versatility he instinctively understood; a three-volume project soon to be published.[2] But David Little's "long and highly congenial affiliation with Harvard and Cantabrigia" — unlike the Garrick — will never be set in type. Nor his honest laughter, his blazing sense of the ridiculous, his courage in adversity. Nor his cheerful deference as in the stimulating days of the great Celebration in 1936 which he helped to manage; nor his presence at Commencement or as the graduate presiding at the 50th anniversary of the founding of Middlesex School, or in the countless unexpected places where he was — or seemed to be — so all at once.

1954

[2] Harvard University Press: autumn 1963.

Of Memory and Hope

THIS issue,[1] which we dedicate simply and with utter respect to the memory of a Harvard man who became the premier citizen of our time, is published as the first half of the battle in which he truly gave his life nears a victorious end. It is one of the fairest measures of the essential greatness of the late President that those who would do and have done him honor in two hemispheres include equally his idolaters, admirers, dissenters, critics, and opponents. Perhaps nowhere more than within the Harvard family itself has death brought together a company of men long so divergent in opinion as to his politics, policies, and leadership. For them, as for all segments and levels and societies of a peace-haunted world, the press of that world has been unitedly articulate in an hour of grief. "Because this war [said the New York *Times*] is a greater war than any war that has ever gone before it, because the central issue of this war has been the very life or death of the civilization we have built, Franklin D. Roosevelt will take the honored role in history that belongs to the chief author of the democratic coalition. Certainly in the eyes of the people of the free world beyond our shores no more towering figure has come upon the American scene in the times of men now living."

All word of him today is praise, and every thought of him is first and last for a courageous leader cruelly fallen in the ranks of a liberal and liberating people. We who are older and have seen two wars, as Dean Buck was humbly explaining to his saddened history class a few hours after the news came, feel in all poignancy a stunning sense of loss. And yet in some ways the longer view and prag-

[1] *Harvard Alumni Bulletin*: 28 April 1945.

matic consideration, which are possible to men and women who have stayed at home, can lessen the shock for them as nothing can lessen it for the generation directly behind the guns. Mr. Roosevelt, as he grew older, grew into younger hearts. He was a symbol, a cause, a reason, and an anvil of strength to youth. He was the only President this fighting generation had ever consciously known. It knew him well. He foresaw; and acted as none but the prescient can act. That is something which youth is supremely fitted to understand. "He belonged to this day," as Dr. Sperry [2] so wisely said. "He spoke the language of the hour and needed no interpreter."

When Hitler's true design was fast becoming apparent to the European nations, if not to us, Mr. H. M. Tomlinson found the equation for it while walking along the south channel coast of England and searching with his eyes the deceptive sparkle of the empty sea. "Out of the viewless comes a corruption of the instinctive loyalties of men." Looking back now, many of us would like to have said that. Mr. Roosevelt was capable of saying it. What matters is that he thought it and understood what it meant to the western world and to the world at large. He acted when few of us wanted to act. A master of timing — another attribute of youth — he took the steps just ahead of us, and on the schedule of divine chance. He hated war, as the generation which is fighting hates it. And he loved and respected that generation which has made and is making the history historians now can never figure without his name. Of his going, some of the circumstances have been likened to those surrounding the death of Lincoln. It is Lincoln's poet, for example, who has been quoted across the land — and not for one poem but for several. Walt would have liked that, for he wrote for the young and the active. Perhaps one measure of a poet is how he comes — or fails to come — to life in a time of crisis. But in a sense Mr. Roosevelt wrote his own poetry. It is written in names: Casablanca, Cairo, Teheran, Quebec, Yalta, San Francisco.

[2] The memorial service at Harvard was conducted by Dean Willard L. Sperry.

Of Mr. Roosevelt's relation to Harvard, Dean Sperry has said the last word in his beautiful and moving eulogy — the delivery of which was poetry itself. We can be proud indeed "that this society was one of the shaping forces which fitted him for his duty and his destiny." Young Franklin was not an unusual student, and he enjoyed in no way unusual privilege. He made a place for himself. He shared in normal undergraduate activities. He graduated in three years, though he stayed on for a fourth in order to devote his energy and interest to the presidency of the *Crimson*. If we examine even cursorily his undergraduate career, we are struck, however, by the fact that his choice of studies was ingeniously fitted to the calling just ahead of him. The *Crimson*, in turn, gave him his first real taste of executive command and the opportunity to write, though his editorials fail to exhibit that ultimate gift for the arresting phrase which made the public addresses of his radio evenings so memorable. All in all he was one of us. Thirteen years out, he was elected Overseer. On his twenty-fifth anniversary of graduation the University honored him with an LL.D. On Harvard's three hundredth anniversary, he honored her by his presence and the delivery of a charming address. Today his Alma Mater mourns the passing of one of her greatest sons.

1945

Early Frost

IN December 1954 Robert Frost surprised an old friend and a new one by recalling something of what he did not refer to as his Harvard Interval. He had left Dartmouth College in 1892 — to get the dates down — in his freshman year, and had married in 1895. Along in 1897 (it must have been) he remembers himself one day as a sedentary poet reading Tacitus in the attic.

"How was I going to earn a living? All of a sudden it occurred to me: Why couldn't I go to college and become a teacher?"

So he wrote to Dean Briggs, and not long after enrolled at Harvard with the Class of 1901 in the autumn of 1897. His teacher in English A was Alfred Dwight Sheffield '96, brother-in-law of T. S. Eliot. His interests (continuing that sojourn in the attic and that letter to the Dean) were Greek and Latin. In Greek he had Frank Cole Babbitt, then a young instructor, soon to leave Harvard to teach at Trinity. Clifford H. Moore, who arrived in Cambridge in 1898 from Chicago as Assistant Professor, taught him Latin.

"He meant a lot to me. A fine first year." But not for long. In his sophomore year his history repeated itself.

"A feeling of suspended animation came over me. I was restless and didn't seem to be liking things again."

He had seen Dean Briggs only once to speak to. A classmate told him at the end of freshman year that Deturs [1] — Harvard's book

---

[1] Given to students attaining for the first time the rank of Group I in academic standing. Robert Frost's father had won a Detur before him. For more information on the subject, see the chapter called "Notes on the Charity of Edward Hopkins." The remarkable painting of Frost by Gardiner Cox '28 is owned by the St. Botolph Club in Boston. Cox later made at least two others, all differing in approach and color; all convincing and convinced of "knowledge beyond the bounds of life."

prizes — had been given out and that there was one unclaimed for him. He went to Dean Briggs to get it.

He then went round again to say good-bye.

"I thought: Now I'm going to get preached to.

"But the Dean simply flipped through a big book.

" 'We're sorry to lose good students. It's a hard world you are going out into. More so because you are leaving here without anything to show for it.' "

And yet there *was* something to show for it. The Dean told Frost he would write a little letter for him which would serve as a kind of diploma. This was done, and the author of "The Road Not Taken" remembers that he carried the letter in his pocket for a long time before he lost it.

A spring-fever kind of puzzlement — his own words — over what to do next.

"In a worldly world I still thought I had better get a degree and teach. I wasn't dedicating myself to poetry or anything."

Frost, of course, was older than his Harvard Classmates.

"One of them said to me: 'You seem very light-hearted about it.' *They* thought it was momentous. Soon after I was farming — that's where I got most of my education."

There was a pause among the fragments.

"Two poems, at least, from *A Boy's Will* were submitted in manuscript in English A. One of them was 'The Tuft of Flowers.' "

The old friend, marveling, thought:

> I went to turn the grass once after one
> Who mowed it in the dew before the sun. . .

Perhaps the new one thought the same. He was lightening a shadow on the poet's face on the large wet canvas in front of him. He lifted his brush. The owner of the shadow moved a little.

"I don't create by the day. I don't write by the week. I write by the year. I milk the cow at midnight and at noon."

1955

Salutary

No man who has, and understands, his own freedom will doubt that Harvard gave to Great Britain's Prime Minister one perfect instance of the collective homage any patriot community would pay to one who has fought so valiantly against such evil. Our founding fathers would say aye to that. And Mr. Churchill in turn, no matter what motives may be assigned to him by other-minded people, gave not alone to his adopting University, but to the Nation, his profound conviction of what the course ahead should be. It is interesting to remember that many thousands of his cheering audience in the Yard were not Harvard alumni but another cross-section of America — young men who happen to be our military guests in the common cause.

Harvard indifference was not in evidence that day. People were at a pitch of enthusiasm. It was easy to see, merely by glancing at faces, that Mr. Churchill in everything he said and did measured up to Walter Lippmann's belief that he is "the one certainly authentic example of greatness in a public man who moves among us". Those privileged to see and hear him went away with renewed faith in the ideals for which we are at war. Mr. Churchill, we sincerely trust, understands that his immeasurable courtesy touched us all.

1943

"If We Are Together"

WITH the suddenness of the coming of autumn leaves, there returned to the Yard on September 6 much of the color and excitement of three historic Harvard events: the Tercentenary celebration of 1936, the memorable Oxford Convocation of June 1941, and the great military Commencement of last May. A blend of these three festivals marked the dignified and delightful ceremony at which, a fortnight ago, the Harvard degree of Doctor of Laws was conferred on the Right Honorable Winston Leonard Spencer Churchill, Great Britain's Prime Minister, and man of the hour. Indeed, the surprise of the occasion brought it sharply into focus; and the time of the year — when the Yard is poised for first flight into fall days — enhanced the sense and feel of adventure. To learn overnight that within a few hours one might see and hear the man whose character and eloquence have been the inspiration of the free world in its darkest hour, brought professors home from vacations, and cheerfully cancelled hundreds of family plans for spending Labor Day away from Cambridge.

Early Monday morning those fortunate enough to hold one of the limited number of Yard tickets began to filter through the main gates. They were still not too sure as to just what was about to happen, for Mr. Churchill's name had so far appeared in print only in a brief announcement in the national press to the effect that he was to broadcast at noon from an unnamed American city. No official word of him had escaped in Cambridge. But the heavy ropes which marked off the large area of the Yard now known as the Tercentenary Theatre, and the battery of microphones on the steps of the Memorial Church, more than confirmed the suspected probability of the impending event. By 11 A.M., Harvard military units were gathering in formations in the old part of the Yard; Overseers and other dignitaries in morning dress were hurrying across diagonal paths, silk hats shining in the sun. Crowds of civilians — mostly women — were finding places on the steps of the Widener Library, members of the Navy Band began to assemble near the west porch of the Church; police were in view. At a quarter to twelve the specially and hurriedly invited to the academic exercises had entered Sanders Theatre; a few moments later began the exercises themselves, in which — now no surprise — the Prime Minister, in the brilliant red of his Oxford gown, played to great applause the leading part. Then the principals emerged from the south door of Memorial Hall, hurried across to the Church, and a minute later from the south steps President Conant was introducing to Harvard's six or seven thousand military, and five or six thousand students, Faculty, alumni, guests, and employees, the man who recently told the world that we have reached "the end of the beginning."

Up to the very last the secret had been well kept. Even those in the next-but-one of the University's inner circles knew nothing whatever of the event until a week before it occurred; and in many cases then there was indication only that an honorary degree was to be conferred. So, in fact, the invitations read to Overseers, alumni officials, the military, and distinguished guests. They were doubly marked *confidential*. The tickets which followed indicated Sanders Theatre, a time, a seat — no more. Yard passes were not generally thought to exist until the Saturday previous. There was suspicion; there were ultimate hints in the public press, such as that of Mr. Churchill's broadcast and something about his keeping "a long-standing engagement." Secrecy extended even to running off the programs late at night. The University Printing Office recalls that when copy was submitted, it appeared that only a Mr. X was to be honored; his name would come later. But at the end of the copy stood the text for *God Save the King!* By and large, one can now half believe that the potential audience *willed* that it prove to be the Prime Minister who was coming to the Yard.

He came. It was a long-standing invitation, to be accepted when opportunity offered. The opportunity had arrived, but there was no time for the University to invite an audience remote from Cambridge. It is remarkable, rather, that the staff in Massachusetts Hall was able to notify the immediate Harvard family; to carry through so many complicated details — from secret service to broadcasting arrangements — in so short a time. But it was done, and here now at a little before noon in familiar Sanders Theatre sat and stood more than 1,200 people in what one man described as "the most exciting fever of a lifetime."

On the platform ranged the empty seats for 118 members of the academic procession. On the floor were set aside seats for the remainder of the procession — the Faculty and the Board of Overseers. At the right and left of the stage, underneath the balcony, sat the higher ranking members of the Army and Navy units at the University. At the back of the Theatre in semicircle stood a group of undergraduates. (Students were permitted to apply for a limited block of tickets, filled in the order of request.) Three or four WAVE officers took seats with the Navy. A number of ladies — wives of members of the Governing Boards and administrative officers — occupied the center balcony. In this group were Mrs. Conant, Mrs. Churchill, and Subaltern Mary Churchill.

A bugle sounded. Three minutes later, to the *Second Connecticut March*, the academic procession entered the Theatre — the Faculty by the south entry, the Overseers and dignitaries by the north. Ascending the platform, the Deans took places in the front row left, facing the House Masters. Robe after robe scattered a rainbow over the stage. Some of the most brilliant were those of the *Emeriti*, among them Professors Merriman and Rand.

At noon sounded the fanfare [1] from the balcony overlooking the

---

[1] Written by Walter H. Piston, Jr. '24, then Associate Professor of Music; first played at the Oxford Convocation in 1941.

transept. This was indeed the moment. The now standing audience broke into prolonged applause and cheers as the Prime Minister, with President Conant, preceded by the Secretary of the University and members of the Corporation, and followed by Jerome D. Greene '96, LL.D. '37, Honorary Keeper of the Corporation Records, the Governor of the Commonwealth, Commander C. R. Thompson of the Royal Navy, and Brigadier General William J. Keville, the Governor's Aide, entered the Theatre and ascended the center steps. From the press bank at the right flashed the camera bulbs. The applause continued. The President and Fellows took seats at the back center underneath the three crimson shields; the Prime Minister found his place at the left between the Governor (on his right) and George H. Chase, Dean of the University. Principals, Faculty, and audience then were seated. Throughout the exercises, six Secret Service men stood inflexible at strategic positions at the back of, and in front of, the stage.

The University Marshal, Dr. Reginald Fitz, said: "Mr. Sheriff, pray give us order"; and the Sheriff of Middlesex County, top-hatted and gold-braided, arose, thrice pounded the stage with his sword-in-scabbard, and said in the tradition: "The meeting will be in order." The Reverend Henry Bradford Washburn '91, S.T.D. '30, offered prayer:

. . . And we most heartily beseech Thee, with Thy favour to behold and bless Thy servants the President of the United States, the gracious sovereign King George, his First Minister, and all to whom Thou hast entrusted the destinies of the United States of America and the British Commonwealth of Nations. . .

The University Choir, in black gowns with broad red facing, seated at the extreme left under the balcony, sang the anthem — the final chorus from Handel's *Samson*, with the resplendent words by Milton:

> Let their celestial concerts all unite,
> Ever to sound his praise in endless morn of light.

Twenty members of the Boston Symphony Orchestra accompanied them, under the direction of Associate Professor G. Wallace Woodworth, Organist and Choirmaster. The Orchestra also played the fanfare and played for the subsequent Seventy-Eighth Psalm and Paine's Commencement Hymn. This was the Orchestra's first participation in a Harvard ceremony since the Tercentenary, and many of those present returned from their vacations just for the one day. Mr. Churchill, it was noted, turned far around in his chair to observe and hear the music.

Leverett Saltonstall '14, LL.D. '42, Governor of the Commonwealth, gave the brief address of welcome. When he had finished and resumed his seat, the Prime Minister turned and laid his hand on the Governor's arm. One could see his lips move. "Very good," he said. The Governor had concluded:

Mr. Churchill: You are an inspiring example of the motto of our great President, Thomas Jefferson:
And ye shall know the truth, and the truth shall make you free.[2]

The audience rose and joined in the singing of the Psalm. When all were again seated, the President stood up in his place and called Mr. Churchill by name. The Prime Minister also arose, and the President conferred on him the degree of Doctor of Laws, reading the citation.

WINSTON LEONARD SPENCER CHURCHILL
An historian who has written a glorious page of British history; a statesman and warrior whose tenacity and courage turned back the tide of tyranny in freedom's darkest hour.

How well it read! When the University Marshal had handed Dr. Churchill his diploma, applause broke out in new strength. It is doubtful if anything in Sanders Theatre ever surpassed it. Again bulbs flashed. Mr. Churchill bowed and smiled, and bowed again. He was visibly touched by the reception.

Taking his manuscript from his pocket, he moved forward to

[2] John 8.32.

the lectern and the battery of five microphones. On either side of him towered the white marble statues of President Quincy and the Colonial patriot, James Otis. He searched for his glasses with hands that reach more happily for a cigar. He looked constantly right and left. His mobile face and restless arms gave fluid emphasis to what he said. Chancellor of Bristol University, honorary Alumnus of Oxford and Harvard, his dramatic address nonetheless led out unerringly from academic groves [3] to Anglo-American relations. There is no need to summarize. The radio and the press of the Nation have already done that and more, and the full and corrected text may be found elsewhere.

[3] The text of Mr. Churchill's address, delivered in Sanders Theatre at noon on Monday, September 6, and printed in the *Harvard Alumni Bulletin* of September 1943 (*q.v.*), was based on the complete published versions in the New York *Times* and *Herald Tribune* of September 7. A note of explanation ran as follows: A transcription of the manuscript was not given to the press, either before or after delivery, and the newspapers which carried the speech in full apparently depended on recording the words of the broadcast itself. As we go to press one week later, the BULLETIN is fortunate in being able to compare the texts in several newspapers, and a few obvious errors have thus been corrected. Students of Mr. Churchill's style of oratory will observe that the *Herald Tribune* reported: "I am once again in academic *robe* — robe is, I believe, the right word." The *Times* had it correctly: "I am once again in academic *groves* — groves is, I believe," etc. But the *Times* elsewhere printed "or be it primitive" (referring to the larger use of basic English), which the *Herald Tribune* rationally took for "albeit primitive." Then said the *Times*, about one-third of the way through the address: "Common conceptions of what is right and decent *mark the gods of* fair play, especially to the weak and poor." Surely the *Herald Tribune* had the sharper ear with "what is right and decent *and marked regard for* fair play." Each of these papers — with similar subheadings, "Regrets Failure of League" — had Mr. Churchill say: "It is *sad* that the League of Nations failed." The context — "If so, that is largely because, etc." — clearly indicates that the Prime Minister said: "It is *said* that the League of Nations failed." The plebiscite authority, Miss Sarah Wambaugh, quoting as correct this sentence with *said* not *sad*, in a letter to the Boston *Herald*, laments the fact that the Boston papers which carried the text in full — and also the Washington *Post* — substituted the word *fanaticism* for *pacifism* farther along in the same paragraph. The two New York papers curiously agreed on "the President and myself as *representatives* of the British War Cabinet." We agree with the Boston *Globe* that it should be "and myself as *representative*."

All of which is more pertinent in the light of an article by Raymond Daniell in the New York *Times Magazine* for September 12: ". . . On those rare occasions when the text of a Churchill address is given out before delivery, the copy always carries a warning that it must be checked against delivery before it is published."

If we are together, nothing is impossible. If we are divided, all will fail. I therefore preach continually the doctrine of the fraternal association of our peoples, not for any purpose of gaining invidious material advantages for either of them, not for territorial aggrandizement or the vain pomp of earthly domination, but for the sake of service to mankind and for the honor that comes to those who faithfully serve great causes.

But beyond the objective, fraternal point of his speech, who will forget this paragraph:

And here let me say how proud we ought to be, young and old, to be living in a tremendous, thrilling, formative epoch in the human story, and how fortunate it was for the world that when these great trials came upon us there was a generation that terror could not conquer and brutal violence could not enslave.

He was cheered to the hardwood echo of the old Theatre. The power of his words had found a mark. He looked pleased.

There followed the Commencement Hymn and the Benediction. To more applause, the Prime Minister, the dignitaries, and Faculty left the platform and the audience immediately followed.

Most of the audience hastened at once across to the Yard and arrived there to find President Conant on the south steps of the Memorial Church introducing the man for whom the massed crowds had patiently waited. The sun was fainting hot. Our visitor saw the whole Tercentenary Theatre filled, the Army and Navy in the center, a large group of WAVES among them. On the steps of Widener stood hundreds. Nearly ten thousand voices cheered him. The Prime Minister, now—robe discarded—in short black jacket, grey trousers, grey unmatching waistcoat, black bow tie with dots, a black Homburg, and a light cane in his hand. This was the familiar figure; no gown to hide his British squareness, no black velvet cap to shield his eyes. The crowd was delighted. Soldier, to soldiers and sailors. The veteran of older wars and this war spoke briefly to young men who had yet to go out. Cameras clicked and whirred. He rapped with his cane to drive home a point. He looked fiercely into the sun. He looked down and smiled. In his talk he was optimistic, but he emphasized that the end of the war was not yet round any visible corner. Closing, he made the sign of the V twice with the first two fingers of his right hand. The crowd voiced mighty concurrence, and V's appeared everywhere in answer.

From there the President escorted Mr. Churchill to the Fogg Museum to attend a small luncheon given by the University. Here he met members of the governing boards, administrative officers, and their wives, and members of the official party. In honor of the occasion, Harvard's seventeenth-century state silverware was used for service. President Conant made some brief remarks:

LADIES AND GENTLEMEN:

Today Harvard welcomes the Prime Minister of Great Britain. We also welcome the Chancellor of Bristol University, a fellow academician. But most significant of all, we welcome a man whose inspiring leadership of a gallant people has preserved for us and our children that liberty without which no university can survive.

Those of us of the Harvard family who are gathered here this afternoon have the special pleasure and high honor of greeting Mr. and Mrs. Churchill and the members of their official party. I trust our guests realize how deeply we appreciate this visit. It is no simple matter for a man who carries Mr. Churchill's burdens to find the time to attend an academic festival. This day will be long remembered in Harvard history. I am sure that I am speaking on behalf of all of you . . . when I express our deep gratitude to the Prime Minister for the honor he has done us.

Mr. Churchill has already spoken twice today. I shall not therefore trouble him by a request to make another speech. I am venturing, however, to take the liberty of asking him to propose the toast to the President of the United States.

Ladies and gentlemen — Mr. Churchill.

A toast and some unrecorded words and a witticism followed.

Crowds trailed to the west entrance of the Museum and waited patiently back of circulating police until the Prime Minister and

President Conant — each now with a long Churchill cigar — emerged. In final response to final cheers, Harvard's newest Alumnus made the familiar sign and hoisted on his stick the familiar black hat.

In the little while that he was long about — to paraphrase a poet — the dominant impression of Mr. Churchill is the kindliness and brightness in his great vitality. It is true that he probably carried in his head that day the knowledge that the first of the Axis partners had given up. But this need not be counted. In a wearied world there was no weariness in that face. He smiled often. He caused his guardians great uneasiness by insisting twice on saluting the crowd through an open window of Memorial Hall before the academic procession had gathered. His informality was continually evident. On the platform he would hitch up the folds of his red gown, and his hands appeared frequently to stray through invisible slits to his pockets. He sat comfortably. When his wife and daughter lingered on the steps of the Museum before entering, he turned around and came out unaffectedly after them. There was no pose to anything that he said or did. He stood equally and foursquare among us, and we shall not forget him.

1943

Tercentenary

"Is that you, John Harvard?"
I said to his statue.
"Aye — that's me," said John,
"And after you're gone."

Notes on the Harvard Tercentenary

Not that the story need be long, but it will take a long while to make it short.   Thoreau

THE first light fall of Cambridge snow is on the ground as these pages are being prepared for the press. Our private New England autumn which Harvard enjoys in fortunate seclusion from the noise and trample of a part-industrial city is virtually over: leaves raked and gathered in ballooning canvas and carried we know not where; the winter guards of pine and burlap in windless position over perishable shrubs; the last of ivy leaf burned red and ruined on so many ancient walls; the smoke of student fires rising thinly from old brick chimneys; a clear cut of November blue to the deepening sky; a jug of cider sighted on an isolated window ledge; elm and oak and bush gone bare; sparrows and starlings in forage at the south side of Grays and Widener; the cawing of temporary crows; and the long eternal business of life and learning steadied to the pulse of youthful blood.

The visitor in the Yard this morning is aware of this pulse and of the normal activity of an academic day. It might be any of a long succession of Harvard days. If he visited the Yard twelve months ago he will note but little change and no more than two new landmarks — both ancestrally old. He will see the College Pump [1] restored to its original site over the old well in front of

---

[1] Dedication exercises for the restored College Pump (heavy oak on flagstones) were held on the morning of June 16. Henry Munroe Rogers '62, Senior Alumnus

Hollis (with a modern bubbler in the interest of sanitation); and the great marble Dragon, presented to Harvard by Alumni in China in honor of her Tercentenary, solemn and perpendicular under the shadow of the Library, wearing for the first time a strange mantle of occidental snow. But our visitor may not be properly aware of one thing of which the Dragon, even more than the pump, persistently reminds us: This is the first snow of the fourth hundred years of Harvard; and this leave-taking of autumn so usual, deliberate, and New England in character is the end of a season of University celebration and "a truly great occasion," as the London *Times* expressed it, unparalleled in the history of our country.

For the passage of two months and the structural clearing of the Yard, much as the autumn winds have cleared her trees, have stripped us clean of all but personal memory of what took place; and it is easier now in retrospect to consider a summer of intense Tercentenary activity and the proceedings of the middle days of September with detached though still fervent delight. The great Tercentenary Theatre whose platform sprang from the steps of the College Church and whose tentative limits were marked by Sever, Widener, and University is gone. The trappings, poles, flags, gonfalons, greens, guidons, seals, crests, lions, and such wonderful paraphernalia, are relics of the past. The last sound through the marvelous mechanics of electrical broadcast is stilled: speaker, orator, odist, poet, chorus, and symphony. The tide of color: gown, hood, cap, fez, turban, mortar board, brocade, braid, silk, velvet, ermine, tasseled gold, all foreign air and grace, all brilliant to the eye, has faded out. Delegates, dignitaries, ambassadors, friends, and strangers who came to do us honor in being honored; spectator, sharer, alumnus, sons; the ten thousand legendary men of Harvard — they have come and departed. The camera lens is dark. The wires which carried our celebration to the ends of the civilized earth are dis-

---

of the College, accepted the first drink with the remark that water had been a great thing for humanity.

connected. Doer and reporter alike have finished their parts. The gates within gates which stood so white and flawless are cleared and themselves removed. The show is over. Reverence, humility, honor, truth, friendship: these remain. As the Sutra of the Lotus of the Good Law in the country of our Dragon has it, the god of the Tercentenary is now "perfectly extinct upon his throne."

II

The Celebration of the Three Hundredth Anniversary of the Founding of Harvard College was a long celebration which commenced officially on Friday, 8 November 1935, with the exercises held in Sanders Theatre in honor of John Harvard's birthday, and ended with a brilliant three-day climax on 16, 17, and 18 September 1936. Preparations were begun as far back as 1924 when Samuel E. Morison '08, Professor of History, was appointed Tercentenary Historian.[2] In 1930 the Governing Boards of the University jointly appointed the first Tercentenary Committee, later associated with a committee of the Alumni. This representative group made its principal report to the Corporation in April, 1934; and on May 14, 1934, Jerome D. Greene '96 was appointed Secretary to the Corporation and Director of the Tercentenary Celebration. His labors to this end, and those of his associates, were long, tireless, scrupulous in detail, and rewarding beyond all expectation.

> I like the scenery
> of the Tercen*teen*ary,
> and behind the scene
> I like Jerome Greene.[3]

[2] His volumes of Harvard History to date (all published by the Harvard University Press) are: *The Founding of Harvard College* (1935); *Harvard College in the Seventeenth Century*, 2 vols. (1936); *Three Centuries of Harvard* (1936); *The Development of Harvard University, 1869–1929* (Editor; 1930).

[3] From the present editor's verses in the Tercentenary Graduates' issue of *The Lampoon*, which also included the quatrain printed on the half-title page of these *Notes*.

Though perhaps it did not occur to him, it must have seemed to his associates and to those on the inside that he worked solely under the aegis of the sundial back of Holden Chapel: "On this moment hangs eternity."

By the spring of 1936 all plans were well on the way to completion, and the advent of summer found Cambridge busy with Graduate School sessions and conferences on such diverse matters as soil mechanics, business, education, and theology. From June 15 till September 25, Harvard held open house, described in attractive posters as "Harvard on View." *Salvete omnes!* A marquee was set up in the Straus Hall Quadrangle where pamphlets, folders, catalogues, Tercentenary history, medals, postcards, photographs, and similar Harvardiana were on sale, and where a free guide service maintained its humid headquarters. A second tent was established also in front of the University Museum; and information desks installed at the entrance to Eliot House and in the cloister of Memorial Hall. Over paths and bypaths marked with white blackletter signs bearing the Harvard arms in red, and under a corps of intelligent and fully informed student guides (red coats and megaphones), in fourteen weeks 66,783 recorded visitors from all parts of our country and beyond the seven seas were enabled to tour the grounds and buildings of the University and to see a multitude of rare and important exhibits[4] in the libraries, laboratories,

---

[4] Under the chairmanship of Charles H. Watkins '09, Chief Marshal for the Associated Harvard Clubs, an important and impressive Exhibition of Furniture and the Decorative Arts "relating to the first two hundred years of the history of Harvard and of the New England community" deserves special mention. With the help of Bertram K. Little '23, Secretary, and the coöperation of many generous lenders, the Exhibition was arranged in Robinson Hall. It was visited by 22,680 persons, including representatives of thirty foreign countries.

In addition: The priceless Tercentenary Loan Exhibition of Japanese Art at the Boston Museum of Fine Arts (Sept.–Oct.) including "National Treasures" from the Imperial Household, the Imperial Museum, the Tokyo Art School, and from the private collection of Prince Takamatsu, and many others. The Boston Public Library, from August through October, exhibited in twenty-four cases a collection of rare books, manuscripts, and engravings relating to the history of Harvard College: a welcome "reënforcement of Harvard's own resources."

museums, observatories, and classrooms of the College and the Graduate Schools, and of Radcliffe. Caleb Cheeshahteaumuck, that recently revived Indian of engaging name, the first of his race to receive (in 1665) a degree from John Harvard's wilderness College, would have fled in terror before the hourly squads of visitors tramping their way about his sacred wood. Indeed, the drone of megaphonic talk seemed never to stop. Cambridge was like a foreign city: Teachers, parents, children, sightseers, old ladies, old gentlemen, tourists, students, professors with horn-rimmed glasses, Nordics in shorts and binoculars, English in tweeds, Latins in berets and slacks, and Blaschka glass flower veterans listened eagerly for the first time to old legends of a new world . . . "and on your left is Wadsworth House, erected in 1726, the second oldest building in the Yard and the home of nine Harvard presidents." . . . One day a young man, more serious and attentive than his companions, walked with a group, turned his head with their heads, his eyes with their eyes, and absorbed with evident satisfaction the fluent exposition of his student-informer. Yes — and the papers made something of the story — he was James Bryant Conant.

During all these weeks an unprecedented and generously sympathetic press kept Harvard in the national headlines and informed the country at large of meetings and symposia wherein historical truth, scientific discovery, mathematical deduction, cosmic theory, medical research, sociological and economic revolution, and the gracious humanities appeared at the breakfast table as vital and important as the citizen's daily dose of crime and disappointment. For the inner circle, a University publication called *The Tercentenary Gazette*, an old-fashioned illustrated broadside, dedicated to "help alumni and friends of Harvard to enjoy their time in Cambridge during September or any of the intervening months," was issued every fortnight.[5] Under an anonymous editorship it delved into amiable recesses of Harvard history and tradition, and provided

[5] 12 June–11 September 1936.

the alumnus with a full and detailed calendar of forthcoming Ter-centenary events. More officially, every Harvard man had received in the autumn of 1935 a letter from President Conant; and in the spring of 1936 this was followed by a formal University invitation to attend the major ceremonies in September. The distribution of tickets, arrangement for accommodations, and all such administra-tive matters followed a rigorous schedule. If any Harvard man re-mained uninformed or uninvited, it was because he had moved to a point on our planet beyond the last lines of communication. At least 10,000 of his fellow alumni were expected back in Cambridge; and the Director's figures show that the estimate was not far wrong: about 10,000 Harvard men, or more than 15,000 people in all, at-tended the concluding exercises in September. One of them was Peter Harvard of England, only son of Lionel de Jersey Harvard '15, and a collateral descendant of the Eponym — our Benefactor, generally referred to as the Founder.

Invitations to all Universities, Colleges, and Learned Societies throughout the world, expressing the hope that they would send official delegates to the Tercentenary, were mailed from Cambridge long months in advance of September. Of the many exhibitions in the University only recently concluded, none was more interesting from the point of view of art, expression, and exquisite taste than that of the hundreds of superbly lettered, printed, illuminated, and inscribed greetings [6] from Harvard's world-wide sister institutions.

[6] In addition to the formal greetings from Universities, Colleges, Learned Societies, and Institutions, certain others are significant as spontaneous expressions of felicitation; one such being an elaborately illuminated vellum from the Mayor, Aldermen, and Councillors of the Metropolitan Borough of Southwark, John Harvard's birthplace. "It is a matter of considerable pride to us that John Harvard was a native of our Borough. We are gratified by the interest which the governing body of the Univer-sity has from time to time evinced in the Borough of Southwark. We express the confident hope that the University will further develop the ideals of its Puritan founders and that thereby the world will be assisted in its development of peace, justice, and honor." A second is from sixty-six of the more than 1,200 Cuban school-teachers who attended the Cuban summer school at Harvard in 1900. The greeting concludes: "Help in war, help in peace, help in honorable living among the nations of the earth, that is a summary of what Cuba owes to Harvard University; and

Many of them startling in perfection and simplicity, they represent a distinguished addition to the archives of the College Library.

The summer passed: actively, excitedly, expectantly. Toward the end of it the Yard, which used to witness annually the brief assembling of fountains and band stands for Commencement, and still knows the temporary Commencement staging in the Sever Quadrangle, became suddenly alive with building operations. The scaffolding of the Tercentenary Theatre, the grandstand for the chorus, strong African machans [7] up in the elms for sound and camera men, gates and flag poles, pedestals and ornaments, flags and bunting, 15,000 collapsible chairs stretching from the Memorial Church (site of old Appleton Chapel) to Widener and past on either flank: carpentry, painting, decoration, and mechanics enough for a fair set in Hollywood; enormous detail, endless minute problems and difficulties — all this represents a story in itself. Not only was the Theatre wired with electrical equipment for amplification, recording, and communication, which the New York *Herald-Tribune* called "the most elaborate ever attempted in the United States," but Sanders Theatre had also to be wired in anticipation of rain, and amplifiers installed in neighboring buildings of auditorium description to accommodate a rainy day crowd. Few people at the exercises could possibly realize the extent of these preparations. Nor did they perhaps consider that without the aid of science such a pageant of the spoken word could not have been held at all. In the final days of tinkering and last adjustment, many visitors to the still open Yard sat on the fringe of its 15,000 seats in the elm shade and listened to flawless reproduction of music or the impromptu conversa-

---

therefore we modest and sincere living witnesses of contemporary history hereby certify and proclaim the paramount importance of Harvard's services to our people and the correspondingly profound gratitude of ours to this glorious living monument to the ideals of the Pilgrim Fathers."

[7] When the *Notes* were first published in 1936, I wrote "aerial bomas" in attempting to describe those platforms in the trees. "Them weren't bomas, were they?" was the way Thomas Barbour '06, Director of the Museum of Comparative Zoölogy, gently corrected me.

tions of workmen testing with private utterance the distributed electric tongues.[8]

It was hot, brown, Cambridge-like post-summer weather. The days slipped on toward the fall; and one day at the end of August seventy-two scholars from all over the United States and from many foreign countries arrived for the Tercentenary Conference of Arts and Sciences held in the College buildings from August 31 to September 12. Sixty-two of this number were to receive honorary degrees from Harvard at the exercises on September 18; the other ten, Harvard had previously honored. These conferences in the four quadrants of learning (Humanities; Physical, Biological, and Social Sciences) were in general open to small groups of spectators, in addition to professors, teachers, and specialists in each field; but there were also public lectures by world-renowned authorities, including many winners of the Nobel Prize: Eddington, Svedberg, Fischer, Jung, Hopkins, Spemann, Krogh, Maunier, Bergius, and others; and the sessions provided in various languages such symposia as: "Authority and the Individual," "Factors Determining Human Behavior;" and such lectures as "Mediaeval Universalism and its Present Value," "Stability and Social Change," "Hellenism and Christianity." President Conant and Jerome D. Greene, Chairman of the Executive Committee of the Conference, made the opening addresses, and many of the papers[9] read during the two weeks were sent out on the air. The Square, the Yard, and contiguous Cambridge appeared brisk with distinguished visitors whose silver Tercentenary medals and grey, green, yellow, and blue ribbons (according to their quadrant) gleamed in the sunlight. Everyone a little excited . . . the sound of French, Italian, German, Spanish, Japanese . . . ritual of the megaphone boys and the footfalls of their charges . . . the final ceremonies rapidly approached.

---

[8] In one of these highly audible official tests, before an audience of astonished transients and arrested squirrels, a second honorary degree was awarded (with variations) to George Washington (LL.D. 1776).

[9] Published in 1937, in three volumes.

NOTES ON THE HARVARD TERCENTENARY

On Tuesday, September 8, a *pro forma* meeting of the Harvard Alumni Association was held in the Faculty Room of University Hall in the presence of President Emeritus Lowell, Professor Samuel E. Morison, Professor R. P. Blake, Director of the University Library, Members of the Governing Boards, Deans, certain Faculty Members, and invited guests. Its immediate purpose was the opening by President Conant of a package sealed by President Josiah Quincy in 1836. Dr. David Cheever '97, Vice-President of the Association, presided. Under a barrage of floodlights and motion picture cameras, the package was unsealed, and found to contain (as Mr. Conant has said) "letters from the Alumni of Harvard College and, unfortunately, nothing else." The Meeting was thereupon adjourned until Friday, 18 September 1936. . . . On Sunday, September 13, at 8 P.M., Professor A. T. Davison '06 and guest organists gave an organ recital in the Memorial Church. . . . On Monday and Tuesday, September 14 and 15, the Tercentenary Session of the Medical School held symposia in Boston in the mornings and afternoons. . . . In Sanders Theatre at 4 P.M. on the same afternoons the Boston String Quartet gave two of a series of three remarkable chamber concerts whose programmes were devoted entirely to the compositions of Harvard Graduates.[10] . . . The next three days will be known to Harvard history as The Tercentenary Days.

III

September 16 was a fair, inviting day. The third and last of the chamber concerts was given and received enthusiastically in Sanders Theatre at 11 A.M. At a two o'clock ceremony in the Widener Library, Alexander Dunlop Lindsay, Vice-Chancellor of Oxford University, presented to President Conant, as Oxford's Tercentenary

[10] Arthur Foote '74; Frederick S. Converse '93; Edward Burlingame Hill '94; Daniel Gregory Mason '95; John Alden Carpenter '97; William C. Heilman '00; Edward Ballantine '07; Randall Thompson '20; Walter Piston '24.

gift to Harvard, a letter [11] by Christopher Columbus concerning "the newly discovered islands," and printed in book form in 1493. This gift out of the great Bodleian Library is one of the only two copies of the first edition known to exist. . . . That afternoon the Undergraduate Delegates from other Universities and Colleges were entertained by Harvard undergraduates in Eliot House Court. In the evening there was a dinner to the Council of the Associated Harvard Clubs at the Harvard Club of Boston; and at 9 P.M. in Symphony Hall the first of the three Tercentenary Concerts by Serge Koussevitzky, LL.D. '29, and the Boston Symphony Orchestra.

But the brilliant event of the day was the reception of Delegates from other Universities, Colleges, and Learned Societies, held in Sanders Theatre at three in the afternoon. To these Delegates the Harvard circle and the friends of Harvard living in Cambridge, Boston, and Greater Boston had opened their doors in generous hospitality and welcomed them as their guests. To their entertainment every possible thought was given, including many private dinners in their honor. The number of Delegates at the reception was 547, and they represented 530 Universities, Colleges, and Learned Societies, and came from forty-six states in the Union, two Territories, and forty foreign countries. Of this number many, of course, were included in the group of seventy-two scholars who had previously participated in the Tercentenary Conference of Arts and Sciences.

The time drew on to three o'clock. The silver medals and ribbons became now but the smallest accents of color in the undulate sea of gowns, hoods, caps, of all hues and fashions, as Dignitaries, Delegates, Fellows, Faculty Members, Presiding Officers, College and University Presidents, and guests of both sexes assembled in Sanders. *Salvete omnes!* No detail of the ceremonial days was more carefully executed than the official reception of these 547 men who had come to do Harvard honor on her three-hundredth birthday. The presentation was ordered by the ranking age of the Institution repre-

[11] *Epistola de Insulis Noviter Repertis.*

sented. If there was more than one Delegate, the Institution was asked to rank them according to its own standard of seniority. The Delegates were accordingly formed in prearranged columns in Memorial Hall. After President Conant, Jerome D. Greene, as Director of the Tercentenary, President Lowell, and all guests had been seated, leaving the floor seats of Sanders Theatre empty, Dr. Reginald Fitz '06, University Marshal, announced the name of each College, University, and Learned Society, and its Delegate (or Delegates in turn) stepped forward from a line entering at the north of the platform and was formally presented to President Conant, who shook his hand. The first Delegate to come forward was Professor Saleh Hashem Attia from Al-Azhar University in Cairo, which was founded in 970, or 666 years before the founding of Harvard.[12]

Past the marble standing figures of Josiah Quincy and James Otis, the learned men of Paris, Oxford, Cambridge, St. Andrews, Rome, Peking, Brussels, Buenos Aires, Tokyo, Havana, Copenhagen, Munich, Rangoon, Beirut, Oslo, Cracow, Madrid, Leiden, Istanbul, Cape Town, and scores beside, descended in rustling silk and chromatic harmony to their places. "As brilliant as the rainbow and as dignified as the Supreme Court," said the Boston *Herald* in its account. But there was another harmony perceived in the printed programme; and this lay in the reverential recital of Saxon and foreign names which could be made to run like a phrase in Sir Thomas Browne:[13] "The Very Rev. Mgr. Francesco Lardone, Prof. Sir Sarvepalli Radhakrishnan, Prof. Jack Henry Sandground."

Professor Conant made the address of welcome; and Professor Elie Cartan, Delegate of the University of Paris, one of the "great Universities from which we are proud to claim our descent," made response for all Delegates present.

"On behalf of the Governing Boards and Faculties of Harvard

[12] Delegate of the youngest University was Dr. Octavio Méndez Pereira of the Universidad de Panamá, founded in 1935.

[13] *E.g.*: "According to the ordainer of order and mystical mathematicks of the City of Heaven."

University," said President Conant, "I bid you welcome. . . . As the President of the most ancient [of American foundations for higher education in the United States], I may claim the privilege of addressing a special salutation this afternoon to those who come from foreign lands. Gentlemen from afar, we receive you gladly not only as Delegates to Harvard's Tercentenary Celebration but as ambassadors accredited to all the universities and colleges of this republic. . . . Ladies and gentlemen, the greetings which you bring to Harvard we thankfully accept. In these messages of good will we read the continued aspiration of mankind toward a universal fellowship based on human reason . . . a fellowship which transcends all barriers of race and nation. . . ."

Professor Cartan, pontifically splendid amid splendor, made his response in French: a response delightful for its grace, sincerity, and singleness of phrase. Of Harvard Alumni he said (in English equivalent): "Here they learned the primacy of spiritual values. . . . If the world, emerging from the trouble and anxiety of the present hour, may at some future time find a spiritual unity more universal and more stable than that which Christendom enjoyed in the Middle Ages, it pleases us to think that Harvard University . . . will have helped us in the search for this unity."

But it is the burst of color in the Delta, whence the dismissed assembly proceeded to tea, that remains in the memory of the spectator as the most magnificent and poetic interlude of all. It was one of those beautiful wine-like middle September afternoons such as New Englanders rightly claim can occur only in New England. The sky, sun, wind, and air were all of one temper to the occasion. Out of Memorial Hall streamed the bright gowns: blue and purple mingling with subtle shades of Oxford, Cambridge, and Sorbonne red; with the dark kimono of Japan, the green and gold braid of the various Academies of the Institut de France; with the fur-edged gown and chain-of-office of the Mayor of the Borough of Southwark, and the uniforms of the service; with what hundred other gowns and hoods showing scarlet, yellow, orange, lilac; with uniforms, medals, swords, pacific and military caps; with plumes and pompons, ermine and velvet; with shades and values as on some great palette: marvelous and romantic as when Stevenson said "but the Camisards had only bright and supporting visions!" Bright and supporting visions of faces, persons, minds; of distinction, cultivation, and individuality. A man wandered about in a kind of mental and rainbow aberration. Many will remember that sight: men and women of all races talking lightly in the fellowship of a common and magnificent interest; brought together in one place in one country over one historical occurrence which perhaps at some time had touched the lives of each of them. Or some will remember it personified in the serenely single figure of Professor Alfred North Whitehead,[14] wrapped in a scarlet Cambridge gown; caught for a moment as solitary as scholarship, yet radiant as a lived philosophy.

IV

On Thursday, September 17, under leaden and vainly threatening clouds, the emphasis changed sharply from scholar to alumnus. The morning opened at 9.30 with a Service of Thanksgiving and Remembrance in The Memorial Church. The audience which came by invitation included members of the Governing Boards, the several Faculties, distinguished guests of the University, representatives of all alumni bodies and of every living College Class, and a delegation of undergraduates. They were deeply rewarded by fine music and a memorable service distinguished for this hauntingly New England prayer offered by The Reverend Charles Edwards Park, S.T.D. (Hon.) '32:

"Almighty God, the God of our fathers, all our blessings come from thee. Without thee there can be nothing strong, and nothing

---

[14] His retirement as of 1 September 1937 had not yet been announced.

holy. In each high moment of life our thoughts turn to thee; and we ask thee to bless unto us the purpose of this hour.

"We come before thee with offerings of heartfelt gratitude for the guidings of thy Providence in the past; for the temper which was in our forefathers, their reverence and godly fear, their quick sense of accountability to thee, which made them eager instruments of thy Will. . .

"We praise thee that in their day of arduous labor a prescience warned them of greater days to come, and instructed them to build a foundation broad and deep. We praise thee that, knowing thy truth to be their only assurance of freedom, and wise to desire more wisdom, they founded this University, to preserve and increase their little treasure of learning, and to guide their rulers in the way of understanding. . .

"We call to mind the wise men who have served it in their generations, their fidelity and unselfish devotion, and the endowment they have left unto it of noble character and integrity.

"We call to mind the rich men who have seen its needs and foreseen its possibilities, who have strengthened its hands and multiplied its resources. . . The fathers and mothers of our land whose love and hope and pride have centered upon this place, who have . . . made their unapplauded sacrifices that their sons might enter upon a fairer heritage. . . The young men in their multitudes who have felt its touch and learned its spirit, whose innocence has been trained to strength and whose strength has been disciplined by wisdom and self-control, and who have gone forth to welcome the task and problems of life with feet that were swift and souls that were jubilant.

"Eternal God, Searcher of hearts, from whom no thought can be hid, if in any way we have done injury to this University, if we have misunderstood its ideal or misused its gifts, if we have tainted its good name by false pride, or narrowed its high spirit by prejudice and jealousy, or if we have betrayed its confidence by unworthy ambition, we beseech thee to accept our penitence and grant us thy forgiveness. . .

NOTES ON THE HARVARD TERCENTENARY

"Grant that each one of us may find a personal reconsecration to all that is fair and true and holy, as we rededicate this University to the years of the Right Hand of the Most High.

"And to thee, O God, be the glory, world without end. Amen."

During the early forenoon members of the Associated Harvard Clubs, many of them fresh in New England for the most important meeting of that organization since the founding in 1897, signed names and collected badges under a temporary marquee in the mall in front of the Harvard Club of Boston. They were out in Cambridge by ten or ten-thirty, and thereupon joined the departing congregation from the Church to find their pick of seats in the great theatre to which their red tickets admitted them. Gray skies meant nothing. It could not rain. It was a day of reunion, of renewal — of revision, even. Many of these men had not been in Cambridge since they were graduated before the War, before two wars; before change had raised so white a spire above the elms, had reared so huge a library, strung so high a fence, or pushed the frontiers of the green Yard down to the river. It was a family day; a day of youth (and not a little sentiment) returned. It was a day of old associations, "hoping for Kitty or Copey or Bliss." [15] *Salvete omnes!*

---

[15] Laurence McKinney '12, in the Tercentenary Graduates' issue of *The Lampoon.* The subjects, of course, were Professors *Emeriti* George Lyman Kittredge '82, Charles Townsend Copeland '82, and Bliss Perry, Litt.D. '25 — all three alive at the time.

> How many years? Why it's over twenty, —
>   We have seen triumphs and treaties go —
> We have come back through want and plenty
>   Looking for scenes that we used to know —
> Gone from the Yard is the Class Day fountain,
>   The Graduate gropes in a strange abyss
> Seeking a landmark, a reckoning mountain,
>   Hoping for Kitty or Copey or Bliss.
>
> Gone the sarcophagus known as Gore —
>   The Library's longer and Widener now —
> The Appleton Chapel stands no more,
>   The Frog Museum is changed — and how!
> Houses have bloomed on the river's brim —

The long gonfalons of red and yellow filled in the occasional breeze; heraldic devices [16] of Lowell, Dunster, Winthrop, Kirkland, Eliot; of Law, Divinity, and Medicine, delighted the modern crusader's eye. The gold lions of John Harvard's Emmanuel stood upright on their white poles. The seats filled rapidly. On the camouflaged platforms erected in the trees — camera, wire, and sound stood ready. The golden weather vane on the Church shifted uneasily. Notables, Dignitaries, Delegates, Officials in morning dress, found their places on the stage. People on the fringe kept drifting in. As amazing as anything else, one thought: that this great sea of life and color walled in to itself could become so utterly remote from the rest of the Yard of which it was now the heart.

> Clear from a far and glowing break of day,
> Harvard, you speak. . . .
> Once more, the wilderness? And a new world?

Eleven o'clock: a simmering quiet . . . the crown-and-pennant weather vane shifted again. . . . Three hundred years! The Reverend Minot Simons '91 ascended the tribune and pronounced the Invocation. Dr. Elliott C. Cutler '09, President of the Associated Harvard Clubs, thereupon called the Meeting to order:

"Mr. President and Fellows of Harvard College, Mr. President

> But what in the name of Conant is this? —
> And what is *that* architectural whim?
>   We'll have to ask Kitty or Copey or Bliss.
>
>   . . . .
>
> Baker is gone to a heavenly setting —
>   And Neilson fled to a flock of femmes,
> The ghost of Wendell we know is getting
>   A gorging of hot conversational gems.
> The crinkled smile on the Dean's kind face is
>   Gone with a myriad smiles we miss;
> So please, dear God, don't fill the places
>   Quite yet of Kitty and Copey and Bliss.

[16] These and other ornaments after the design of Pierre la Rose '95, were part of the decorative setting designed by the late Charles A. Coolidge '81 and his partner, Henry R. Shepley '10, architects of the Tercentenary Theatre.

and Members of the Board of Overseers, Your Excellency the Governor of the Commonwealth, our Host the Harvard Club of Boston, distinguished and honored Guests, Gentlemen of Harvard, Ladies: I now call this gathering to order. Lest there be some doubt as to why I, whose life is spent in hospitals, should preside today, let all recall that a doctor is usually present at birth, and I come to you as a physician to initiate this Tercentenary occasion in its first steps.

"We meet today as part of a great session to honor the Universities of the World, to acclaim the value to humanity of the scholarly and inquisitive mind, to uphold free speech, and in particular to do service again to Harvard University. Nothing created by man has had a more vigorous, useful, and prolonged existence than the universities. They have had their ups and downs; political, social, and religious upheavals have pushed them from their forward course, but always they have returned to assume their certain duty — the grouping together of students and teachers to inquire, to investigate, to study for the benefit of mankind.

"No graduate ever repays in any sense his obligation to the university that assisted his awakening spirit, so that this great gathering can be taken as another gesture of our Alumni expressing their gratitude and devotion to Harvard. That Harvard has grown in size and has assumed a leading role in the destinies of our people should make us very happy, and that these, our distinguished colleagues, have gathered from the ends of the earth to assist us on this occasion should emphasize to each and every graduate both his good fortune in being an element of Harvard, and his desire to be of greater service to the Harvard of the future.

"The Associated Harvard Clubs was formed by an ardent band of Harvard graduates in 1897 in the middle western states. The spirit of the pioneer has helped its personnel to a deep devotion to Harvard. As President of the Associated Harvard Clubs for this year I preside today, and now have the pleasure of calling upon our Regional Vice-Presidents for a report of the greetings they bring to

Harvard from the clubs within their district. Will the delegates of the respective clubs please rise and stand during the presentation of their greetings by their Vice-President."

The delegates of the respective clubs each rose in turn as the Regional Vice-Presidents [17] presented greetings to Harvard amid much applause.

Dr. Cutler then introduced President Conant, and the audience rose in spontaneous applause. For many it was the first intimate glimpse of this graduate of the Class of 1914, the internationally known young chemist who had succeeded President Lowell in 1933, becoming the twenty-third holder of Harvard's highest office. Mr. Conant ascended the tribune almost as if aware of this. The crowd fell doubly silent. He began to speak clearly and without effort, his voice and sharp enunciation carrying, as through previous and impending speeches, to the outer edges of the crowd. He welcomed the Associated Harvard Clubs to Cambridge: "The future of this republic will be affected in no small measure by what you think and by what you believe. . . . At this time of our celebration Harvard men might well look backwards not only at Harvard's history but at three centuries of human activity. . . . If we can learn anything from such history it is surely that in the past patience and courage have won victories for the life of the spirit. Can we believe that in the future it will be otherwise?" This in extract; but the full conclusion of President Conant's remarks is important here for two episodes of sentiment on which it turns:

[17] New England: Thorvald S. Ross '12; Eastern, H. V. Blaxter '05; South Central, Ralph H. Hallett '04; Southern, Harold Bush-Brown '11; Central, W. O. Batchelder '05; West Central, Philip Little, Jr. '09; Southwest Central and Southwestern, Fermor Spencer Church '21; North and South Pacific and the Orient, Rudolph Altrocchi '08; Canadian, Herbert L. Sanborn '08; European, F. Herman Gade '92. The collected greetings filled fifty-six typescript pages, and their tenor of devotion and homage is reflected in this sentence from the Harvard Club of Western Pennsylvania: "Your spirit is ever conscious of the amazement of the questioning stars, the ceaseless challenge of events, the inexhaustible appetite for adventure; and as your faith, your confidence, and your hope are ever strong and enduring, you will always wear the crown of immortality."

"And now I shall seal a package which will be placed in the Harvard archives to be opened in the fall of 2036. This package contains letters from some of the officials of the University addressed to their successors a hundred years later and certain material collected by the Director of the Tercentenary Celebration."

The package was then handed to President Conant by David M. Little '18; and with proper ceremony and some adhesion difficulty this was sealed by him, to be opened by the President of Harvard University in 2036 (and not before). Mr. Conant continued:

"As you all know, President Quincy sealed a package of letters a hundred years ago and wrote on the outside of the package in his own hand the following inscription:

Letters from Alumni of Harvard College written in August 1836; responding to the invitation of the Committee of Arrangements for the Centennial [*sic*] Celebration commemorative of the foundation of that institution.

To be opened by the President of Harvard College in the year 1936 and not before.

Pursuant to Josiah Quincy's directions, I had the privilege of opening this package at the small meeting of the Alumni Association held in the Faculty Room of University Hall on September 8 this year. An inspection of the contents showed that the package contained, indeed, letters from the Alumni of Harvard College and, unfortunately, nothing else. The letters from the Alumni have been examined by our official historian, Professor Morison, and he will publish a report in a few days. I have been permitted by him to quote from certain sections of his summary. In the first place, Professor Morison points out that although the package may have been closed in 1836 it could not have been sealed until 1844, as the seal used was the one adopted by the Corporation on December 30, 1843. This seal was the first actual die ever cut with *Veritas* on the books. I have just used this same, identical seal in closing the package which is to be opened one hundred years hence. Mr. Morison reports that in the package sealed by Quincy there were 436 letters from the Alumni of which about sixty per cent were acceptance of Mr. Winthrop's invitation to attend the Bicentennial meeting. A number of these letters are of interest because of the autographs,[18] and others are interesting because of the contents. Time permits me to read only a few. One of the most striking and optimistic is that of the Reverend Peter Eaton of the Class of 1787, minister of West Boxford, who wrote as follows of his Alma Mater:

As a literary institution she stands preëminent; but, a combined effort has been made by religious intolerance to crush her. Although this effort has been successful in diminishing her numbers; she still lives and flourishes. I put a persuasion, as knowledge is increased, free inquiry indulged, (in which, she leads in the march,) as truth is more clearly displayed to view, from ye rubbish in which it has been buried, she will assume her former prominence, for "great is the truth and strongest of all things." Its progress is hard, for it has to encounter early education prejudice, ignorance, the pride of party; yet its triumph is, ultimately, certain. That Harvard may live & flourish — the day rendered pleasant to her Sons, is the sincere desire & prayer of your humble servant

P. Eaton

"Samuel Atkins Eliot of the Class of 1817, who was later Treasurer of Harvard College, writes about certain arrangements for the celebration which he had agreed to undertake for President Quincy, and apologizes for his lateness in attending to the matters because of the serious illness of his two-year-old boy. As Professor Morison remarks in his report: 'It was lucky for Harvard that this baby recovered, for his name was Charles William Eliot.'

"It is comforting to know that among the Harvard Alumni of one hundred years ago there were those who wished to enter a protest. It has, apparently, always been a characteristic of Harvard College that among its graduates one can count on an ample number of critics. As a representative of this important branch of the Harvard

---

[18] Four are those of Francis Parkman, Class of 1807; Edward Everett 1811; Ralph Waldo Emerson 1821; and Wendell Phillips 1831.

family one hundred years ago, I may put forward a gentleman from Philadelphia who wrote as follows:

> Excuse me for this frank expression of my feelings. I owe nothing to the President, professors and tutors of Harvard College in office from A D 1810 to A D 1814.

"But almost all the replies were in a different vein, and although Harvard individuality is shown by the language (no two replies being alike), the general sentiment is perhaps summed up by Samuel Wragg of the Class of 1790, of Charleston, who concluded his letter with this sentence:

> May the Sons of Harvard University celebrate her centenial [*sic*] anniversaries to the end of time, each celebration witnessing her encreasing prosperity and reputation.

With this sentiment which we are glad to echo on this occasion, I conclude my report on the contents of the package sealed by President Quincy.

"In addition to this package [continued the President] there has been reposing in the Harvard archives for one hundred years another object of perhaps even greater interest to this gathering this morning. The last speaker at the alumni meeting on 8 September 1836 was Josiah Quincy Jr., Class of 1821, vice-president (of the celebration) in the chair. He began his address with these words: 'The occasion and the place on which we are now assembled, connect us with the past and the future.' Referring then to the fact that none of his hearers would be present at the Tercentenary Celebration, and that even the memory of a great majority would have perished, he said:

> [But] it is a boon [for us] to be permitted to see, even with the eye of the imagination, that promised land which we may not enter. Creatures of a day, it is delightful to multiply our associations with that distant time. In this spirit, the banner that floats over us had been prepared. It will be deposited among the archives of the University. Our

hope is, that a century hence it will collect under its folds the Alumni of Harvard. Over what a scene will it on that day display its blazonry! What a feeling of relationship will it establish between that age and the present!

"That banner, Gentlemen, which was deposited indeed in the archives of the University, is now ready to be raised over this gathering of the Alumni of Harvard. Dr. Cutler, will you raise the flag!"

Dr. Cutler issued a brief command. The old flag, gray-white against the dull sky, shook out of its century folds as it was slowly raised by Charles H. Watkins '09. It hung lifeless in the still air, but its meaning was alive.

"Gentlemen," concluded the President, "the hope of a hundred years ago has been fulfilled."

Threat of rain, but no rain fell. Music — "Ten Thousand Men of Harvard" — followed by three undergraduate addresses: Rendigs Thomas Fels '39, of Cincinnnati, "Freshman Life in the Yard Today;" Norman Lee Cahners '37, of Bangor, "The Changing Aspect of Harvard Athletics;" Edward Oehler Miller '37, of St. Louis, "The Undergraduate of Today." Edward Miller, last of the three to speak, said in part — and in example of the modern undergraduate mind at work:

"Prominent among the changed attitudes of the undergraduate today is a marked increase in social responsibility. The inertia implied in resignation to a system of laissez-faire is being challenged by a scientific search for that form of society most conducive to the common good. The undergraduate's zeal for earning a living is being replaced by a desire to participate intelligently in later civic activities.

"In this increased sense of undergraduate social responsibility, Harvard has shown that she must avoid aloofness from the outer world. She has, with fluctuations, been a dominating force in the past in national and international affairs. Today she is trying earnestly to face the new problems which have arisen. We may confidently predict that, in doing so, she will avoid the evil of attempting to teach her future social leaders what to think, instead of how to think. . . .

"Another change in the undergraduate of today is his attitude toward extra-curricular activities. He does not, in general, feel that a crowded social and extra-curricular calendar is necessarily a mark of distinction, or of collegiate success. More and more, he is choosing his extra-curricular activities to supplement his college training as a whole — to suit him better for his later, more practical life. . . . This is a tendency that is becoming more and more pronounced. It indicates the undergraduate's feeling that extra-curricular activities should be treated as a means to a chosen end, rather than as an ultimate end in themselves.

"These are some of the more important consequences of the recent changes in the social and academic life of Harvard College. Other accomplishments, equally important, might be mentioned, but there still remains much to be done. Consider, for example, the House Plan. The Houses, equipped with ample libraries, comfortable common rooms, billiard rooms, squash courts, and music rooms, to say nothing of the dining halls which offer the most valuable means of acquaintance, have been of great value in giving purpose to the undergraduate's scholastic pursuits. He is now made to feel, by his very surroundings, that he is part of a vast intellectual activity, and that even his recreation may be directed toward the common goal. They make him realize his increased social responsibility. But, although the Houses have been a true blessing to undergraduate life, they have fallen short of their goal in several respects. Instead of integrating the College into one great whole, they have tended to break it up into separate units. They have restricted friendships, to a great extent, to members of the same House. Paradoxical as it may seem, the Houses might well serve to integrate the College as a whole, if more individual House spirit were developed. For a developed House spirit would lead to an increase in competition between the Houses — and such wholesome rivalry would tend to bring the diverse parts of the College together. . . .

"A conspicuous characteristic of the past decade is a growing feeling of intimacy on the part of the young generation with their elders. In the College, this has revealed itself in an ever-increasing desire among the students to have more personal acquaintance with the members of the faculty. The Houses, where faculty and students may dine together, have done a good deal toward meeting these demands, but much is still desired by the students. The older members of the faculty, with large courses and heavy administrative duties, as well as with the guidance of graduate students and with their own research work, have too little time for personal contact with the undergraduates. This represents one of a very few instances where the College has not succeeded in adapting itself to the changed spirit of its new generation. Through the increased coöperation of both the faculty and the undergraduate members, the Houses must be utilized to the fullest as educational no less than as social units, for only thus can Harvard College's future be planned and ultimately determined, by the mutual efforts of students and teachers. . . .

"The undergraduate of today is gratified at the great measure of freedom which the college authorities now allow him. The effect of this freedom on the student is his assumption of a large share of the responsibility for his own education. And it is safe to predict that this freedom will be no less when the College celebrates its four-hundredth birthday. Harvard has had a brilliant past. The recent developments show that Harvard, aware of the great changes that are taking place in the society of which she is a part, is prepared, now as always, to furnish that intellectual leadership which has invariably been her glory. . . ."

64

NOTES ON THE HARVARD TERCENTENARY

Looking back to the 250th Celebration in 1886, we find Dr. Oliver Wendell Holmes looking forward to our own 300th. He is looking, of course, in autocratic verse (of the order of 450 lines):

> So when the third ripe century stands complete,
> As once again the sons of Harvard meet,
> Rejoicing, numerous as the sea-shore sands,
> Drawn from all quarters, — farthest distant lands . . .
> These tinkling lines, oblivion's easy prey,
> Once more emerging to the light of day,
> Not all unpleasing to the listening ear
> Shall wake the memories of this bygone year. . . .

But further back than such days of "reckless and swaggering prosperity," as James Russell Lowell viewed Dr. Holmes's time, went Hermann Hagedorn '07 in his Tercentenary Ode [19] here quoted in part:

HARVARD, WHAT OF THE LIGHT?

Light is not light, that lights the mind alone.
Clear from a far and glowing break of day,
Harvard, you speak: "Light is not light, that lights
Only a part, with cold moon-brightness, leaving
The rest to darkness and the whole to the storm.
Light, that is light, is light for the whole man."
Oh, light, complete, creative, shining, kindling!
Flame in the mind, flame in the heart, white flame
Upreaching infinitely to white flames,
Austere, obedient in their ordered gyres:
The light you bore, the light that bore you, Harvard!

Three hundred years, Harvard, three hundred years!
Out of your light, like fiery birds upspringing,

[19] Both the Ode and the Phi Beta Kappa Poem were to be given by Robert Frost '01, who withdrew because of illness. At Commencement, 1937, Frost received from Harvard the degree of Litt.D.

Runners, runners, with torches! The wilderness upreared,
Monstrous, with talons raised. The wilderness, blinded,
With head averted, withdrew.

Out of your light, Harvard,
A fire on the hearth, a lamp on the hill, a crackling
Beacon, proclaiming to darkness, the deathless
Creator of light!

Out of your light,
Brave hearts, large minds! Out of your light, heroic,
Indomitable souls! Forerunners, captains, upholders!
Rebels and sages! Prophets! Breakers of idols!
Delvers in darkness! Watchers by lonely headlands!
Contrivers of magic! Summoners of the invisible!
Kindlers of fires!
Out of your light, Harvard!

Out of your light,
Cities and states! Out of your light, resounding
Bells in high towers! White beams, exploring the hidden
Interstices of electrons, the secret
Vagaries of stars!
Out of your light, light! Out of your faith, faith!
Out of your love, the open hand, the outstretched
Encompassing pity. Out of your listening spirit,
A word, a way! Out of your hushed obedience,
Harvard, a new world! . . .

With appropriate ceremony, and to "keep alive to future genera-
tions the wit, the love, the holiness, of his face," a bust of the late
Dean Le Baron Russell Briggs '75 was unveiled by his grandson,
L. B. R. Briggs 3rd, and presented to the University by Professor

NOTES ON THE HARVARD TERCENTENARY

Joseph H. Beale '82 in behalf of a few of the Dean's legion of friends. It has since been placed in the Faculty Room of University Hall.

Presentation to Harvard of the Chinese stone Dragon, gift of the Harvard Alumni in China, was made by Fred C. Sze '18, President of the Harvard Club of Shanghai. Many of the audience on their way to the southwest theatre gate had paused to observe it in its present location just off the path along the west side of Widener and in front of Boylston Hall.[20] To the occidental eye it appears half tortoise, half dragon, towering twenty feet, supporting on its back a black stone tablet in which is cut in beautiful Chinese characters the appropriate oriental dedication. A monument out of the Ch'ing Dynasty (1796–1821), it was originally presented by the Emperor to a Governor of his provinces. President Sze, in a graceful and moving speech, concluded with a quotation of an ancient Chinese poet:

> Take this not as a fair repayment
> But as a pledge of enduring love.

Dr. Masaharu Anesaki, Delegate of the Imperial Academy of Japan, and one of the sixty-two recipients of honorary degrees on September 18, presented the University with a Japanese stone lantern,[21] unveiled in front of the platform. This lantern, "of nearly the same age as Harvard, perhaps a little younger," was placed in the garden of the Fogg Art Museum. It stands about six feet high, and was selected by Baron Ino Dan of Tokyo, a Harvard graduate student, '18–'19. To the Japanese a lantern "symbolizes light, the light that dispels the darkness of illusion, and it is dedicated everywhere in Japan to the deities of earth, or to the souls to be loved, or to . . . spirits of the mountains, forests, rivers, and gardens." It symbolizes here "our sense of admiration of *veritas*," said Dr.

[20] Boylston Hall at the time contained the Harvard-Yenching Institute and the Chinese-Japanese Library.
[21] Gift of the Harvard Club of Japan.

Anesaki. "May it . . . serve as a link of affection and gratitude binding us to Harvard forever."

There followed then a stirring tribute to Harvard from non-Harvard men, delivered by Dr. Stephen Duggan, Professor of Political Science at the College of the City of New York and Director of the Institute of International Education. After addressing his audience, he turned from the speaker's lectern in the Tercentenary tribune to hand President Conant a letter "together with a check for five thousand dollars and a list of those who have joined in this greeting." No individual subscription to that gift was permitted to exceed fifty dollars; and "we whose names are subscribed to this message," said Dr. Duggan in behalf of his fellow contributors, "may assume to speak not only for ourselves but for a vast number of men and women who, like ourselves, have been reminded by this celebration of the incalculable services which our colleges and universities render to our civilization."

More music: "Tercentenaria" by the Harvard band; clouds lowering in the sky; the great weather vane idle and unprophetic. And then John Harvard came a step nearer the present when Dr. Cutler introduced Dr. Thomas S. Hele, Master of Emmanuel College, Cambridge, and Delegate from our Mother University: "But in the University of Cambridge we do not only remember John Harvard, John Cotton, Thomas Hooker and those other thirty Emmanuel men, but we remember also Dunster of Magdelene, Eliot of Jesus, Norton of Peterhouse, Chauncy and Winthrop of Trinity, and we do not forget the men from Oxford. . . ."

Dr. Cutler announced the election of officers of the Associated Harvard Clubs for the year 1936–1937: Mackey Wells '08, the new President,[22] received from him the President's Cup. The band played "Fair Harvard," which the audience sang, and the first of the great meetings of the Celebration was over.

There followed a luncheon in Memorial Hall given by the sev-

[22] Secretary, Nathan Pereles Jr. '04; Treasurer, Clarence B. Randall '12.

eral Faculties in honor of the Delegates; a buffet luncheon for the Associated Harvard Clubs in the Memorial Hall Delta Pavilion; luncheon for ladies, in Sever Quadrangle; for alumni, in various rooms of Hollis, Stoughton, and Holworthy — headquarters, as at Commencement, of returning classes; luncheon in the Houses for Undergraduate Delegates. A single but important ceremony: dedication of the new Eliot Gate on Quincy Street (north of the Dudley Gate and opening on the grounds of the President's house). A gift of the Class of 1908, John Richardson '08 made the presentation. This gate completes the final link in the iron fence which encloses the Yard. On one side of it is cut

IN MEMORY OF

CHARLES WILLIAM ELIOT

1834–1926

Given by the Class of 1908

On the other side, the final lines in the Henry James biography of the true Olympian:

HE OPENED PATHS FOR OUR CHILDRENS FEET TO FOLLOW

SOMETHING OF HIM WILL BE A PART OF US FOR EVER

At 4 P.M. the second Symphony Concert was given in Sanders Theatre. The series concluded [23] in Symphony Hall on Friday evening at 9 P.M., when the orchestra was assisted by a Harvard and Radcliffe Chorus.

Evening: celebration continues: (*Salvete omnes!*). A dinner was given by the Council of Radcliffe College in honor of the Delegates

---

[23] President Conant's last official Tercentenary word was uttered toward the close of this concert, when he went to the stage and said to Dr. Koussevitzky: "You and the members of the orchestra have given so much pleasure to the guests of Harvard during the past three days, that I venture to intrude at this point . . . to say just two words: 'Thank you.' "

of the Colleges for Women. The Harvard Chapter of Phi Beta Kappa held in Sanders Theatre its meeting postponed from Commencement week: Professor Bronislaw Malinowski, Delegate from the London School of Economics and Political Science and recipient of the degree of Doctor of Science on the following day, was the orator. Associate Professor [24] Robert Hillyer '17 read the poem. From 9 to 11 P.M. in the Isabella Stewart Gardner Museum in Boston the Trustees of the Museum gave a reception in honor of the University and its guests, the Delegates from other Universities, Colleges, and Learned Societies.

But the public of Greater Boston will remember Thursday for the nine o'clock display of fireworks and illumination of the Charles River. A phantom census, which has never failed to supply the newspapers with accurate figures of parade and demonstration attendance, said that "350,000 people jammed their way into positions on both sides of the Charles between the Anderson and Weeks bridges as well as on the bridges." In the memory of one spectator this seems for once a wilful tabloid understatement: 3,500,000 is more nearly correct. But whatever the number, alumni and the public got the University's money's worth. Under clearing skies, rain seemed a thing remote. The cosmic scene-shifters were doing their best. But for us? . . . *In cælo quies.* . . . Be that as it may, they were quiet enough until one of two barges starting from the West Boston bridge in the wake of secular tugs suddenly shot the night with fire in a mighty brilliance of bursting stars and miniature comets. For two hours, at an acceleration of from two to six a minute, mine after mine was twice exploded — once on the powder barge and then in the local stratosphere. The second barge bore on its prow a plaster cast of John Harvard and was trimmed with Japanese lanterns. Members of the Harvard band were also on board, but the honors for sound lay heavily on the side of the aerial bombs. Noise and light continued terrific. Flooded by thick color

[24] Boylston Professor of Rhetoric and Oratory, 1937–1945.

of red fire along its banks, the river shone like the crater of some equatorial volcano. It was Harvard's show for the public who could not attend the alumni festival. The Friday newspapers waxed rhapsodic: "The earth seemed to shake . . . after the deafening bursts of the bombs; and green, gold, and orange streaked the blackness, poised for a moment high in the sky . . . then floated slowly downward to fall hissing into the many colored waters." . . . "Continual cheers from a crowd whose size was almost as impressive as the scene." . . . "Not the arrival of the President, not the climactic finale when President Conant makes his speech . . . can touch this scene tonight for almost incredible pictorial beauty." So much for the press and for the fact.

The fireworks ended with a *Veritas* set piece — more modest, we may be surprised to discover, than the display at the 250th Celebration when in Jarvis Field there was "a representation of the statue of John Harvard, *standing in the midst of a gorgeous temple.*" But like that festival, the 1936 show was capped by a torchlight parade which passed singing and cheering up Boylston Street to the Yard, to the real statue (cheers), to the President's House (more cheers), and to a pop concert and dance in Memorial. *In cœlo quies* — and still the chance of rain.

V

The weather forecast [25] for Friday, September 18, was issued

[25] RAIN CHECK: A post-Tercentenary letter to Jerome D. Greene from Charles F. Brooks, Professor of Meteorology and Director of the Blue Hill Observatory, records an exciting weather drama, and shows how carefully the meteorological factor was considered in deciding to hold the Friday morning exercises as originally scheduled: *"For* rain, was the inexorable and increasing rate of advance of the hurricane, centered Friday morning close to the Virginia Capes and moving northward. *Against* rain, was the steady high pressure here, the high and rising pressure and dry air on Mt. Washington, and the well-known tendency of morning sunshine to weaken cyclonic rainfalls. I have never known a more difficult problem in weather forecasting, nor, while successful, seen an important forecast coming so close — a matter of only a quarter of an hour — to failure. You saw how it poured just after

Thursday evening by the Blue Hill Meteorological Observatory as "cool and overcast, no rain." (Sighs of relief.) In the Friday morning paper (late city edition) the tone had become more pessimistic: "Cloudy today, followed by rain tonight and tomorrow." No one cared about "tomorrow." Some 200 Tercentenary Aids and Marshals went to their windows early, fingered silk hats and looked out: Very doubtful. By 8.30, when most of them were arriving at University Hall to receive their red and silver batons, a few drops were actually falling. It fell intermittently during the early forenoon, but not hard enough by 9.30 o'clock to call for a rain programme. It may be, as Donne says, that

> We are scarce our fathers' shadows cast at noon,

but it shall not be said of that ineluctable morning that any son of Harvard was afraid of the elements.

In what is always designated as the *old* Yard [26] the alumni procession began to form at 9.30. Bugles blew then for Assembly; for "Ready" at 9.40; for "March" at 9.45. Charles Francis Adams '88, was Chief Marshal of the Day; Joseph R. Hamlen '04, Deputy Chief Marshal; G. Peabody Gardner Jr. '10, Chief Aid; and Henry C. Clark '11, Chief Flag Marshal. Flags for all living College Classes and for the Graduate Schools had been placed in advance in their designated sockets round the complete inner quadrangle bounded

---

the end of the procession got into Widener! The rainfall of the storm, practically ending at 3 the next morning, was 3.40 inches in Cambridge and 5.78 inches at Blue Hill (B. H. was closer to the center)."

The specific forecast for Friday morning was given over the telephone to President Conant (9.37 A.M., E.D.S. time) by Salvatore Pagliuca, Chief Observer at Blue Hill: "Rain will be light and intermittent until 12 noon. Increasing thereafter. Less than 0.1 inch (probably 0.05 to 0.06 inch rain in Cambridge by 12 noon). No downpour before noon." President Conant asked if this could be "guaranteed." Mr. Pagliuca said that it could.

The Blue Hill verification record justifies that guarantee: "Intermittent light showers began at 8.03 A.M., E.D.S. time, at Blue Hill, giving a total of 0.08 inch rainfall by 12.30 P.M. (0.05 inch by 1.00 P.M. in Cambridge)."

[26] The *old* Yard is bounded on the north by Holworthy; south by Wadsworth House; east by University; west by Massachusetts and Harvard Halls.

by Holworthy, University, Grays, and Massachusetts Halls. The Governing Boards, Delegates, Distinguished Guests, and Professors and Associate Professors of the University, assembled in Widener Library; all other officers of Instruction and Administration, between Thayer Hall and the Memorial Church. Undergraduates formed their procession in Sever Quadrangle. Outside in the Square, the umbrella business throve. All areas about the Yard were policed and kept clear of cars. Harvard families, guests and friends of the University began thronging the theatre, spreading newspapers on the wet chairs, opening and closing umbrellas, settling themselves with the greatest fortitude and cheerfulness, by a few minutes past nine. The gates were crowded with arrivals for over an hour.

In the old Yard graduates old [27] and young formed in fours behind their flags, chatting with each other; optimistic, patient, wet. "The manhood and offices they brought hither today seemed masks; underneath we were still boys." It drizzled in spells. Those who had raincoats had two companions under them. Over in the theatre reporters and movie operators climbed to their simian retreats. Telegraph boys ran in and out with copy. Somewhere in the crowd the President's secret service men from Washington mixed themselves into the assembly. Streamers and gonfalons hung motionless and held fast to their primary colors. The outlook for the possibility of rain had changed to an outlook for the possibility of cessation. And from time to time there were lulls — readjusted collars, reshaken hats, and reorganization of self against September weather.

The parade started, not many minutes late, with a lift of flags and jovial, undampened spirit. The band played, feet stamped, collars were buttoned tighter, handkerchiefs appeared; men talked again like undergraduates as the moving classes passed the waiting.

---

[27] Of the youngest we do not know the names; but the names of two elders we know and record: Henry Munroe Rogers '62, oldest living graduate of the College; and John Torrey Morse Jr. '60, sole survivor of the oldest living College Class. In the procession these men marched directly behind the Chief and Deputy Chief Marshals.

They seemed to take endless minutes circling the old Yard to enter by the Tercentenary gate past the battery of relentless lens and un-reeling film and into the swarming humanity gathered for the climax. But once in, things moved fast enough; for while the last and youngest classes were still finding seats and the audience rose and clambered upright on its chairs straining for a view, the doors of Widener opened and the academic procession began to descend the steps. An anxiously awaited moment! Down they came in twos, headed by President Lowell and President Conant, moving in measure through the parted Cambridge sea and the Marshals in a double wall of flags, to proceed directly to their places on the stage — behind the tribune and to the right and left. Rain fell upon them in gusty release. Dignitaries, Delegates, Judges, Ministers, Officers, Faculty. "Like moving day in the ark," as some wag has put it since; but exciting-solemn on that day, and wonderful alike for academic color and for the crowd in "veneration of their visible images," as Pater elsewhere said. Such living drama was utterly new to the majority, who had not seen the earlier pageant in the Delta. It seemed new even to those who had. Down they went. We saw them ascend the stage. Under the pillars of the Church they settled finally like a flock of iridescent birds.

The wet weather had also turned cold. In the front rows, after stacking their flags in two flower-like clusters bordering the tribune, the Marshals retired under the smaller and less reliable trees. Rain fell into silk hats during prayer, or was shaken from the leaves whenever a breeze came up. As the end of the academic procession arrived on the platform and the audience rustled into a prelude of repose, the alert observed that Franklin D. Roosevelt '04, President of the United States, had slipped in from the back to his seat, front center. Others remarked the fact, and then the audience was on its feet in first applause. It was the Boston *Herald*, referring to this moment, which reported that "the rain spattered upon him with as much abandon as if he were a Republican." And "the world scholars," said the Boston *Globe* . . . "must have been impressed . . . by the informality with which the President of the United States took a seat and sat through the exercises . . . as though he were just one more of the many distinguished men upon the platform."

The University Marshal rose to make some magical prediction, and immediately the air was filled with a peal of bells transmitted across the Atlantic from the Tower of Southwark Cathedral. In a generation all but impossible to astonish, few of those assembled can have escaped some feeling of awe that this singularly moving circumstance could be. For a few minutes the bells rang in honest glory of sound: two worlds as one, John Harvard's land brought home. One listened, but humbly. When at last they faded out, and the Sheriff of Middlesex bright in blue uniform pounded his sword-in-scabbard three times and commanded traditionally: "The Meeting *will* be in order!" — the Meeting *was* in order; and the breach between us and our own American past which we had come to celebrate mysteriously healed.

On the platform, final courtesies were extended: umbrellas offered and refused. Three Presidents sat but a few feet apart declining all such protection; though for a time (on photographic evidence) Mr. Lowell shared the umbrella of Bishop Lawrence. A mushroom growth of Jonas Hanway's unimproved invention sprang up all over that acreage of listeners; most of these umbrellas were black, leaving color to the stage alone. . . . "*Salvete . . . vos certe feminae ornatissimae et venustissimae (quarum pulchritudo pluviae causa umbraculis nunc nimis operta est).*" . . . The rain went on steadily about its business.

Dean Willard L. Sperry, Chairman of the Board of Preachers, pronounced the Invocation. As the bells had drifted in, his words floated off through the tribunal microphone, repeated in two hemispheres. An uncanny business, used to it as one was: Word of John Harvard's God, not now from England to his wilderness, but

75

from his wilderness to England. Following the Invocation the Pope Professor of Latin, E. K. Rand '94 delivered in Latin the Salutatory Oration.

"*SALVETE OMNES!* Praeses magnifice, cum coetu Sociorum et Inspectorum Universitatis Harvardianae, patriae nostrae Praeses illustrissime cum Summorum Conciliorum legatis praeclarissimis, gentium nobis amicissimarum legati primarii, patriae et civitatum et urbium magistratus huiusque civitatis et legati et supreme dux, venerabiles quoque ecclesiarum pastores, accipite vobis debitam salutationem. . . .

"Nunc salutemus etiam mortuos illos immortales qui a parvo collegio condito ad universitatem instauratam magnam doctrinae urbanae et bonae vitae principia velut cursores lampada tradiderunt. . . .

"His igitur ominibus corroborati, non superbo sed pio et humili animo Deum optimum maximum precemur ut hanc universitatem tantae hereditatis nobis commissae haud indignam in nova et meliora semper saecula producat."

Between speeches, the speechless on the platform shifted a little under the weather. Once Mr. Conant was observed to wring the water from the gold tassel of his mortar board (an act preserved in the Tercentenary film). Stoics all! It was only the speaker who experienced momentarily the drier blessing of tribunal escape. "We of the audience [said an editorial philosopher later in the *Harvard Alumni Bulletin*] . . . were drawn together by our shared sense of the nobility of the occasion, not less than by a feeling of pride in our relationship, however humble, to the Harvard family. The ties that united us were almost as tangible as the rain itself, which bound us even more closely, perhaps, than the sun could ever have done.

"We saw the rain beating gustily in so many venerably beautiful faces; we saw it pattering down on rank on rank of grey heads which we knew contained as precious an agglomeration of brains as the world has ever seen gathered in one spot; we saw it splashing and staining their blazing silks and ermine; and — even as we hitched our drab trousers and turned up undistinguished collars about our humble necks — we noted the truly aristocratic disdain with which the demigods on the platform met the dull fury of the heavens. A remarkable demonstration of the power of mind over wet clothes, felt we, and gloried in imitating their noble indifference; pleased, too, in memory of urchin days, at the sight of so many silk hats preparing to meet their makers."

Professor Morison, as the Tercentenary Historian, delivered an address, "The Founding of Harvard College," which concluded: "From the small college here planted 'in sylvestribus et incultis locis,' on the verge of the Western Wilderness, Harvard University has grown, and higher education in the United States is largely derived. So we are gathered here to commemorate our founders and early benefactors; to thank God for the faith, overriding all prudent objections and practical difficulties, that sustained them through poverty and struggle, in so ambitious and so excellent an enterprise." The Tercentenary Chorus [28] sang Gabrieli's *"In Deo Salutari Meo."* His Excellency James M. Curley, Governor of Massachusetts, brought Greetings from the Commonwealth. There followed then a ceremonial tribute by President Conant to our three ancestral Universities: Paris, Oxford, and Cambridge. As the names of these Universities were spoken by him, the Chief Delegate [29] of each arose and was escorted by an Aid to a position side by side in front of, and facing, the President. After receiving in turn from the University Marshal the engraved addresses to each University, President Conant delivered orally their several words and presented them to

[28] At least one member, George W. Wheelwright '90 had also sung (as a freshman) in the Anniversary Chorus of the 250th Celebration, 1886.

[29] Paris: Professor Cartan; Oxford: Vice-Chancellor Lindsay; Cambridge: Dr. Hele.

the three Delegates. It was a mediaeval ceremony, still strangely fresh in the minds of many of that audience.

John Masefield, Litt.D. '18, Poet Laureate of England, and a poet to behold, in slow and enchanting voice read his poem [30] composed for the occasion:

Lines on the Tercentenary of Harvard College in America

When Custom presses on the souls apart,
Who seek a God not worshipped by the herd,
Forth, to the wilderness, the chosen start
Content with ruin, having but the Word.

So these, abandoning the English scene,
As spirit's solitary surety bade,
Ventured the wrath where Christ had never been,
Facing both sea and savage unafraid.

And here, amidst what then was desolation
Of marsh and forest, these prepared and sowed
The spiritual seed-corn of a Nation
For life to harvest, when the Summer shewed.

They were three thousand miles from help of kind,
Supply of tool or skill, support of store;
Their help was certainty within the mind
That, where the danger lurked, God went before.

Yet, when the certainty obscured, when doubt
Staggered the courage and made dumb the call,
When all the chaos of the waste without
Glared at the tired spirit to appal,

[30] Copyright, 1936, by John Masefield. All rights reserved.

Then, to those setters forth, in their despair,
The need was grim for any rallying place,
That might give comfort from God's being there,
Or, if not He, a brightness from His face.

Then they remembered quiet far away,
Quiet and piety and bells in chime,
Among old college dwellings, long gone grey,
Built by the love of learning of old time;

And knew, that as that city had inspired,
Moulded and helped themselves, so they should found
Such blessed seeking-place for truth desired,
There in that thoughtless waste beyond the bound.

So, from their common will, they planned to raise
A spiritual house, that should inure
The white youth and the red youth to God's praise,
That, so, should prosper and be ever sure.

There was a preacher in that little band,
JOHN HARVARD, son of one from Stratford town,
Who may have shaken William Shakespeare's hand;
He, in himself, has title to renown,

For, when he preached, his earnestness would pierce
Beyond the bounded tenement of sense,
Into that living love, forever fierce,
Whose glory makes our stammering eloquence.

And it was he, who, with his dying gift
Of books and money, set this noble vine,
With roots too deep for ignorance to shift,
Its boughs aloft, in light, with living wine.

There is no record of his form and face.
One praised his preaching; little more is known.
He cast the spirit seed-corn of a race,
And died at barely thirty, having sown.

Untimely, to an unrecorded grave,
The unlimned ruins of his body passed;
This living monument of what he gave
Stands builded here in triumph, to outlast.

It has outlasted every other seed
Flung by the men and women of his day,
This excellence, the harvest of his deed,
Being divine, shall never know decay.

His act has brought us here; his dead hand brings
These thousands in his honour and his praise.
Which of our many peopled planet's kings
After three hundred years so surely sways?

In admiration and devote consent
Of gratitude to him, our thousands come
From Asia's age, from this new continent,
From Europe's all, and from his English home.

Would that his human eyes, untimely dead,
Freed from that quiet where the generous are,
Might see this scene of living corn made bread,
This lamp of human hope become a star.

Again the bond with our beginning tightened a little; the spirit perhaps burned brighter. The Poet bowed and withdrew, and the clapping swept away. But even poetry could not entirely dissemble

the blackened character of the sky, though for an hour and a half
— now almost forgotten — there was no rain at all.

The Tercentenary Chorus sang Bach's "Hymn of Praise," and
President Conant ascended the tribune to deliver his oration on
"The University Tradition in America — Yesterday and Tomorrow." Several times in its course he was interrupted by applause;
once, so vigorous that for a minute or more, smiling and vainly
protesting, he was unable to proceed. At the end he received an
ovation. He began on a note of affirmation; and what he said there
is quoted here not quite in full:

"Such a gathering as this could come together only to commemorate an act of faith. This assembly honors a vision three centuries old and in so doing reaffirms an intent of perpetuating an
ideal. A hundred years ago President Quincy, writing of the founding of Harvard, used these words: 'On recurring to the origin of
this seminary, our first feelings impel us to wonder and admire.'
From such admiration grew the celebration of the two hundredth
anniversary; with no less reverential feeling the sons of Harvard
have once again met here to mark the turn of another century.

"The passage of a hundred years has enabled us to see more
clearly the events which occurred between 1636 and the granting
of the charter to the President and Fellows in 1650. Thanks to the
labors of the historians we are able to appreciate more fully than
did Quincy the spirit of the founders and to understand more completely the significance of their bold plan. And with the increase
in our knowledge comes a more than proportional increase in our
admiration. As you have heard, the Puritans' ambition was none
other than to transplant to an untamed forest the ancient university
tradition. They would be satisfied with nothing short of duplicating
here in New England at least one college of Cambridge University.
Carried forward by the strong tide of Puritanism, the enterprise
was at first blessed with almost miraculous success. The goal might

well seem to be in sight when, within twenty years of the founding, Oxford and Cambridge (then in the hands of dissenters, to be sure) recognized the Harvard degree as equivalent to their own. But many changes in both the mother country and the Bay Colony were yet to come. The enthusiasm for education in a new land waned, and even the second President of Harvard complained of those who desired 'to pull down schools of learning, or which is all one to take away the oyl from the lamps, denying or withholding maintenance from them.' The acorn had been planted, the young tree was alive, but its growth was slow beyond the expectation of those who had brought the seed to a wild, new continent.

"In the middle of the last century, in 1867 to be exact, the head of one of the Oxford colleges, an eminent scholar and educational reformer, saw no evidence that the university tradition had ever taken root in the United States. 'America has no universities as we understand the term,' he wrote, 'the institutions so called being merely places for granting titular degrees.' Taken literally this harsh judgment is undoubtedly false, and yet I venture to think that it is not a gross exaggeration of the situation which then existed. The new spirit moving within the educational institutions of this country had not become evident to those outside the academic walls. Another decade was to pass before a university was opened in Baltimore, national in its scope, and proclaiming boldly that 'all departments of learning should be promoted . . . and that the glory of the University should rest upon the character of the teachers and scholars . . . and not upon their number nor upon the buildings constructed for their use.'

"We commemorate today the daring hope of a group of determined men — a hope the fulfillment of which was long delayed; delayed, indeed, until within the lifetime of many now present here this morning. With feelings of gratitude we turn back through three centuries to pay homage to the faith that could see no obstacles and to ideals which are indeed eternal. But the real past which we salute is but yesterday. Harvard, together with all the other universities in this country, stands just beyond the threshold of a new undertaking. It is towards the future of our common enterprise that on this occasion we must direct our gaze.

"The future of the university tradition in America — that is the problem that must concern all of us who are assembled here today. But what is this tradition; indeed, what is a university? Like any living thing, an academic institution is comprehensible only in terms of its history. For well on a thousand years there have been universities in the western world. During the Middle Ages the air they breathed was permeated with the doctrines of a universal church; since the Reformation in Protestant countries these have undergone a slow and varied metamorphosis. But the essence of the university tradition has remained constant. From the first foundations to the present, four main streams have watered the soil on which the universities have flourished. These ultimate sources of strength are: first, the cultivation of learning for its own sake; secondly, the general educational stream of the liberal arts; thirdly, the educational stream that makes possible the professions; and, lastly, the never-failing river of student life carrying all the power that comes from the gregarious impulses of human beings. All four streams are easily discerned bringing life to the English universities in the first half of the seventeenth century. For this reason Oxford and Cambridge flourished; and because they flourished, their sons who migrated to this strange land desired to cultivate the same sturdy tradition even in a wilderness.

"The plans of President Dunster and his collaborators reveal clearly what the university tradition meant to the Anglo-Saxon world of the seventeenth century. Harvard's founders insisted on the 'collegiate way of living,' thus recognizing the importance of student life. They knew the educational values which arise from the daily intercourse between individual students and between student and tutor. Their concept of professional training was, to be sure, largely cast in terms of the ministry, but they envisaged also training in the law and medicine. The liberal arts educational tradition they transplanted *in toto* from the colleges which they had left behind. And finally, their zeal for the cultivation of learning is made evident by the reference in the charter of 1650 to 'the advancement of all good literature, artes and Sciences. . . .'

"Such, it seems to me, was the properly balanced plan of a university in a time when universities were flourishing; such, it seems to me, must be the idea of a university if institutions of higher learning are to fulfill their proper function in the times that are to come. But there have been periods of sickness, even of decay, in the history of almost every academic foundation. If one of the four vital streams I have mentioned either fails or swells to a torrent, thus destroying the proper balance of nourishment, then the true university tradition may perish. The cultivation of learning alone produces not a university but a research institute; the sole concern with the student life produces an academic country club or merely a football team manœuvering under a collegiate banner. On such abnormalities we need not dwell, but I should like to take a few moments to consider the disastrous effects of an overemphasis of either the liberal arts educational tradition or the element of professional training. This is a real danger at all times. For a university nourished exclusively from either one of these two educational streams always seems to the uninformed to be most healthy because they believe it to be most useful.

"Let us consider, first, the situation created when the proper balance is upset by disproportionate concern with general education. In this case the stream of learning and research inevitably dries up; indeed, some have contended that it should. Newman defined his idea of a university as 'a place of teaching universal knowledge, for the diffusion and extension of knowledge rather than the advancement.' In his famous essay he recommended 'a division of intellec-

84

tual labor between learned academies and universities.' (In twentieth century terminology we should substitute the words 'research institute' for 'academy.') He believed that 'to discover and to teach are two distinct functions.' Newman's proposal amounted to eliminating one of the four vital ingredients evident in the life of the universities during their healthy periods. Unconsciously he was reflecting the condition of the English universities as he knew them before 1850 when they were still suffering from the long sleep of the eighteenth century. His proposition was in reality but a concise description of a disease. A few years later a prominent member of his own University, recognizing the condition as pathological, expressed himself in the following words: 'The colleges [of Oxford and Cambridge] were in their origin endowments for the prolonged study of special and professional faculties by men of riper age. . . . This was the theory of the university in the Middle Ages and the design of the collegiate foundations in their origin. Time and circumstances have brought about a total change. The colleges no longer promote the researches of science, or direct professional study. . . . Elementary teaching of youths under twenty-two is now the only function performed by the university, and almost the only object of college endowments. Colleges were homes for the life-study of the highest and most abstruse parts of knowledge. They have become boarding schools in which the elements of the learned languages are taught to youths.' When we read this indictment penned before the completion of the nineteenth century reform of Oxford, we may well ask: If the intellectual division of labor which Newman advocated and which still finds proponents in our time is to be desired, why were the English universities in so unsatisfactory a condition? The accidents of time had destroyed the ancient function of advancing knowledge, and yet the institutions did not flourish.

"As further evidence, listen to what the Royal Commission of inquiry into the condition of Oxford had to say on this subject in 1850: 'It is generally acknowledged that both Oxford and the country at large suffer greatly from the absence of a body of learned men devoting their lives to the cultivation of science and the direction of academical education. . . . The presence of men eminent in various departments of knowledge would impart a dignity and stability to the whole institution, far more effectual against attacks from without than the utmost amount of privilege and protection.' Attacks from without — the phrase has a modern ring. Events proved that the Commission of 1850 was correct in its statement; the changes which they advocated restored the confidence of the nation in its two ancient institutions. They could not foresee, however, the reluctance of certain sections of public opinion to welcome the restoration of the true university tradition. They did not realize how willingly the public often follows those who argue for a separation of teaching and research! No better illustration could be found than an article in the London *Times* published in 1867. The writer endorses the general view that 'the university is mainly a place of education for young men just before they enter upon life and should confine its whole administration to this practical aim.' (Please note the word 'practical'!) 'We are confident,' the article continues, 'that this view is the one from which Englishmen in general regard the universities. It is a growing subject of discontent among the public that the tutors and professors of both Oxford and Cambridge are becoming more and more absorbed in their own scientific pursuits.' And these remarks at the time when the two ancient universities were undergoing that revolution which restored them to health and enabled them to take the position of intellectual leadership which they now enjoy! So shortsighted is often the popular reaction to matters of education. Would the English public today wish to turn back to the years when the professors and tutors rarely yielded, indeed, to the temptation to cultivate sound learning and pursue new knowledge?

"There is comparatively little danger, however, that in the years ahead there will be any effective movement to turn the universities of this country into boarding schools. The cause for apprehension seems to me to lie in a different quarter. Even the most idealistic of those who lead public opinion too often insist on examining educational institutions through the dull glasses of immediate utility. To be sure, the promotion of learning usually appears to be worth saving even when viewed through such an unfavorable medium. The most relentless reformers are at least partially convinced that at some time almost all research may be materially rewarding. There is, however, a growing demand for more and more professional training, and there is a tendency to stretch the word 'profession' until it comprises every vocation. The utilitarian demand for specialized vocational training and the practical man's contempt for useless knowledge go hand in hand. When such influences gain control, an institution of higher learning supplies training, not education, and the promotion of learning is degraded to a vehicle for providing material well-being. The liberal arts conception of a general education disappears and with it the institution's most important contribution to the land. The universities of a country are the sanctuaries of the inner life of the nation. When they cease to be concerned with things of the spirit, they cease to fulfill their most important function.

"If I am correct, then, in my interpretation of academic history, the future of the university tradition in America depends on keeping a proper balance between the four essential ingredients — the advancement of learning, the liberal arts college, professional training, and a healthy student life. None must be neglected; no one must be allowed to predominate unduly. If this balance can be maintained, the universities of this country, privately endowed and publicly supported alike, will function both as instruments of higher education and as centers for developing a national culture worthy of this rich and powerful land. . .

"Those of us who have faith in human reason believe that in the next hundred years we can build an educational basis for a unified, coherent culture suited to a democratic country in a scientific age, no chauvinistic dogma, but a true national culture fully cognizant of the international character of learning. In this undertaking the schools are involved quite as much as the universities, but the latter must lead the way. The older educational discipline, whether we like it or not, was disrupted before any of us were born. It was based on the study of the classics and mathematics; it provided a common background which steadied the thinking of all educated men. We cannot bring back this system if we would, but we must find its modern equivalent. Like our ancestors we must study the past, for 'he who is ignorant of what occurred before he was born is always a child.' In my opinion it is primarily the past development of our modern era which we must study, and study most exhaustively and critically.

"For the development of a national culture based on a study of the past, one condition is essential. This is absolute freedom of discussion, absolutely unmolested inquiry. We must have a spirit of tolerance which allows the expression of all opinions however heretical they may appear. Since the seventeenth century this has been achieved in the realm of religion. It is no longer possible for some bigoted Protestant to object if any person within the universities or without expounds sympathetically the philosophy of St. Thomas Aquinas. It is no longer possible for a member of the Roman Catholic Church to take offense at a critical discussion of Galileo's trial. Statements believed to be erroneous are met openly and fairly by counter arguments. But there is no persecution; there has been an end to religious bigotry in this country, and there are no signs of its return.

"Will the same conditions prevail in the future when political and economic problems are examined? Unfortunately there are ominous signs that a new form of bigotry may arise. This is most serious, for we cannot develop the unifying educational forces we so sorely need unless all matters may be openly discussed. The origin of the Constitution, for example, the functioning of the three branches of the

Federal Government, the forces of modern capitalism, must be dissected as fearlessly as the geologist examines the origin of the rocks. On this point there can be no compromise; we are either afraid of heresy or we are not. If we are afraid, there will be no adequate discussion of the genesis of our national life; the door will be shut to the development of a culture which will satisfy our needs.

"Harvard was founded by dissenters. Before two generations had passed there was a general dissent from the first dissent. Heresy has long been in the air. We are proud of the freedom which has made this possible even when we most dislike some particular form of heresy we may encounter . . .

"The university tradition in this country has been sustained through three centuries by the courage and sacrifice of many men. An ever-increasing number of benefactors have followed John Harvard's example. Patrons of learning have not only favored Harvard with their gifts but have established and aided other universities throughout the nation. In cities and states, institutions have been founded and supported from the public funds. In all our colleges learned men have labored with little material reward to 'advance learning and perpetuate it to posterity.' Teachers of the young have so lived their lives that the coming generations might be inspired with a love of wisdom. All this devotion on the part of those concerned with higher education stands as a clear witness to the significance of what was here envisaged three hundred years ago. He who enters a university walks on hallowed ground. . . .

"During the coming century of academic history what gifts will the American people bring to further this great advance? A hundred years from today the record will be read. With humility but with hope we look forward to that moment. May it then be manifest to all that the universities of this country have led the way to new light, and may the nation give thanks that Harvard was founded."

Music again by the excellent chorus under Professor A. T. Davi-

son: Händel's "Let Their Celestial Concerts All Unite." And following this, the impressively brilliant spectacle of the conferring of
sixty-two honorary degrees. Forethought once more lent mechanical
precision to an aesthetic end. What might have lasted long never
seemed to drag. President Conant read each citation, handed the
diploma (which had been handed to him) to one of four active Aids
who conveyed it to the recipient. The Delegate so honored rose
from his seat in a flash of color, received it, and sat down amid applause. Sixty-two men:[31] the pick of the world's most learned,
recognized elsewhere and before, but here gathered as one body
representing nearly all the important fields under the Arts and
Sciences, for the sole purpose of honoring Harvard and receiving
in turn her highest pronouncement of merit. As the list was read,
and man after man of different race and nation, thought and training, bowed response, the layman leaned obviously to names like
Jung and Eddington; and yet seemed no less cordial in applauding
the scholar of whose reputation he was doubtless politely ignorant.

The list is too long for this account, but a few of President
Conant's citations in the tradition of Commencement may be quoted
in illustration:

EDWARD JOSEPH DENT: Doctor of Music. A professor of Cambridge
University famed for his historical studies of that melodious art which
is the common heritage of all western nations.

SIR ARTHUR STANLEY EDDINGTON: Doctor of Science. A student of the
cosmos who peers within the atom and surveys the expanding universe,
an expounder to the multitude of the poetry of modern science.

WESLEY CLAIR MITCHELL: Doctor of Letters. An American economist
whose influence has extended far, noted for his study of the business
cycles which, despite all efforts, still revolve.

LEOPOLD WENGER: Doctor of Laws. A lawyer deeply versed in the
origins of his profession, a man of learning profound in his knowledge
of the legal systems of antiquity.

[31] None of these men had previously held any Harvard degree.

90

NOTES ON THE HARVARD TERCENTENARY

WERNER WILHELM JAEGER: Doctor of Letters. A critical student of that great master who once dominated the universities, an eminent teacher of the eternal wisdom of Aristotle.

HU SHIH: Doctor of Letters. A Chinese philosopher and historian, the inheritor of the mature wisdom of an old civilization, who guides with courage and understanding the spirit of a new age.

CHARLES GUSTAV JUNG: Doctor of Science. A philosopher who has examined the unconscious mind, a mental physician whose wisdom and understanding have brought relief to many in distress.

KARL LANDSTEINER: Doctor of Science. The master of the science of immunology, the discoverer of those fundamental principles which made blood transfusion possible, saving countless lives.

MICHAEL IVANOVICH ROSTOVTZEFF: Doctor of Letters. The social and economic historian of the Roman Empire, whose fruitful study of antiquity accumulates for all who read centuries of rich experience.

ETIENNE GILSON: Doctor of Letters. An expounder to these chaotic days of the serene and ordered philosophy of the Middle Ages, that great synthesis of faith and reason.

The audience sang properly "O God, Our Help in Ages Past" (Isaac Watts), and after Benediction by Bishop William Lawrence '71, the Meeting concluded — now in a downpour which lasted the rest of the day. One happy corollary not well understood is that Dignitaries, Delegates, and other guests were ushered immediately back to Widener where the Corporation's Ganymede had provided what the *Bulletin* in thin disguise called "comforting nectar." But not to know, of course, was not to envy.

The principal one o'clock luncheons that day were the Chief Marshal's to the Governing Boards and their Guests (Memorial Hall), and that of the Harvard Alumni Association (Memorial Hall Delta Pavilion). Those farthest in kept the driest. It was obvious even then that the Meeting of the Alumni Association scheduled for the Tercentenary Theatre that afternoon would have to be held in Sanders. To lose, at the last minute, the open-air advantage of vividness and size seemed hard. But with apparently no effort the right switches were thrown, the right mechanical changes made, the right notice given, the public address system plugged in for the Memorial Church, Memorial Hall, the New Lecture Hall, Music Building, Jefferson Physical Laboratory, and the Continental and Commander Hotels (by broadcast), where the now divided congress of the morning might convene. As with everything else, the afternoon exercises were also released on the air. One could stay at home and listen.

Sanders Theatre will accommodate some 1,200 people. By two-thirty it was practically filled with an audience admitted only by ticket, and composed largely of Officials, Dignitaries, Delegates, and University guests. Officials and Dignitaries crowded the stage. Such an intimate gathering, after one so vast, bore even closer to the heart of things. President Lowell presiding carried most of us back to another administration. When all tests for the broadcast were completed and the doors locked safely Symphony fashion, the familiar figure rose and went to the lectern. Did a strange thing seem to happen? One almost fancied that he held back for a second as if indrawn by some old reluctance. But "the Greek agility" of his mind, as Professor Morison has called it, must have persuaded him even as he persuaded at once his seen and unseen audience. With the freshening memory of what had transpired that day and for many days before, it was impossible to see and hear him now and remain unmoved. He began in what familiar style! shaking his head characteristically in emphasis:

"As wave after wave rolls landward from the ocean, breaks and fades away sighing down the shingle of the beach, so the generations of men follow one another, sometimes quietly, sometimes, after a storm, with noisy turbulence. But, whether we think upon

92

the monotony or the violence in human history, two things are always new — youth and the quest for knowledge, and with these a university is concerned. So long as its interest in them is keen it can never grow old, though it count its age by centuries. The means it uses may vary with the times, but forever the end remains the same; and while some principles, based on man's nature, must endure, others, essential perhaps for the present, are doomed to pass away.

"Education is as old as man; and many of the arts of life were learned and taught long before any historic record. All the domestic animals we use today were tamed no one knows how long ago; the planting of seed goes back to a past invisibly remote; so do many of the modes of preserving food; and each of these advances must have been carefully taught to children, or they would have perished with their inventor. Teaching cannot be less ancient than the oldest art that ever was transmitted; and with the growth of knowledge it has become more and more important for the public welfare; yet we now know less about it with certainty than of many other arts of later origin.

"The inevitable breakdown of the ancient fixed curriculum, coupled with larger openings for enjoyment, on one side, and on another the vast expansion of knowledge, have raised two of the serious questions of our time. The first has made it hard to impress upon youth the value of scholarship. Apart from a definite, visible application that value has seemed to them difficult to measure — pale as compared with athletic and social achievement. Its significance for the man himself, for the development and attitude of his mind appears so vague, the fact that all real attainment comes by personal effort, — a process of self-education under guidance so contrary to his ideas of how teachers should labor and students absorb, — that it is not easy to make him see these truths.

"Some years ago a class orator [32] remarked that only as they near graduation do students learn what the real object of college is, and

[32] Edward C. Aswell '26.

93

this seemed very unfortunate until we reflect that when they do know it they are educated men. With the problem of inciting scholarly ambition all institutions of higher learning have been wrestling; happily by different means, for there is no single formula for solving it, and all experiments, if judged by their results, are good.

"The vast increase of knowledge has raised obstacles of a different kind for the professors, and for all others bent on contributing to learning. The first result was a division of the field of thought into self-contained sections under separate departments; but that has proved defective because there are no natural barriers to knowledge. It has overflowed and undermined the fences, rushing as a flood across them, and hence the later effort has been to bring the various laboratories, the whole contents of the libraries and the professors themselves into as close contact as possible, so that every man may draw whatever he needs from the great supply.

"A university is, indeed, a thing that moves and grows. In deepest gratitude to its progenitors we recall on this occasion that three hundred years ago Harvard College was born, a brave babe, with only one teacher — the President himself — who at first gave all the instruction, and possessed all the learning, it contained. Now it is one of the great universities of the world; one of the reservoirs and springs of knowledge that, beginning in the Middle Ages, have developed into what they are today.

"The vast learning stored on the shelves of the libraries, and in the minds of all the scholars, in a great university no single man can compass; of the channels leading to new knowledge, one can explore but a small part. The treasures are well-nigh inexhaustible, the opportunities limitless; and open not to the members of the institution alone, but almost for the asking to anyone who has the desire and the capacity to use them. From our forebears, who in less propitious times have taught and labored and hoped here, we have inherited a priceless trust which will be fostered until, as the Arabs say, the stars grow old, the sun grows cold, and the leaves of the judgment book unfold.

"The generation that have now retired, hoping in their own time to have made their contribution, have passed the torch that burns here to you, President Conant, and your colleagues, to bear farther and higher on the way."

Mr. Lowell then introduced President Conant whose remarks rested largely on Harvard's plans for the future and on the Tercentenary Gifts already received.

Mr. Lowell rose again and spoke for perhaps six minutes, glancing once or twice at his watch. It is not likely that many were aware of the identity of the next speaker until his name was pronounced. As though he were in the same room and had himself risen from a seat on the platform, The Right Honourable Stanley Baldwin, Chancellor of the University of Cambridge and Prime Minister of England, responded as Mr. Lowell ceased. His message, for the second time in the celebration, united miraculously the new world and the old. Precise as that electric appointment, his message carried clear:

"As Chancellor of the University of Cambridge it is with special pride that I send greetings to Harvard University on the occasion of its Tercentenary. The Cambridge men from the beginning identified themselves with Harvard; and graduates from Trinity, Emmanuel, and Kings were on the first governing body three hundred years ago.

"Above all, it was an Emmanuel man, John Harvard, who supplied the funds for the outward and visible sign of the new College and his admirably chosen library for its inward and spiritual grace.

"Nor can I forget that it was a graduate of Harvard — his father and grandfather were Cambridge men — who gave his name to Downing Street [33] in which I live.

"May God's providence, which has watched over Harvard since

[33] Sir George Downing, Bart., M.P., Class of 1642.

its first home had to be fenced in to keep out the wolves, continue to bless it, adorned as it now is with magnificent buildings and celebrated throughout the world as a great center of learning.

"May Harvard men remain faithful to the great traditions of liberty which are the common glory and heritage of all the English-speaking people of the world, and may we all, as university men, though we cannot hope for the special fame that is John Harvard's, aspire to be remembered in our time in the moving words applied to him by a contemporary:

" 'The man was scholar and pious in his life, and endeared to the country in life and death.' "

When he had finished speaking, Mr. Lowell replied:

"If a university can have one mother, Cambridge is our mother; for Harvard was founded mainly by her graduates. Six year after landing on these shores our forefathers set up a college, and named the town after the place where they were trained. The University of Cambridge fostered our early days by granting to our degrees equality with her own. From her we have drawn inspiration and example — not least in these latter times. To her sons we owe a vast debt in science and in letters. In the light she has shed we have rejoiced.

"If she be the mother of Harvard, she is, through Harvard, the ancestress of most of the universities and colleges in the United States. It is right that we should turn to her in gratitude this day; and, now when we have prospered, should seek her approbation.

"Therefore, in behalf of the thousands of Harvard graduates here assembled, I thank you for the kind words you have said in bringing to us, on this our three hundredth birthday, the greetings of our parent University."

Following the singing of the Seventh-Eighth Psalm, and a speech by Judge Learned Hand '93, President of the Harvard Alumni Association, Mr. Lowell came forward. "The next speaker it would be impertinent for me to introduce to you, or to any American audience. He is the fourth graduate of Harvard College to hold the office of Chief Magistrate in our nation — two of them named Adams, and two Roosevelt. Gentlemen, The President of the United States!" The audience rose in great applause. President Franklin Delano Roosevelt '04, LL.D. '29:

"I am here today in a joint and several capacity. First, as the President of the United States. Second, as Chairman of the United States Harvard Tercentenary Commission, which is composed of five members of the Senate, five members of the House of Representatives, a representative of the United States Army and one of the Navy, and two representatives of the universities of the United States, the distinguished Presidents of the Universities of California and North Carolina. Finally, I am here as a son of Harvard who gladly returns to the spot where men have sought truth for three hundred years.

"The roots of Harvard are deep in the past. It is pleasant to remember today that this meeting is being held in pursuance of an adjournment expressly taken one hundred years ago on motion of Josiah Quincy.

"At that time many of the alumni of Harvard were sorely troubled concerning the state of the nation. Andrew Jackson was President. On the two hundred and fiftieth anniversary of the founding of Harvard College, alumni again were sorely troubled. Grover Cleveland was President. Now, on the three hundredth anniversary, I am President.

"In the words of Euripides:

> There be many shapes of mystery.
> And many things God makes to be,
> Past hope or fear.
> And the end men looked for cometh not,
> And a path is there where no man sought.
> So hath it fallen here.

"In spite of fears, Harvard and the nation of which it is a part have marched steadily to new and successful achievements, changing their formations and their strategy to meet new conditions; but marching always under the old banner of freedom.

"In the olden days of New England, it was Increase Mather who told the students of Harvard that they were 'pledged to the word of no particular master,' that they should 'above all find a friend in truth.'

"That became the creed of Harvard. Behind the tumult and the shouting it is still the creed of Harvard.

"In this day of modern witchburning, when freedom of thought has been exiled from many lands which were once its home, it is the part of Harvard and America to stand for the freedom of the human mind and to carry the torch of truth.

"The truth is great and will prevail. For centuries that grand old saying has been a rock of support for persecuted men.

"But it depends on men's tolerance, self-restraint, and devotion to freedom, not only for themselves but also for others, whether the truth will prevail through free research, free discussion, and the free intercourse of civilized men, or will prevail only after suppression and suffering — when none cares whether it prevails or not.

"Love of liberty and freedom of thought is a most admirable attribute of Harvard. But it is not an exclusive possession of Harvard or of any other university in America. Love of liberty and freedom of thought are as profound in the homes, on the farms, and in the factories of this country as in any university . . .

"Many students who have come to Harvard in the past have left it with inquiring and open minds, ready to render service to the nation. They have been given much and from them much has been expected. They have rendered great service.

"It is, I am confident, of the inner essence of Harvard that its sons have fully participated in each great drama of our nation's history. They have met the challenge of the event; they have seen in the challenge opportunity to fulfill the end the university exists to serve. As the Chief Executive of the nation I bring you the felicitation of our people. In the name of the American nation I venture to ask you to cherish its traditions and to fulfill its highest opportunities.

"The nation needs from Harvard today men like Charles William Eliot, William James, and Justice Holmes, who made their minds swords in the service of American freedom.

"They served America with courage, wisdom, and human understanding. They were without hatred, malice, or selfishness. They were civilized gentlemen.

"The past of Harvard has been deeply distinguished. This University will never fail to produce its due proportion of those judged successful by the common standard of success. Of such the world has need. But to produce that type is not, I am sure, the ultimate justification that you would make for Harvard. Rather do we here search for the atmosphere in which men are produced who have either the rare quality of vision or the ability to appreciate the significance of vision when it appears.

"Where there is vision, there is tolerance; and where there is tolerance, there is peace. And I beg you to think of tolerance and peace not as indifferent and neutral virtues but as active and positive principles . . .

"Harvard should train men to be citizens in that high Athenian sense which compels a man to live his life unceasingly aware that its civic significance is its most abiding, and that the rich individual diversity of the truly civilized State is born only of the wisdom to choose ways to achieve which do not hurt one's neighbors.

"I am asking the sons of Harvard to dedicate themselves not only to the perpetuation but also to the enlargement of that spirit; to pay ardent reverence to the past but to recognize no less the direction of the future; to understand philosophies we do not accept and hopes we find it difficult to share; to account the service of mankind the highest ambition a man can follow, and to know that there is no calling so humble that it cannot be instinct with that ambition; never to be indifferent to what may affect our neighbor; always, as Coleridge said, to put truth in the first place and not in the second; these, I would affirm, are the qualities by which the 'real' is distinguished from the 'nominal' scholar.

"It is only when we have attained this philosophy that we can 'above all find a friend in truth.' When America is dedicated to that end by the common will of all her citizens, then America can accomplish her highest ideals. To the measure that Harvard participates in that dedication, Harvard will be justified of her effort, her purpose, and her success in the fourth century of her life."

"The Shores of Harvard," by M. A. De Wolfe Howe '87 (music by Holst), previously a part of the Commencement service, was sung by the Tercentenary Chorus. Mr. Lowell then introduced James Rowland Angell, President of Yale University.

"Despite my possession of two Harvard degrees [said Mr. Angell], it is with no little astonishment that, as a simple Vermont Yankee representing conservative Connecticut orthodoxy, I contemplate my temerity in appearing here — *in partibus infidelium*, as it were. It may be a case of fools rushing in where angels should fear to tread. In any case, it is with peculiar pride and gratification that Harvard's eldest daughter, her nearest of kin, is permitted upon this festal occasion to join with all the learned world in singing her praises and in wishing her yet many centuries of invaluable service to mankind. One cannot possibly add anything to this chorus of acclaim, couched in most felicitous phrase, with which for days these halls have been ringing.

"Founded, and in her early years largely guided, by men of Harvard lineage, Yale has always felt herself bound by ties of special intimacy to the parent institution — albeit cherishing at times toward Harvard sentiments of more than doubtful moral elevation, sentiments almost always warmly reciprocated by Harvard. It is not without reason that each speaks of the other as its dearest enemy. But today Yale comes bearing only the olive branch and a garland of bay leaves.

"I cannot quite repress the temptation to pause and pay a purely personal tribute to a group of great Harvard men to whom I shall always stand indebted. I came here as a young man in the early '90's to study under William James, Josiah Royce, and George Herbert Palmer. These brilliant scholars left on my mind an indelible impress, and, together with John Dewey, then at Michigan, gave me the essential *Weltanschauung* with which I have gone through life. I command no words which will adequately convey my obligation to them.

"I have also enjoyed most delightful relations with three eminent Presidents of Harvard. Charles William Eliot offered me my first academic job and at a time when I much needed it. When I came to preside over Yale, President Lowell greeted me in the most generous and cordial manner. During his administration no suspicion of tension between Harvard and Yale ever arose which he and I in frank conference could not quickly banish. Yale could ask no more sincere friend than he. For President Conant, in the few years I have had the pleasure of knowing him, I have come to entertain the most genuine admiration and a very warm regard. In his great address this morning the sturdy and vigorous qualities of his mind and character were in striking evidence. Incidentally I may say that, as I was drawing about me my bedraggled robes at the close of the ceremonies, I overheard one of your distinguished graduates,[34] who was exhibiting a condition of complete saturation, remark: 'This is evidently Conant's method of soaking the rich.' I naturally feel a purely academic interest in the fate of the Harvard rich, but I want to put in a plea for your indigent country cousins, whose endurance is fast approaching its limit. But let me turn back from these more personal matters.

[34] Laurence McKinney '12.

"No one can view the history of universities without being profoundly impressed by their amazing vitality and longevity. Nations come and go, dynasties rise and fall, civilization itself is radically transformed, but the great universities live on. Clearly they minister to enduring needs which men will not allow to go unsatisfied; and Harvard, for all her relative youth on the roster of the world's great seats of learning, — and even in the western world three exceed her in age — has abundantly exemplified some of the noblest of the traits to which the university as an institution owes its preservation . . .

"Incident to the execution of her ends she has assembled one of the world's most magnificent libraries, where are preserved the imperishable treasures of the human spirit manifest throughout the ages, and has supplied to her scholars all the technical facilities which superb laboratories and exhaustive collections afford. For all these achievements and many more that must here go unnumbered the world owes Harvard a lasting debt of gratitude, and especially are the colleges and universities of America, and whosoever loves learning and books, debtor to her . . .

"Would that we could turn away from this feast of felicitation with no feeling but one of joy in a great achievement and placid confidence in what the future holds in store for Harvard and for all other universities. But to do so would argue us completely oblivious to certain of the most tragic happenings of our time. I have no appetite for playing the part of Banquo's ghost, but there is another picture of the learned world, unhappily all too true, which ought not wholly to escape us and for a brief mention of which I beg your indulgence.

"In three of the great nations of the world the university as the home of intellectual freedom, of truth for truth's sake, is essentially extinct. Some of the most revered seats of learning have overnight been transformed into propaganda factories. How much further the process may go no one can foresee, much less predict. But almost in the twinkling of an eye one great set of values for which generations of men had struggled and sacrificed, and to which men paid the tribute of deep and sincere reverence, have been wiped out. . . .

"Perhaps most often in our own educational history it has been the attack of sectarian bigotry which our colleges have had to resist. Harvard history reveals not a few such episodes. But today the most menacing attack comes, as it has repeatedly in the past, from the political side. In one form it is precipitated by allegedly patriotic organizations committed to maintain in schools and colleges their own particular conception of loyalty. The motives of these misguided folk are, I doubt not, often excellent. But they have opened the cover of Pandora's box and we may well be fearful of the issue. For example, in many schools American history may now be taught only in terms these self-appointed patriots deem desirable. Teachers who will not prostitute their knowledge and convictions to the often ignorant bias of these worthies must find other jobs. Sometimes the results desired are sought through the imposition of teachers' oaths. Sometimes by more direct methods, but the outcome is always the same, i.e., the assignment to busy-bodies, often moronic in mentality, of the power to terrorize able and honest teachers, with the ultimate ruin of the morale of the teaching force. Few teachers would object to taking a loyalty oath if other citizens did the same, especially editors, priests, preachers, radio speakers, playwrights and actors, and the directors of movies, all of whom exercise a far more direct and potentially corrosive influence on public opinion. But as now applied, the oaths inevitably reflect upon the character of the teaching profession . . .

"In this connection I wish I could share the belief expressed by President Conant this morning that we have little or nothing more to fear from religious bigotry. But I cannot wholly forget the Ku Klux and the Black Legion of Detroit and the Scopes trial and the fact that in several states it is against the law to teach the doctrine of evolution.

"Pernicious and dangerous as are these trends in their ultimate possibilities for simple honesty and truth in education, the attack through taxation is far more immediately serious. This assault takes two general forms: — one, the attempt of local governments to impose real estate and other taxes upon endowed institutions which are tax exempt by legislative enactment. . . .

"President Conant's encouraging report on Tercentenary gifts to Harvard makes such anxieties seem rather groundless here. Apparently Harvard men have not heard of the depression, but your poor relations are faced with quite a different situation.

"The second threat to endowed institutions from taxation arises from the relentless impositions on income and on legacies of benevolent individuals, two sources from which the endowed institutions have in the past secured a large part of their essential resources. . . . Men high in authority have been of late quoted as intimating that taxation would shortly be so used as to compel all endowed colleges and universities to come under state or federal control.

"Now I am myself a product of the public high school and the state university, for both of which I cherish the most profound gratitude and respect. I only regret that I do not represent them more worthily. But I say with the most solemn conviction that to strangle the endowed educational institutions, or to convert them into mere creatures of the state, would be to destroy supreme and irreplaceable values into whose creation centuries of the most devoted and unselfish human effort have been poured. It would be a tragedy different in kind from, but comparable in character with, the ruin of the great universities abroad . . .

"To fair and stately Harvard her devoted sons offer their most profound and affectionate homage. May the Almighty continue to shed upon her the light of His favor that in all the centuries to come she be ever found marching on to new victories of the spirit with the torch of truth held high in her blessed hand."

NOTES ON THE HARVARD TERCENTENARY

Following President Angell, Alexander Dunlop Lindsay, Vice-Chancellor of Oxford University and Master of Balliol, spoke briefly in gracious tribute to Harvard and her place in "this strange Utopian flower, this free commonwealth of universities all over the world." The chorus sang "*Laudate Dominum*" (music by Frederick S. Converse '93); and after George Russell Agassiz '84, President of the Board of Overseers, had made his address, President Conant called on Jerome D. Greene to stand up: "The name of one man who will be forever connected with this Anniversary, the man whose loving care has been reflected in every detail." Long and affectionate cheers; and then the meeting was prophetically adjourned, after the example of 1836, to the year 2036. President Lowell, as Chairman, called on President Conant for the motion. President Conant made the motion, adding a word of explanation: "Yesterday morning we connected the present with the past; this afternoon we look toward the future. . . . One of the undergraduate speakers referred to Josiah Quincy Jr.'s prophecy[35] that 'a century will soon roll away and there will be another clan-gathering of the sons of Harvard. They will come rushing, as it were, on the wings of the wind, from every quarter of our land.'

"Gentlemen, I repeat Quincy's prophecy and venture to extend it by changing one simple word: 'On the wings of the wind' from every quarter of the globe will throng the Alumni of this University when America celebrates the beginning of the fifth century of higher education.

"Mr. President [to President Lowell], I move that this assembly of the Alumni be adjourned to meet at this place on the eighteenth of September, 2036."

Mr. Lowell said:

"Before putting the motion I want to say a word in its favor. If I have read history aright, human institutions have rarely been killed while they are alive. They commit suicide or die from lack of vigor,

[35] Bicentennial, 1836.

and then the adversary comes and buries them. So long as an institution conduces to human welfare, so long as a university gives to youth strong, active methods of life, so long as its scholarship does not degenerate into pedantry, nothing can prevent it from going on to greater prosperity. In spite of the condition of many things in the world, I have confidence in the future. Those of you, therefore, who believe that the world will exist one hundred years hence, and that universities will then be faithful to their great purpose, will say 'Aye'; contrary-minded, 'No.' "

It was a unanimous vote.

The Meeting was adjourned.

The assembly sang "Fair Harvard," and with that the Tercentenary Celebration was formally closed.

VI

By that adjournment the sense of conclusion was not complete. It was certain only that the mediaeval color had disappeared. The alumni population of Cambridge and Boston suddenly fell to normal; in a week or ten days the College would open the 301st academic year. Something was over, and something was about to begin. But it was not certain that the festival which we had shared, to which so many had lent their fellowship, had not clarified the future equally in clarifying the past. If this were so, the ennobling spirit of those three days must remain with us long after the events shall have been forgotten. Perhaps now — like the Puri Indians — for yesterday, today, and tomorrow we have only one word. We have looked back and found new strength; shall we look forward and keep it?

The consideration of "this homespun past of ours" at any time, during any celebration, can only be a good and cleansing thing. Lowell recommended it fifty years ago — "to remind ourselves how poor our fathers were, and that we celebrate them because for themselves and their children they chose wisdom and understanding and the things that are of God rather than any other riches." We have considered it again, in all humility and in fortifying company. Harvard is still her own proof "that there is true ascension in our love." We may take that phrase from Emerson, who was one of us.

When Harvard celebrated in 1936, the Alumni did not gather alone. We shall remember with pride that there were others and greater to do her honor. Nor did we for our part (let us hope) merely fumble with sentiment. The many alertly persuading elements of costume, companions, voice, and music absorbed our attention, but significance cut deeper than sight or sound. Something of that final week is still unadjourned; something of that meeting will continue independently, and in strange and far-off places. And so long as such is the fact, we may start the count of another hundred years and evoke in the name of courage what was really our ancestors' worth.

1936

Notes on the Charity
of Edward Hopkins:
1657-1957

PERHAPS the real way to insure tradition is to endow it by name. There is a long and honorable tradition about the Harvard College Yard, but it is not endowed by name. Today in Cambridge the word College has all but disappeared. Thirty or forty years ago the Goodies, now vanished both in name and flesh, used to say that they worked in the Colleges (plural), meaning in Hollis, Stoughton, Thayer, and the like. The College, it seems, is now a School. There are also termites in the Yard, and in due course of time, unless something drastic is done, the golden word itself will have crumbled to a campus. Harvard indifference in these matters is depressing. The site of old Beck Hall should be marked by a stone, for which I would gladly supply the legend:

> *Spread* is dead.
> Let the dance thrive.
> Long live King Jive.

All this saddens me, of course, but I take comfort in the Charity of Edward Hopkins which has endowed the word *Detur* by salting it down in a bookplate. And although the Detur as a book or books given to undergraduates who attain for the first time the dignity and distinction of classification in Group I is not as old as the Charity of

Edward Hopkins which dates from 7 March 1657, it is old enough to stand as the established symbol of that Trust which is the subject of these brief remarks.

It is amusing to reflect that this single word *Detur* — let it be given — from the Latin phrase *detur digniori*, or (as it stands on the current bookplate) "Detur . . . pro Insigni in Studiis Diligentia," represents an early shortening or abbreviation characteristic of a nation which jeeps its way to Sears, eats cukes, spuds, grass, and dogs, drinks cokes and fraps, dwells in Capes and walk-ups, grows glads and mums, watches TV, flies in jets, reads paperbacks, and vibrates between OK's and KO's. Let there be given then *Detur:* one word in the Harvard language not likely to disappear, since it functions under the aegis of a legally constituted body. You will find it in *The Shorter Oxford English Dictionary:* "A prize of books given annually at Harvard College, U.S.A., to meritorious students. So called from the first word of the accompanying Latin inscription."

Like most things long familiar through use and usefulness, the Detur at Harvard is today a mildly coveted undergraduate prize which might conceivably gain in luster if something of the history behind it were more generally known. It is neither an obscure history nor uninteresting. It is surely not a definitive history, since there are certain moments and motives in the fabric which remain to this hour none too clear. It is far from my purpose in these casual remarks on a commemorative occasion — implicit in the title — to rehearse in detail what has already been written and rewritten, published or not published about Edward Hopkins, Esquire, and his somewhat remarkable bequest. There are four principal documents readily available, the first of which is *An account of the Trust Administered by the Trustees of the Charity of Edward Hopkins* by Charles P. Bowditch, sometime Secretary of the Trustees, privately printed for that body in 1889, following a vote of authorization passed on 6 May 1886. This is amplified by a *Supplemental Account, 1889 to 1943*, written by Roland Gray, whose trusteeship began in

1908. His supplement was privately published in 1948 and brings the official history down through the year 1943. Then there is an excellent paper (to which I am particularly indebted) entitled "Edward Hopkins, Seventeenth Century Benefactor of Education," by Cecil Thayer Derry '03, first read at Deerfield Academy on 20 March 1953 before the 47th annual meeting of the Classical Association of New England, and subsequently read at a meeting of the trustees of the Charity of Edward Hopkins at the Harvard Club of Boston on 7 May 1953. The fourth paper of which I have any knowledge is called "Harvard, Yale, and Governor Hopkins' Bequest," constituting the remarks made by Mr. Sidney Withington '06 early in 1955 before a group of New Haven people. Neither of these last two articles, I am reasonably certain, has as yet been published.

Now the Edward Hopkins history, so far as we are concerned with it, falls into three parts: the man himself, his will which was proved at London 30 April 1657, and the somewhat complex interpretation of that will. The brief summary which follows derives in fair measure from all four of the papers I have cited.

It is generally agreed that Edward Hopkins was born in or near Shrewsbury in England in 1600, making him some seven years senior to John Harvard. He was educated in the Royal Free Grammar School, became a merchant in the East India Company, and dealt with India and the Levant "in such products as figs, raisins, carpets, and damask." He married Ann Yale, widow of David Yale; and his mother-in-law was, by a second marriage, Mrs. Theophilus Eaton. Elihu Yale, it will be remembered, was the grandson of Mrs. Eaton by her first husband. Edward Hopkins' marriage was a tragedy almost from the beginning. Mr. Withington says that Ann Yale Hopkins "had a sad mental collapse while the Hopkins were still in England." Mr. Derry says that she "became hopelessly insane." There is no doubt, however, that Edward Hopkins remained throughout his life a remarkably devoted huband, and bore his cross as not many men could bear it. Governor Winthrop (who would not have sanctioned the founding of Radcliffe College) speaks of Ann as a "goodly young woman of special parts, who has fallen into a sad infirmity, the loss of her understanding and reason which had been growing on her divers years by occasion of giving herself wholly to reading and writing, having written many books. . . . Her husband being very loving and tender was loath to grieve her; but he saw his error when it was too late. For if she had attended her household affairs and such things as belong to women and not gone out of her way and calling to meddle in such things as are proper for men whose minds are stronger, etc., she had kept her wits, and might have improved them usefully and honourably in the place God had set for her." Edward Hopkins "diligently sought the meaning of his tragic affliction. He thought that perhaps he was being punished for expecting too much worldly happiness in his married life. There seem to have been no children." Ann lived until 1698 — or for more than forty years after her husband's death.

II

It is obvious from the first that Edward Hopkins had the head and vision for business. Very early in England he became connected with some eminent Puritans; and having suffered by 1636 "some financial loss in speculative ventures in the New World, he was appointed purchasing agent in London for the Saybrook Colony." He apparently sailed from England in the *Hector*, reaching Boston in 1637. Theophilus Eaton, John Davenport, and possibly John Harvard, were among his fellow passengers. A single winter in Boston being sufficient, if not too much, Hopkins proceeded to Hartford where he rapidly became a leader in commerce and public affairs. He held numerous offices: member of the Assembly of 1638; magistrate and first secretary to the colony in 1639; second governor of Connecticut in 1640, to which office he was re-elected no less than six times — the last in absentia in 1654. In some of the intervening years he served as deputy governor. He was also president of the Federation in 1644 and 1650, acted as judge, as commissioner for public defense, set town boundaries, settled disputes over contested lands, and negotiated with the Indians. He was equally successful in his personal affairs — particularly in general shipping. It is presumed that he amassed a considerable fortune.

He returned to England in 1652 — ostensibly for a visit, but actually for good. Being prescient in the matter, he sent for his wife, who had been cared for by her mother Mrs. Theophilus Eaton, and made every provision for her welfare. Edward Winslow wrote of Hopkins as one "whom we all know to be a man that makes conscience of his words as well as of his action." Cotton Mather called him "devout . . . and fervent in prayer." In the England of Oliver Cromwell he appears to have flourished about as well as he did in the country to the south of us. He was appointed a Navy commissioner in 1652; and in 1655 became, on the death of his brother, Warden of the Fleet and keeper of the palace. Mr. Derry has been quick to point out that Fleet in this sense meant Fleet Prison, and that keeper of the palace signified Honorary Curator of Westminster Palace.

If Edward Hopkins' name is irrevocably associated with Harvard, it is amusing to recall that it was likewise connected with the name of Yale, not destined to become a college until 1701; and also with Dartmouth whose date of founding is 1769, or one hundred and twelve years after Hopkins died of tuberculosis — 5 December 1657 — for in 1656 he was elected to Parliament from the Borough of Dartmouth in Devonshire. Mr. Derry has discovered that, when he died, a friend in England wrote, "Mr Hopkins [is] gone to God . . . at a time wherein we have great need of the presence and prayers of such men." Edward Hopkins, says Mr. Derry in summation, "exemplified many of the finest traits of the Puritans. He was enterprising, energetic, practical-minded, public-spirited, devoted to the interests of both New England and old England, tenderly affectionate towards his invalid wife, foresighted in his provision both for her and for the interests of education, and deeply devout in thought and deed."

The opening sentences of Edward Hopkins' will give further evidence of his character; "The Sovereign Lord of all Creatures giving in Evident & Strong Intimations of his pleasure to call me out of this transitory life unto himself, It is ye desire of me, Edward Hopkins, Esqr., to be in a readiness to attend his call in whatsoever hour he cometh, both by Leaving my Soul in the hand of Jesus who only gives boldness in that day & delivers from the wrath to come, and my body to a comely Burial according to the discretion of my Executor and Overseers, and also by Settling my small Family (if it may be so called) in order, and in pursuance thereof do thus dispose of the Estate the Lord in Mercy hath given me."

Now the interesting and important item in the will is this: "*And the residue* of my Estate there [in New England] I do hereby give & bequeath unto my ffather Theophilus Eaton, Esquire, Mr. John Davenport, Mr. John Cullock, and Mr. William Goodwin, in full assurance of their Trust and Faithfullness in disposing it according to the intent & purpose of me, Edward Hopkins, which is to give some Encouragement unto those forreign Plantations for the breeding up of Hopefull youth in the way *of Learning* both at ye Grammar School & Colledge for the publick Service of the Country in future times."

Approximately three hundred words farther on, there occurs a codicil of sorts: "My further mind and Will is That within Six Months after the Decease of my Wife five hundred pounds be made over into New England, according to the advice of my loving Ffriends Major Robert Thompson & Mr. Francis Willoughby, and conveyed into the hands of the Trustees before mentioned in further prosecution of the aforesaid public Ends, Which in the Simplicity of my heart are for the upholding & *promoting* the Kingdom of the Lord Jesus Christ in those parts of the Earth."

III

It is now generally agreed that the word *Colledge* in the will refers to Harvard College, since this was the only one at that time in existence in New England. Mr. Bowditch cites Professor Francis J. Child as saying that the grammar school and college in the will "undoubtedly meant a school and college in more or less intimate connection." To Edward Hopkins the writing of this will undoubtedly was a simple matter, for he was direct and unequivocal in all things. It is difficult, therefore, to conceive of the complicated construction put upon his sentences, of the curious way in which his wishes were carried or half carried out, and of the bitter arguments that attended the whole settlement from beginning to end. In the first place there was a time lag, since the General Court at Hartford sequestrated the estate "and ordered that it should be secured within the Colony until an inventory of the estate was presented and administration was 'granted according to law.'" Messrs. Goodwin and Cullock, two of the original trustees, joined forces against Theophilus Eaton Esquire, pastor of the church in Hartford, the outcome of which was that Mr. Goodwin and a large number of the church members moved to Hadley where they proceeded to settle. Thus Genesis faded into Exodus; and with one trustee in New Haven and a second in Hadley — the others having already departed this world — the General Court decided to hold on to the estate. Not until 1664, after threats to take up the matter in England, was the restraint removed. In April of that year John Davenport and William Goodwin, one still in New Haven and one in Hadley, divided the residue of the estate as follows: £400 to Hartford and the balance divided between Hadley and New Haven, "only provided that £100 will be paid to Harvard College out of that half of the estate which Hadley had." I think at this point of a verse about Bishop Potter quoted in Mark A. DeWolfe Howe's *John Jay Chapman and His Letters:*

> Then sleek as an otter rose Henry C. Potter,
> And smiled with the smile of his race.
> "My friends," he said calmly, "I reckon you've gotter
> Accept with your usual grace
> The *altered conditions* . . ."

Conditions having altered suddenly in favor of Harvard College, approximately £100 in the form of corn and meal was transported to Cambridge for the nominal fee of £7-0s-6d, or about 7 per cent. Furthermore, the produce was consigned to Deputy Governor Willoughby, a merchant who credited the College with the amount agreed, but proceeded to live until 1671 still owing the College for this and other items. The score at this point was considerably in favor of New Haven.

Now the second part of the bequest of the property in England, dependent (as we have seen) on Mrs. Hopkins' life, was still undistributed when she died in 1698. By this time all the original trustees were dead, as well as the executors, and one Mr. Henry Dally, Overseer of the will. But the case of the "Edward Hopkins bequest of £500 for propagation of Y^e Gospel" was revived in England in 1708, probably through the efforts of the Society for the Propagation of the Gospel in New England. The result, in brief, was that £500 with interest at 5 per cent starting six months after Mrs. Hopkins' death were produced, amounting to some £800 in all. The master of the Court of Chancery issued an order on one Mr. Exton, Mr. Dally's executor, to lay it out "in the purchase of lands in New England in the name of the Corporation for Propagation of the Gospel, for the benefit of the College and Grammar School at Cambridge." Long before this the town of Hadley had established a Hopkins grammar school, now known as Hopkins Academy, and acceptance by the court in May 1660 had already marked Mr. Davenport's plans "for the contemplated college preparatory school . . ." the beginning of the Hopkins grammar school in New Haven. A board of trustees of that school [1] has, like the trustees of the Charity of Edward Hopkins, held continuity through nearly three centuries. Only Hartford, so closely identified with the Benefactor, has now no secondary school bearing the name of Hopkins.

Thus it came about that in 1712 agents for the Cambridge grammar school and Harvard College agreed "humbly to propose to Mr. Attorney General that three-fourths of the said £800 and the produce thereof shall be for the benefit of Harvard College at Cambridge . . . for bringing up students in Divinity for the service of the country, and that the other fourth part and produce thereof be for the benefit of the grammar school at the town of Cambridge for the bringing up of youth to be sent to the said college. . . . That three-fourth parts of the Charity proposed to be appropriated to the Colledge be for ye encouragement of four Batchelors of Art to reside at the College and perform publick Exercises in Theology in such manner as shall be approved by the president and corporation of the colledge. . . . That every Ma[ster] of art or batchelor of art who shall be Entituled to receive part of this Charity shall be obliged to pay after the rate of two shillings in ye pound for what he shall so receive to the Trea. of Ye Colledge for the time being towards a ffund for ye use hereafter mentioned. Namely, to Buy Books and reward the Industry of such undergraduates as shall distinguish themselves by application to their studys." This is the prelude to the Detur as we know it today. The Cambridge Grammar School has long since given up the ghost; and its portion of the Charity now goes to the Cambridge High and Latin School.

The land which the trustees of the Charity of Edward Hopkins purchased belonged to the Natick Indians, the tribe to which the Reverend John Eliot had ministered. The specific tract which they proceeded to purchase was "commonly known by the name of Maguncoog." Toward the close of the eighteenth century some acreage in Upton was added. Mr. Bowditch remarks in his Account, "That

---

[1] Walter Camp, incidentally, was one of its alumni.

the purchase was not profitable to all concerned" as shown by the following extract from the same diary [that of Judge Sewall]:

Oct. 12. Solomon Thomas acquaints me that Isaac Nehemiah, one of the committee, had hanged himself. Ask'd what they should doe. I sent him to the Crowner. . . . hang'd himself with his girdle, 3 foot and 4 inches long, buckle and all.

Mr. Withington has observed that the signatures to the purchase of land which subsequently became the town of Hopkinton "do not indicate a high degree of learning among the Natick Indians. . . . Only two . . . wrote their names themselves and that not very well." The land proved something of a headache: collection of rents, collection of taxes, and so on. In 1823 the tenants on the land were persuaded and agreed to pay the trustees $2,000, to which the State added $8,000 in full settlement of all claims for past and future rentals. From that time on, the Charity of Edward Hopkins has remained an invested fund.

IV

At this point we should return to New Haven for a moment to consider what President Timothy Dwight of Yale wrote in his travel memoirs. His presidency extended from 1795 to 1817. "Munificent donations [he says] have been given to Harvard College by several opulent gentlemen, both in Great Britain and America. About two thousand pounds sterling plainly intended for Yale College by the Honorable Edward Hopkins, once Governor of Connecticut, fell, through a series of accidents, partly into the hands of her sister seminary and partly into the hands of the trustees of three grammar schools; one at New Haven, one at Hartford, and one at Hadley, Massachusetts." Now it is true that Governor Hopkins had written to Mr. John Davenport, April 1656: "If I understand that a college is begun and like to be carried on at New Haven for the good of posterity, I shall give some encouragement thereto."

But since he died some forty-five years before the founding of Yale, it is difficult to understand how Dr. Dwight could validate his words: "plainly intended for Yale College by the Honorable Edward Hopkins." In 1948, for no accountable reason, save the editor's privilege, I printed in the *Harvard Alumni Bulletin* a little verse about Dr. Dwight. At that time I was not a trustee of the Charity of Edward Hopkins. This is the verse:

> Ah, Timothy Dwight
> Was short of sight.
> But at the time
> And in his prime
> They thought him right.

What results, then, has the Charity of Edward Hopkins achieved across the years? First of all, I would remind you that it is undoubtedly the oldest trust fund in America. The original £800 today amounts to about $174,000, market value.[2] In the year 1956 the sum of $438 was paid to Harvard College to provide Deturs; $3,949 paid to the Divinity School to provide six scholarships; and $1,462 to the Cambridge High and Latin School to be used for prizes and awards.

What sort of people has the Charity of Edward Hopkins benefited? The first Deturs in Harvard College were apparently given in the year 1756 — possibly a few years later. Prior to this, the income from the Hopkins legacy was used to help poor students. The first printed list of students to whom Deturs were awarded appears in the faculty records of 1759. In that year there were 16 awards. In 1800, forty-one years later, there were 20 awards. In 1850 there were 40; in 1900, 26; in 1925, 22; in 1935, 34; in 1940, 41; in 1945, 27; in 1950, 79; in 1951, 83 (the highest number to date); in 1955, 64; in 1957, 60. For many years it was the practice of the College to print the list of Detur recipients in the catalogue, but this practice was abandoned after 1947.

[2] Market value by 1962 had risen to $199,442.

THE CHARITY OF EDWARD HOPKINS

In the eighteenth century, books given as Deturs in the main included classical authors, textbooks, grammars, dictionaries, scientific and philosophical works — for example, Locke's *Essay Concerning Human Understanding*. In the nineteenth century the standard English authors, and particularly the poets, predominated; but there were also translations —Montesquieu, for one — and certain of the specialized works like dictionaries.

In the light, or at least in the twilight, of history, it would be interesting and even instructive to compose a list of the twenty graduates and former students of Harvard College most likely to have received a Detur in the last two hundred years. Out of the names I have arbitrarily selected there will be perhaps a few surprises: Justice Oliver Wendell Holmes, for example, but not his equally famous father; Henry D. Thoreau, but not Emerson; Charles William Eliot, but not A. Lawrence Lowell; Robert Frost, but not his poet classmate Wallace Stevens. Among the notable recipients: Timothy Pickering 1763, William Ellery Channing 1798, Washington Allston 1800, Edward Everett 1811, Cornelius Conway Felton 1827, Benjamin Pierce 1829, Henry D. Thoreau 1837, James Russell Lowell 1838, Francis Parkman 1844, Charles W. Eliot 1853, Phillips Brooks 1855, Justice Oliver Wendell Holmes 1861, William Vaughn Moody 1893, Edward Kennard Rand 1894, Julian Lowell Collidge 1895, Walter Bradford Cannon 1896, Robert Frost 1901, William Ernest Hocking 1901, John La Farge 1901, Percy Williams Bridgman 1904, Lee Simonson 1909, Walter Lippmann 1910, Frederick May Eliot 1911, James Bryant Conant 1914, Charles E. Wyzanski Jr. 1927, John Updike 1954.

The records are not clear as to what books were given in each instance. But we do know that Channing received Watson's *History of Phillip II*; Edward Everett, Campbell's *Rhetorick*; President Eliot, Milton's *Prose Works*; Phillips Brooks, Southey's *Poetical Works*; and Justice Holmes, Bryant's *Poems*. Theoretically I suppose that Thoreau ought to have received *Das Kapital*; but unfortunately —

or fortunately — the author was but nineteen years old when Thoreau was graduated.

As to the selection of Deturs: it is only in this century, so far as I can discover, that the students have had any real choice in the matter. I have at hand as I write a copy of James Thomson's *The Seasons*, 1830. This is apparently a centennial edition published by William Pickering, since the book first appeared in 1730. It is handsomely bound in leather with the College seal in gold impressed on front and back — but who would have asked such elegance? From 1933 to 1951, for example, when students were given a list of books from which to choose, one notes with interest that only once was a set of books containing more than four volumes ever selected: this was Goethe's *Works* in six volumes. But Augustus, it seems, followed Tiberius.

In the period 1951 to 1957, recipients of Deturs were privileged to choose from certain sets of books bought by Mr. Philip Hofer during the years 1951–1953. These were handsomely bound volumes — a deluxe offering to a lucky few. The Detur winners in the early nineteenth century, could they know of it — Thomson's *Seasons* in leather notwithstanding — might feel somewhat envious of the young gentlemen in 1957 who may select (and have selected) an 1845 *Chaucer* in six volumes, a *History of British India* in nine volumes, Tolstoy's *Works* in fourteen volumes,[3] *The Life and Works of George Herbert* in six volumes, *The Memoirs of Napoleon* in eight volumes, and so on.

Among the most popular titles in recent years, one notes with pleasure Kittredge's *Shakespeare*; Cushing's *Life of Sir William Osler* in two volumes; Walton's *Compleat Angler*; Samuel Eliot Morison's *Three Centuries of Harvard*; *The Oxford Book of English Verse*; Frazer's *Golden Bough* — presumably a one-volume selection; a two-volume Boswell's *Life of Johnson*; Professor Jaeger's *Paideia* in three volumes; Louis Untermeyer's *A Treasury of Great Poems*;

---

[3] Tolstoy, it would seem, is leaner in 1957 than in the Farnsworth Room in 1921.

THE CHARITY OF EDWARD HOPKINS

The Copeland Reader; de Tocqueville's *Democracy in America*; and Newton's *Principia*.

The Bowditch and Gray accounts contain what purports to be a complete list of Divinity students upon the Hopkins Foundation. The earliest award is that of 1730; the last is 1944. Some 570 names are on the combined lists. Not all of those who shared in the largesse of the Foundation became ministers of the Gospel. Among the distinguished and well-known names, I note (with their College classes) Horatio Alger 1852 (the novelist) and his father who preceded him in the Class of 1825; George Bancroft 1817; Edward Everett 1811, last of the nine Harvard presidents to live in Wadsworth House; Ebenezer Gay 1737, Samuel Gilman 1811, who wrote in Fay House — now the administration building of Radcliffe College — the words of "Fair Harvard"; John Farwell Moors 1842, Edward Rowland Sill, who became a well-known poet in spite of not having attended Harvard College; Benjamin Wadsworth 1769, son of the builder of Wadsworth House (1726) who was the first Harvard president to live in it; Joseph Willard 1793, son of another Harvard president; Frederick Winthrop Alden, present chairman of the Board of Trustees of New England College; the late Ralph Barton Perry; and the late Edward Kennard Rand. There is also, parenthetically, one Perkins and one Palfry, but not one Palfrey Perkins.

V

The Trustees of the Charity of Edward Hopkins, whose number has never exceeded (as indeed it may not exceed) twenty-one members, has existed as a body at least since 14 January 1713, the date of the first meeting recorded in the Diary of Samuel Sewall. There are twenty-one on the board at this moment. The odd thing is that the trustees have enjoyed over this span of 244 years no fewer than twenty-seven separate titles. Except for one word, the present title of "The Trustees of the Charity of Edward Hopkins," as established in 1827, was in existence in 1743. But prior to 1743 the body was known under four different titles; and in 1743 began a series of twenty-one changes of refreshing and even astonishing variety. I remember very well once having in my hands for some days the manuscript of a dictionary of Indian Place Names of New England, assiduously and reverently gathered by the late William B. Cabot. He had listed no fewer than sixty-seven variants in the spelling of Massachusetts, so that at times the word resembled itself about as closely as Connecticut resembles Carolina. And so it is with the titles by which the present body of Edward Hopkins' trustees has been known. Furthermore, if the Natick Indians were unlettered, several of the scribes or secretaries of the Trustees (in the dim past, if you will) were enchantingly notional in the matter. I am suspiciously reminded of a relevant item which Mr. Walter M. Whitehill has called to my attention. It is taken from *The Public Records of the Colony of* [Governor Hopkins'] *Connecticut*, dated 3 June 1647: "Tho. Newton, for his misdemeanor in the vessel cauled the Virgin, in giveing Phillipe White wyne when he had to much before is fyned 5 *l*." So then:

The original title in 1717 was The Trustees for Managing the Charity of Edward Hopkins, Esq. This was simple and effective and not far from the title today; but within one year they were both honorable and geographic — even disturbingly insular: The Honourable Trustees for the affairs of The Town of Hopkinston. Too much and too long. In 1726 it was abbreviated to The Trustees of Hopkinston. Perhaps the year 1728 was a wet one; at any rate, the name expanded as a tree ring might under aqueous conditions, and the new title became The Honourable & Reverend Trustees for the Charity of Edward Hopkins, Esq. Two years later a drought set in, and it shrank to the brief Trustees of Mr. Hopkins' Legacy. Then in 1743 we find The Trustees for the Charity of Edward Hopkins, Esq.; but in the same year the reverends returned, and the title expanded to The Honourable & Reverend Trustees of the Charity of Edward

Hopkins, Deceas'd, Esq. But there was something obviously wrong about the order of Deceased, Esq. So in 1748 we find the Honourable & Reverend Trustees of the Charity of Edward Hopkins, Esq., *Deceased*. What became of the legacy? It was restored somewhere between 1748–1751: The Honourable & Reverend Trustees of the Legacy of Edward Hopkins, Esq. It was a lean year in 1751, and we now find simply Ye Trustees of Hopkinston. In 1753 we are back at the old stand with The Honourable & Reverend Trustees of the Charrity of Edward Hopkins, Esq., only this time a second "r" has been introduced into Charity. The year 1754 finds the word Hopkinton for the first time without an "s." Five years later the "s" was restored.

Then in 1760 the name of Mr. Hopkins changes unaccountably: The Honourable & Reverend Trustees for ye Charity (with two "r's" in it) of ye Honourable Ez. Hopkins, Esq. In 1761 the word Legacy was substituted for Charity, with or without two "r's"; the Esq. was dropped entirely. In 1763 we find The Honourable & Reverend Trustees for ye Legacy of ye Honourable Ezek. Hopkins, Es. We have gained a vowel and a consonant for Ez., but we have lost a consonant from Esq. In 1764 the transition is complete: Ez. *to* Ezek. to Ezekiell; and at the same time an extra "p" is dropped into Hopkins. Now in 1770 the whole concept suddenly changes: Honourable Trustees of Hopkinston Colledge Land. In 1771 it is The Honourable & Reverend Hopkinston Trustees. The Legacy is back with us in 1772, but in 1781 another new word appears: The Trustees of the Hopkinton Donation — the legacy has become a gift, though not for too long. In 1797 we have The Honourable Trustees of the Estate of Harvard Colledge; but later in the year we progress to The Honourable Trustees of the Hopkinston and Upton Land. 1808 has a forward look with Trustees for *perpetuating* the Legacy of Edward Hopkins. The word Donation returns in 1809 and perpetuating goes out. In 1822 perpetuating is back and Charity has replaced Donation. Also Edward Hopkins, deceased these now 162 years, suddenly becomes "the late Edward Hopkins." Between 1822 and 1826 we are perpetuating again; but in 1827 at last we emerge Gentlemen Trustees of the Hopkins Donation to Harvard College. It reminds one of Robert Frost's "The Gift Outright" beginning:

The land was ours before we were the land's . . .

In that same year 1827 we became the Trustees of the Charity of Edward Hopkins and have now stayed put for more than 130 years. *Esto perpetua!*

The Trustees of the Charity of Edward Hopkins have numbered more than 350 since 1712, though the Bowditch account acknowledges some imperfection owing to the loss of the records in 1825. Among the distinguished names we may note those of Waitstill Winthrop, Samuel Sewall, Increase and Cotton Mather, John Leverett, Thomas and William Brattle, Benjamin Wadsworth, John Quincy Adams, William Ellery Channing, Samuel Atkins Eliot, Josiah Quincy, James Walker, Jared Sparks, Cornelius Conway Felton, Charles Eliot Norton, Francis Parkman, Francis Greenwood Peabody, Abbott Lawrence Lowell, Judge Robert Walcott, LeBaron Russell Briggs, Samuel McChord Crothers, and Chester N. Greenough.

Any trustee of the Charity of Edward Hopkins who happens to live on the wrong side of Commonwealth Avenue in Boston must admit that the 19th of April, although it is R-Day for Paul Revere, and D-Day for General Dawes, is also H-Day for Hopkins. For the Detur of Patriots' Day is a crown of bay leaves offered by His Honor the Mayor of Boston to that gentleman of whatever nationality who has not galloped on four legs but has run on his own mare's shanks from Hopkinton to Boston, a distance of some twenty-six miles. On the morning of that day, the south side of Commonwealth Avenue is roped off, vehicular traffic diverted elsewhere, and the town of Hopkinton brought forcibly to mind. It seems a pleasant thought. If Marathon is a flowering word like

THE CHARITY OF EDWARD HOPKINS

Anthology out of the Greek, surely Hopkinton and Hopkins deserve consideration and respect in the lexicon of Harvard. Tradition and devotion have lost some of the firmness with which they once were spoken. The Charity of Edward Hopkins was born out of generosity and vision. It is now a part of our Cambridge heritage. Those of us privileged to help prolong its life are twice fortunate. Like the Boylston Professor who may tether his cow in the Yard, and the Poet Laureate who has his butt of sherry, so we possess and enjoy the right to sit on the Commencement platform. There is something mysterious about this right — which is quite as it should be. The year 1781 is the earliest year in which we have a record of the line of march at Commencement. The Trustees are not there. They first appear on the records in 1896. Whence and when came this privilege? That is our one and closely guarded secret.

1957

Commentary

What have I been doing all my life? Have I been idle, or have I nothing to shew for all my labour and pains? Or have I passed my time in pouring words like water into empty sieves. . . Is there no one thing in which I can challenge competition, that I can bring as an instance of exact perfection, in which others cannot find a flaw? The most I can pretend to is to write a description of what this fellow can do. I can write a book: so can many others who have not even learned to spell.

William Hazlitt

Then he drew off his glove, produced a small book from his waist, licked the lead of his pencil and made ready to indite.

James Joyce

Alembic in Limbo

QUO ANIMO (*"By what mind, with what intent"* — *hereafter Q.*): Driving a car or shaving or falling asleep, haven't I heard you somewhere before?

Alter Idem (*"Second self"* — *hereafter A.*): I have many disguises: conscience, inspiration, *élan vital*, the inner check, Monday-morning quarterback, the brass-tack salesman, echo, the private I. You are asking my help?

Q. What can you tell me about the *general* use of *higher* education? Please observe that I emphasize the adjectives.

A. Something — just possibly. I have lived in three different college towns.

Q. A man might live in Camembert, and not know how to make cheese.

A. I spent four years *in* a college.

Q. And then?

A. I hung round for another forty just to see what I had got out of — pardon me — derived from it.

Q. You have steeped yourself in Alma Mater? You must reek of the place!

A. I am unaware of that. Apart from accurate estimates of my true vocation, I have been taken for a chess player, an orchardist, a reporter at large, a patent lawyer, print collector, past president of a narrow-gauge railroad, editor of a defunct quarterly, and a dealer in movable type. It is only in Greek and German restaurants that I am sometimes called professor.

Q. You know you are not a professor.

A. In extended argument, some of my friends will say that I missed my calling, though not by much. No: I am a lifelong student. Do you remember what James Bryant Conant said in 1936, at the time of the Harvard Tercentenary? "He who enters a university walks on hallowed ground."

Q. But a college or university surely is not life.

A. Perhaps. But at least it is a stage; and on the stage, says Thornton Wilder, "it is always *now*." The only difference is that on Broadway or in London you have the same actors in different dramas; in college you have successive actors in the same dramas. Take your choice.

Q. All right; you have taken yours. Am I correct in suspecting that you are puzzled by the current popular image of the college? We all know what that is: the passport to a better job — where "better" is an unrequited comparative; a package deal of contacts-that-will-help-me-in-later-life, organized or spectator sports, bull sessions, desultory reading, dates unlimited, freedom of supervision, and the technical mastery of an early warning system against the examiners' attack. College is also a place to go back to, a football team, a target for stray criticism, a box of dreams in camphor, an experiment in architecture, a prestige name to boast of, an annual-giving Fund.

A. This isn't everyman's indictment, even among the young.

Q. I called it the popular image: largely in the minds of the unacquainted.

A. "All music [I am quoting Whitman] is what awakes in you when you are reminded by the instruments." When the mind awakes, the student — and then only — has a right to be so-called. He has found himself.

Q. Has it ever crossed your mind that a Maine guide's license — not to be come by lightly — is in one respect worth more than the A.B. degree? It is, in fair part, a guarantee against getting lost. The A.B. guarantees nothing. . . .

A. Think that through. Anyone who does not commit himself to being lost in college will never know what he's really there for. And what is he, may I ask you, if not for the joy of discovery?

> I take the red lance of the westering sun
> And break my shield upon it; who shall say
> I am not victor? only that the wound
> Heals not, and that I fall again.

Something to tilt against: something to win from or win in, and lose to and win from or in again. It matters not whether the light breaks through in poetry, linguistics, acoustical theory, choral composition, Sanskrit, engineering, steroids, heavy water, or mycology. Call it revelation, if you like. It may tremble in the turn of phrase on a teacher's tongue; it may lie hidden in an oil or water color hanging in the college museum; it may settle as yellow substance at the bottom of a test tube, or break forth in a single chord of Palestrina. G. M. Trevelyan has spoken of "the *poetry* of handling old Mss. which every researcher feels." Harlow Shapley, the astronomer, has said that on opening a book on mathematics he was sometimes moved by the same emotions he had when he entered a great cathedral.

Some day (and I regret to predict it) there will be a monitor station, with a dean in charge, in every college in the land: a light will flash, and Freshman X will be credited with his awakening. "Three years, Mr. Y, and I must inform you that as yet your light has not come on." But enough of that! To be young and in college, if only the young and in college knew it, is looking up at the night sky, mobile under scattered clouds, when no two stars are of one constellation. Now and then the heavens will open wide; but oftener not. Consider Mr. Frost's poem, "Lost in Heaven," from which I draw my star-talk:

> Let's let my heavenly lostness overwhelm me.

Q. That seems an elaborate metaphor for one who frequently quotes Ellis, what? "Be clear, be clear, be not too clear." In the popular image, of course, there is no room for footnotes like the one that Christopher Morley's father, Professor of Mathematics at the Hopkins, appended to a tough examination paper he had set. "If an exact answer does not suggest itself, an inspired guess will not be without value." To the image makers, college is . . .

A. Colleges, if we adhere to the prefab image of so many young matriculants, would feed the dream direct to the computers. But this will never be, make no mistake; for somewhere on some campus there is always coming up an Emerson, Webster, Brandeis, Milliken, Jane Addams, Thurber, Cather, Cushing, Carson, Salk, De Voto, or Marquand who find exactly what they need, flourish often in creative loneliness or at variance with tradition. In the renewal of achievement, they will mend the leaks in the true legend of what a college is. And please to note here that the legend is always better than the popular image, just as in poetry the metaphor is stronger than the simile. Observe with pleasure that the legend is always *of the college.* Longfellow of Bowdoin, for example.

Q. We are not forgetting (a) that the awakening process frequently occurs at the grade-school level; (b) that for many remarkable individuals college was and remains outside their ken: witness Franklin, Whitman, Mark Twain, Winslow Homer, Edison, Burbank, Hemingway.

A. We are not forgetting that to the early-awakened the college is a paradise. For the writer and the artist it helps provide an intelligent, widening audience. As to inventors: it is unlikely in the future that the great ones will not be trained in universities or technical institutes. It is quite a day's journey to the frontier of science.

Q. You will grant that in spite of inflation, internecine war over who gets whom among the teaching giants, and the magnified problem of balance between the humanities and the sciences — our colleges survive as islands of light across the nation. The young ones struggle toward accreditation; the old ones to keep their place, or to better the peck order in achievement and endowment. At the same time they are beginning to function as the cultural centers of their communities and sometimes (as in particular with certain state universities) of their states. They are the new patrons of the arts — and of the sciences, too; on the air and on the screen and on the public platform. Faculty, students, facilities — all are variously involved.

A. But still the tragic failure of our colleges involves the average alumnus — and I am using the masculine by grammatical convention. He is like a three-stage rocket: the first takes him up through the 12 grades into college, the second takes him through college and even through graduate school; but the third one frequently fails to ignite, or flames out before he goes into orbit. "All the little time I have been away from painting [wrote Edward Lear in 1859, when he was 47] goes in Greek. . . . I am almost thanking God that I was never educated, for it seems to me that 999 of those who are so, expensively and laboriously, have lost all before they arrive at my age — and remain like Swift's Struldbrugs — cut and dry for life, making no use of their earlier-gained treasures: whereas, I seem to be on the threshold of knowledge."

Q. Well. . . .

A. Let me say it for you. The average men or women of 35, graduated from college, many of them having sensed the land fall or having seen the beacon; well aware of benefits — of doors that opened, of books that pointed on toward other books, of speculation promising delight — can only say with Coleridge: "My imagination lies like a cold snuff on the circular rim of a brass candlestick." If they learned to haunt old bookstores, did they continue the habit until they had put together a self-selected library of two or three thousand volumes? Very few of them. Do you think they really know and value and re-examine the heart of a dozen great books? I strongly doubt it. Do they read 12 worthwhile books a year? I doubt that, too — more strongly. When they learn that Johnny can neither read nor write, do they ever stop to listen to the sound of their own speech? read the letters which they themselves have written? think before they parrot back clichés that figure like I'm telling you?

Have they acquired a modest judgment respecting prints or water colors, etchings, aquatints, or wood engravings? In most cases, no. Do their homes and offices reflect in taste what a hundred dollars or so a year for fifteen years would gratify? Make a mental check of the next ten of each you visit. Music I except because the stereo mind was likely developed independent of the college years; and this is the one art truly catholic in our time. As for the drama, I cannot even guess. It is surely strong in the colleges, and the stock companies (freshly stocked) are witness to that strength. I am minded, rather, of Dorothy Parker's account of a Benchley-Ross exchange in the *New Yorker* office. "On one of Mr. Benchley's manuscripts Ross wrote in the margin opposite 'Andromache,' 'Who he?' Mr. Benchley wrote back, 'You keep out of this.' " Perhaps I should have kept out of this dialogue.

Q. Not at all. Someone may shift Mr. Benchley's "Who he?" to plain "Who? Me?" Someone who thinks that the ethos of college is still with him; who is rusting (I *mean* rusting) on his undergraduate laurels for whatever they were worth; who has neither found the time nor taken the trouble to form an exemplary taste for anything — in anything.[1] You remember what a character in *H. M. Pulham, Esquire* said? "On leaving college [25 years ago] I started Gibbon's *Decline and Fall of the Roman Empire* and Nicolay and Hay's *Lincoln*. I am still working on them in my spare time." Amusing, yes; but sadder than amusing — and pathetic in its sadness.

[1] See Jowett's *Introductions to Plato*: "The want of energy is one of the main reasons why so few persons continue to improve in later years. They have not the will, and do not know the way. They 'never try an experiment' or look up a point of interest for themselves; they make no sacrifices for the sake of knowledge . . . hardly any one keeps up his interest in knowledge throughout a whole life."

A. The prevailing notion is that one passes through college on the way up — toward success, achievement, or some satisfying approximation. Under this assumption, the college appears as a point — a little gold star — on the curve: about 21 years out on the X (horizontal) axis. Interpretation? Enter, exit the college. Agreed? No, that is wrong. It is, in truth, the basic tragedy.

Ideally, the college remains a *function* of the curve and not a point upon it — a determining factor of its ultimate character or direction. For example: if against the X life-span you plot the vertical Y as the sum of special knowledge — what the individual *knows in detail* respecting many subjects — the peak of the curve may well remain at 21, since after graduation most diversified special knowledge tends largely to decrease.

An honors student — a good student, for that matter — may never know again so much in several fields as he does in the final week of senior examinations. On the other hand, remembering Whitehead's disclaimer anent the value of "scraps of information," Y may (and should) assume a much nobler role — intellectual power, for one. Granting that, then, any moment on the curve will reflect the increasing functional share of the college in the value of the individual to himself and to society. For want of a better name, let's call that function "the habitual vision of greatness."

Q. Since many have a natural distaste for graphs (graphobia), why not choose the river symbol? The curve suggests a river.

A. Bear in mind that the curve (ideally) runs up, the river down. But fortunately the river runs toward bigger and even better things — the fertile valley and the sea, for instance. You may flow with it or let it float things past you, as you wish. Poets frequently stand close to fishermen in thought. "Poets," says Archibald MacLeish, "are always wading and seining at the edge of the slow flux of language for something they can fish out and put to their own uses." Let me argue, then, that if we think of the college as a river in the slow flux of being, we shall always find something to fish out of it.

To this day I remember my high school teacher of German — rich in the culture of the Jewish race — shaking her finger at us, saying: "Never let a day go by without looking on three beautiful things." Trying not to fail her in life meant trying not to fail myself.

Q. Are you suggesting that it is only between the best teachers and the most responsive students that this flux of being can be perpetuated?

A. Not at all. The great critic, George Saintsbury, said of Oxford: "For those who really wish to drink deep of the spring — they are never likely to crowd even a few Colleges — let there be every opportunity, let them indeed be freed from certain disabilities which modern reforms have put on them. But exclude not from the beneficent splash and spray of the fountain those who are not prepared to drink very deep, and let them play pleasantly by its waters." Almost a hundred years ago, Andrew Preston Peabody, Acting President of Harvard, plead publicly for all those of "blameless moral character" who stood scholastically at the bottom of their class. "The 90th scholar in a class of a hundred has an appreciable rank," he said, "which he will endeavor at least to maintain, if possible to improve. But if the 10 below him be dismissed or degraded, so that he finds himself at the foot of his class, the depressing influence of this position will almost inevitably check his industry and quench his ambition."

Today, under the pressure of increasing competition, some reasonably good minds will function somewhere near the foot of every class. Provided that they see the light, who else will be more avid to enjoy what Justice Holmes has called "the subtle rapture of a postponed power"?

Q. Perhaps it is largely the city which stands between the college and the disciples. Within its arcane babel it is hard to distinguish echoes from that other world. And with days pressing in and time running out — in the city, in traffic, in confusion — doubly hard to remember that the physicist has room for Andrew Wyeth, the classicist for *Tarka the Otter*, the Bauhaus architect for *Walden*, the musicologist for Freya Stark, the masters of Univac for the sight of *polygonella articulata* burning in the autumn wind by sandy edges of expressways into Maine, the floundering economist for spotting Indian watermarks in southernmost Wyoming.

A. No wilderness bewildered Academe a hundred years ago; but megatropolis is something else again. Man on his plundered planet, in his silent spring, must come to terms with nature long before his packaged plankton supersedes the boxtop cereal. The colleges, backwater stations as they once were called, are all we have here on the last frontier. Alumni who support them ask and take too little in return. It is their own fault, to be sure.

As Samuel Butler could lament that there was (and is) no Professor of Wit at Oxford or Cambridge, so one may deplore — why not? — the lack in all our colleges and universities of an Emerson Chair of the Spirit. You may take that small suggestion indirectly from Matthew Arnold. And a Henry Thoreau Chair of Self-Sufficiency. "It is time that villages were universities," said Henry. The time is coming when they will be. Better than that: when man will be a college to himself, not least of all lest "things grown common lose their dear delight."

1963

Arrival at Xanadu

A GRADUATE of the late John Livingston Lowes' remarkable course on the Romantic Poets (English 72) turned up like an old flame at the New Lecture Hall on Wednesday, November 10, to hear the present Charles Eliot Norton Professor lecture on *The Ancient Mariner*. Professor Lowes would undoubtedly be pleased to know that his former student had firmly in hand his battered but annotated copy of Page's *British Poets of the Nineteenth Century* (1921), with a twenty-seven-year-old marker against page 73.

> The Bridegroom's doors are opened wide,
> And I am next of kin;
> The guests are met, the feast is set:
> May'st hear the merry din.

He heard it clearly, for that would be in part the large number of Radcliffe girls in *restless gossameres*. He was early — earlier than he used to be in the old Emerson D days — not because he has necessarily grown more punctual than the Wedding-Guest, but because he was reasonably sure that the doors, if locked at 8 P.M., would stoppeth a good many more than one of three. Outside it was raining lightly.

> And the rain poured down from one black cloud;
> The Moon was at its edge.

As a matter of curious conjunction, there *was* a moon faintly showing along the edge of Memorial tower. He noticed that and shuddered a little in anticipation.

138

ARRIVAL AT XANADU

Inside the old familiar room the visitor found a seat up somewhere near the back and toward the right, conveniently located next to one of the several lally columns supporting the gallery. It was not until he had been sitting there for several minutes (*"and forward bends his head"*) that a strange thought crossed his mind: he had taken his place instinctively. The gratuitous friendly support of the black post in the dark hours of undergraduate life is one of the many mixed memories of Harvard College common to all students. He nodded to himself as he remembered the deep well in *The Road to Xanadu*: "The deep well knows it certainly." He opened the book and turned to page 77. . . Five minutes of eight. People were still coming in, wet and out of breath.

> They moved in tracks of shining white,
> And when they reared, the elfish light
> Fell off in hoary flakes.

Twenty-seven years fell away too. "Compare," he murmured, "*Job: 41, 32*."

C. M. Bowra,[1] Warden of Wadham College and Professor of Poetry at Oxford, is the present incumbent of the Charles Eliot Norton chair. His general subject is *The Romantic Imagination*, and his lecture that night was number three. Four minutes of eight. Professor Bowra, the only man visible in a dinner coat, was down there at the right, just below the platform. He was looking up and across the room, anxiously, with the unionized frown of a train dispatcher wondering what has become of the Twentieth Century Limited. He took a short, nervous turn and searched again the sea of faces, for the room was nearly full.

> I watched their rich attire:
> Blue, glossy green, and velvet black. . .

[1] Now Sir Maurice Bowra, who returned to Harvard in 1963 to receive the degree of Doctor of Letters. It was his tribute to my friend and teacher which led me to the Lowes counterpoint above. And it is precisely that tribute which assures me that John Betjeman's peal for Sir Maurice in *Summoned by Bells* is splendidly deserved.

Memorial struck eight. He heard the loud bassoon and moved to the supernatural mike.

For an hour Professor Bowra lectured and they listened like a three years' child. He spoke slowly and beautifully: a strong clerical voice with fine modulation, joking but once or twice, when "Gramercy! they for joy did grin." He began with a candid tribute to Professor Lowes and *The Road to Xanadu*: the road has been traveled; there are no by-roads to explore. Professor Bowra dealt with the poem itself: its meaning, its allegory, the achievement of "that synthetic and magical power . . . the imagination." A careful analysis led him to find it a myth of crime and punishment, of guilt and redemption. He called attention to Coleridge's prophetic insight into himself. He read only fragments of the poem, but very movingly the stanza beginning

> Like one, that on a lonesome road
> Doth walk in fear and dread . . .

Again the years rolled back. "No voice did they impart?" But, yes . . . "*Inferno, xxi*," supplied the visitor (to himself eftsoons) with no apparent hesitation whatsoever.

1949

Marmalade, Sausages, and Books

Here will I dream on garth green shaven lawns
And last enchantments of a middle age.

OXFORD and enchantment are two words with an old affinity. Their immediate association is of course with Arnold, but the relationship proves to be centuries older than the poet. "Our most noble Athens, the seat of the English Muses, the prop and pillar, nay the sun, the eye, the very soul of the nation: the most celebrated fountain of wisdom and learning, from whence Religion, Letters and Good Manners, are happily diffused thro' the whole Kingdom. A delicate and most beautiful city, whether we respect the neatness of private buildings, or the stateliness of public structures, or the healthy and pleasant situation." So wrote William Camden, who died not long before the founding of Harvard. Two and a half centuries later nothing much had changed or suggested change. "The prospect is pleasant enough, on an autumn morning, with the domes and spires of modern Oxford breaking, like islands, through the sea of mist that sweeps above the roofs of the good town." That was Andrew Lang, and he used the word *modern*. To Hazlitt, somewhat earlier, Oxford was not only the Sacred City; it was the dream city too.

Let him who is fond of indulging a dream-like existence go to Oxford, and stay there; let him study this magnificent spectacle, the same under all aspects, with the mental twilight tempering the glare of noon, or

141

mellowing the silver moonlight; let him not catch the din of scholars or teachers, or dine or sup with them, or speak a word to any of its privileged inhabitants; for if he does, the spell will be broken, the poetry and the religion gone, and the palace of enchantment will melt from his embrace into thin air!

Even in our own time Edward Thomas — whose courage to become a poet owes much to his friendship with Robert Frost — continually saw the countryside in Oxford, which accounts for part of the charm of his lively book on the university city, which John Fulleylove so richly illustrated. "Nowhere is green so wonderful as at Magdalen or Trinity," said Thomas. "But their sweetness is no more than the highest expression of the privacy of Oxford. Turn aside at the gate that lies nearest your path; enter; and you will find a cloister or cloistral calm, free from wolf and ass." Thus do we think of Oxford; thus we read of Oxford; thus do we refer to her; thus do we suppose the beautiful city still to be, exactly as Arnold described it: "so venerable, so lovely, so unravaged by the fierce intellectual life of our century, so serene!"

Unfortunately a change has come; the dream is shattered, and illusion all but fled. The ugly details of fact are assembled in an impressive article called "The Future of Oxford," by Robert Newman, published in the January issue of *The American Oxonian*. "If Oxford dreams today," says the author, himself no idle dreamer but a member of an important body called the Oxford Preservation Trust, "she dreams feverishly, and under forced draft."

The Rhodes Scholar of 1910, returning now, would hardly know the town. The buildings would be there, so would the gardens. Christ Church Meadow, the Parks, the Cherwell Valley have not as yet been altered. All that is barred off and protected still seems to be the same. But astride the academic body, there rides an industrial giant; and where once the major product was learning, today the major product is cars. Beyond the cloistered walls, and in between them, thunders the "faculty" of the new dispensation. As effectively as by a full-scale air raid, the peace of Oxford has been shattered. Nor is quiet secured with the retreating squadrons; more take their place, and heavier, and louder, until Oxford seems quite like Birmingham, and Magdalen Bridge bears the second-heaviest concentration of vehicular traffic in all of England. Industry has arrived, and an industrial population of 50,000 is superimposed on the groaning, constricting medieval framework.

This is outrageous! This is not true! But alas, apparently it is. The change, of course, did not come overnight. Americans have heard the rumors; travelers and war veterans have returned with stories of the black industrial conquest. What was it that Max Beerbohm said back there in *Zuleika?* "Oxford walls have a way of belittling us." Well, we in turn would belittle the black little stories. But we may not belittle this one. The impact of Mr. Newman's well-documented argument on those of us who have not seen Oxford in the past twenty years is much as if a comparatively recent graduate of Harvard, now living in North Dakota, were to learn that the abattoir had been moved from Brighton to the site of Jarvis Field. "Few Americans," says Mr. Newman, "realize that Oxford is now the Flint, if not the Dearborn, of England. But the British realize it."

Now the population of Oxford at the turn of the century was 50,000. Fifty years before that it was 27,000. This notable increase was due to a combination of factors: the freedom of dons to marry, the influx of retired colonial civil servants, and the rise of light industries such as marmalade, sausages, and books. There is nothing alarming in marmalade, sausages, and books. In 1927, however, the Pressed Steel Company was established in Cowley to supply automobile bodies to the Morris Motor Works, and the population of Oxford by 1940 had risen to 100,000. Mr. Newman's recital of the resulting monuments of ugliness, including the presence of a gas works "only 470 yards from Tom Tower," is more than distressing. But that it comes as a shock to us of another university is remarkable testimony to the power of the legend of last enchantments in a city of lost causes. Says Mr. Newman: "Even the multitude of writers who have considered Oxford in recent years (Hobhouse, Waugh, Betjeman, Dale, Buchan, Roberts, etc.), though each has pointed the virulent expansion, can do little to jar former Oxonians into a realization of how fast and how far this scholarly city, once 'at anchor in the stream of time' has come." What can be done about it? Oxford looks to her very active Preservation Trust — composed almost equally of City and University elements — to restore something of an old composure, a notable silhouette, and original dignity. May it be restored!

The bricks of Harvard are not yet shaken as the stones of Corpus Christi are shaken. The Oxford walls to poet Edward Thomas were tufted with ivy-leaved toadflax, wallflower, and inelegant ragwort. To us they are lasting grey reminders of the industrial and decibel disaster that could easily overtake us here at home.

1948

Beyond the Dewey
Decimals

O N the little hill that was always a hill, in the far southeast corner of the College Yard, the effective light of two thousand modern slim-line tubes ushered in the first Monday of the new year with the opening of the Lamont Library. Designed primarily for the use of undergraduates, it was built through the generosity of the late Thomas W. Lamont. All day, from 8.45 A.M. to 10 P.M., the undergraduates flocked in by the thousands. A steady stream of visitors followed them. A century ago the Dana house on the site of the new Library was more concerned with the baleful flicker of Betelgeuse and Arcturus and the daylight streaming in through the transit fixed on Milton's Blue Hill, the other terminal of the local Greenwich line. All is changed. The renovated building that housed the first Harvard observatory now stands on the opposite side of Quincy Street, and where its trees grew green, a shifting thousand undergraduates daily and nightly apply their individual minds to several thousand widely varying problems.

> Out of your light,
> Brave hearts, large minds! Out of your light, heroic,
> Indomitable souls! Forerunners, captains, upholders!

These words of Hermann Hagedorn in his *Tercentenary Ode* find suddenly a new application. The Lamont Library is first of all a building of light. Every last functional and functioning corner of it was planned and executed with equalized light as the controlling factor. A plain building not so tall as to overpower and not so huge as to dominate by mass alone, it somehow manages to lend tremendous new life and accent to this corner of the Yard largely by the area of glass set in the finest brickwork [1] to be found in any Harvard building. Behind that glass is light: continual, visible, and warm. Early armchair and even sidewalk critics, seeing the building rise, or glancing hastily at construction photographs and artists' drawings, have differed sharply as to the artistic value of what they saw. It seems now to the layman (call us average) that the Lamont Library, built as it is into the side of a hill, suggests a unit of which the exterior must be appraised largely in terms of the interior. Detractors of its geometric external lines, so far as we can judge, are electrified on passing through the big bronze-glass doors into the light within. "Glory it is," observed the *Crimson* in its eighteen-page Lamont issue. "No mistake about that, once you get inside." As someone has said: The Lamont Library has rendered nearly every other building in Harvard obsolete.[2]

There is no flight of steps of any consequence. The undergraduate enters at either of two different levels, on the level, through triple bronze-glass doors to the west, or through multiple bronze-glass doors to the north. He doesn't walk in — on either level — to Gothic emptiness or Georgian hall. He walks straight into a bright world of books — *his* books, to examine, read, or retreat with as he pleases. To open one of those big doors is to open a book itself. He can lay hands on one almost before the door has closed behind him.

Two years ago an undergraduate described the reading conditions in overcrowded Widener in no uncertain terms: "A disturbed vastness about as conducive to study as the waiting room in the Grand Central Station. . . Like a cafeteria in the Square at noon. . .

---

[1] Waterstruck brick: apt to have and to show rough edges which catch the light.

[2] A silly remark in 1963 as one contemplates the Carpenter Center for the Visual Arts. Sillier still, I predict, by 1984.

146

Like the belt line at Willow Run. . . Close to a hundred men are searching for about the same books in the space of five or ten minutes. . . There's somebody in your seat. . . There's somebody in every seat." On the day Lamont opened, a cheerful young man, heading home to his room, loosed this fragment of conversation in passing: "It used to take me an hour or two to get my books in Widener. Today I went into Lamont and had them in just four minutes."

What is the secret? If one individual could follow a quartet of undergraduates into Lamont Library the question would be answered. Suppose we try it. They are just ahead of us now, swinging up the path from Emerson, past the northeast corner of Houghton Library, leaving the President's house on the left. At this point they turn on to the temporary board walk leading past the main entrance of Lamont toward the new, unfinished gate and the Union. They pause at the porch entrance and glance about. Several new trees (they look suspiciously like elms to us) have been planted very recently with the aid of tree-truck and special derrick. A large and bushy mountain laurel[3] in leaf is taking root near the west end of the porch. The rest of the planting will wait till spring. The ground is wet and muddy.

II

The four boys have entered. They find themselves in the main lobby — much wider than it is deep, and beautifully lighted overhead by slim-line tubes concealed above a continuous aluminum grill resembling nothing so much as one vastly enlarged separator for a box of inverted ostrich eggs. If your era was old Gore Hall, you will surely look at it ten times. Our young friends survey it carefully: it is just as remarkable to them as to you. They inspect

---

[3] It was old and healthy and had a North Shore heritage; but it died very soon from overwatering.

other things. At their left is the long charging desk, with a few shelves of books in "closed reserve" behind it. These would be books for which there is great demand. To the right is a smaller charging desk; and beyond (through a door) the reference room, catalogues, and the like. The air is warm and fresh. Windows do not open: the whole building is air-conditioned — but not in the manner of a Pullman car or a cocktail lounge. Native Cambridge air, except in May or October, is rarely so good as this. In the reference room — we observe by peering through the glass door — a young man may smoke. Shades of Sibley!

Our quartet divides and subdivides. We follow in four easy stages. We are on the third level (as conveniently located stairway signs will tell us); and our first young man, being a Classical scholar, heads for the alcove area. There are twelve alcoves (forty in the building) on this third level. They are all to the right and left in front of him. At one stride in that even, shadowless light comes the alcove and Horace: *Ficta voluptatis causa sint proxima veris* (which translated might mean: a little fiction is not a dangerous thing). The young man selects two or three books, sits down at the table in the center of the alcove, leafs them through for five minutes, returns one, and moves on through the corridor a few steps and into the reading area. He has a choice of cubicles with chair, desk, and a peg for his coat (he wears no hat), a seat at one of the six long tables, a straight but comfortable chair apart from all this, or one of twenty-four deep upholstered chairs. But he is Spartan and has notes to take, and he moves into an available cubicle. He observes that the room is approximately full — but there is still a sense of freedom in it and no air of crowding. He is aware, too, that another reading room lies below him, and yet another above. He would find them equally used with no appearance of crowding. He thinks back to Widener.

Our second undergraduate is after a certain bound periodical. He crosses the lobby to the far righthand corner, disappears down a flight of stairs, turns into a stack area just under the alcove of his classical roommate, finds his periodical, and makes off for the smoking room in the southwest corner of the building on the same (second) level. He has a passage to type from the periodical he has found so easily. He sits down, opens to the passage, smokes a cigarette, reads another passage as he smokes, gets up and crosses the room to one of the five sound-proofed typing cubicles. He has his portable with him: the light in the cubicle (he discovers) is exactly the same in intensity as the light in every square foot he has covered since he entered the building.

The third member of the quartet is an undergraduate interested in philosophy and social relations. His first mission takes him down two flights from the third level to the first. He knows, of course, that under him even so are two additional floors of storage stacks for Houghton and Widener. He visits a pair of alcoves, spending a little more time with philosophy than with social relations (as perhaps more of us should, for does not one presuppose the other?). The practical side of his mind approves the simplicity of book cataloguing in Lamont. In the Open Reserve stacks a large, legible label marked *Social Relations* is on the spine of every book in that field: no numbers, no decimals, no confusion. And so with Philosophy, Science, Music, and the rest. Under each subject the books are arranged alphabetically by authors. In the alcoves, each in general devoted to a single subject (American History, Physics, Economics, Fine Arts, and so on), the books are arranged by subcategories, with a simple library number on each, but again alphabetically by authors. When he has finished with Pareto and Kant our undergraduate quietly deposits the books on a return-book shelf in the corridor. He observes with pleasure the duplication of books in which there is a multiplication of interest. No more mass panic when it comes to finding books at examination time. Sixteen copies of Cantril's *The Invasion from Mars*, for example, which would please the late Mr. H. G. Wells! Browsing in a strange field, his eye spots at once most of the important volumes simply because there are several copies of them.

His first-level mission over, our Middletown philosopher explores the first-level reading room for a moment, observing the open-closet coat racks at each end. These are made of half-round unfinished wood, which gives the pleasant appearance of a closed picket fence. This screen-like motif is current throughout the building — at the charging desks, at certain corners, round pillars and columns, at stair terminals, and so on. He leaves the first-level reading room at the west end, briefly inspects (for the heck of it) the charging desk and diminutive lobby at the west entrance to the building, and ascends the stairs to the fifth level. There is a small elevator at hand, to be sure, and another at the east side of the building; but these are for the physically handicapped and for Library personnel. His aim now is the Farnsworth Room, and this he elects to enter by a glass door from the east-west corridor rather than through the smoking room which it adjoins. One can smoke in the Farnsworth Room, for that matter. The compression air-check on the door isn't working properly. The door bangs: boys notice it. Queer, how one trivial imperfection screams aloud amid perfection!

III

The Farnsworth Room,[4] of which Thomas Wolfe once said reflectively, "few places have meant more," has been moved from the Widener Library. It is now a fine, distinguished corner room, finished in cherry wood, broken by projecting shelves, almost carelessly, into three alcoves. The five windows are all large, but the one facing west rises from the floor level and commands both the room and the late afternoon sun. Few places in Harvard, likely, will mean more to future generations of undergraduates than this retreat.

After browsing for five minutes, our third undergraduate takes

[4] Memorial to Henry Weston Farnsworth, Class of 1912, killed in World War I.

down a copy of Beerbohm's *Seven Men,* of which he has never heard, and retires to an appropriate Victorian chair to read it. May his friendship with the incomparable Max outlast the association of the old furniture with the modern room in which he sits! However that may be, an old room with a new look will continue as an oasis and retreat for undergraduates in search of recreational and purely cultural reading. It will continue to cater to that need of the sequestered and adventurous which the House Libraries, in their more functional spheres, do not quite supply.

In one notable respect the Farnsworth Room will effect a gradual change on its handsome shelves. The long sets, such as Tolstoi in 28 volumes, Bulwer-Lytton in 32 volumes, Scott in 48 volumes, and Purchas in 20 volumes will likely be reduced to a preferred selection. The larger categories of history, the novel, and biography will remain; but other smaller categories will be established for the purpose of inviting inspection of new fields and new areas. For example, there will be a small shelf of books on college and schoolboy life, another on spectator sports, one on sports for solitaries, one on walking, one on traveling. There will be a shelf for hobbies, indoor and out. The naturalists will be together under some such title as *The Ancient Wood*; New England as a playground and skiground will be selectively displayed. There will be a shelf of Utopias; and another on loneliness, since no man's education is in any sense rounded unless he has learned to live in his own company.

Tales of detection will be reduced to the accepted classics with, of course, a gradual turnover. Books of voyage and travel will fall under some such heading as *Landfalls and Departures*; a shelf called *Multitude and Solitude* and another called *The Sea and the Jungle* will concentrate such titles as these words themselves suggest. In this way it is hoped (if not expected) that undergraduates may enter easily into new fields of thought and speculation and perhaps acquire some lasting avocational interests. Creature comfort will remain a part of the Farnsworth Room: future chairs, like the present Victorian, will be comfortable; and the editions of the books themselves are and will be chosen, at least in some part, for their physical attractiveness.

Somewhat sensitive to the artistic, the fourth member of the quartet does not fail to observe the skill with which the library walls on every level have been painted in pleasing variation so as to utilize to the full the important factor of light. The ground-glass screen, extending over the east-west length of the fourth level — which is in reality a mezzanine floor — shelters a long row of cubicles, the occupants of which may look over and down at the third-level reading room itself. The architects are worried about a fractional segment of glare reflected from this glass into the reading room below, but it is not at all obvious even to the critical layman. Exploring further, the fourth member notes the use of the main lateral corridors on all levels for exhibition cases, with exhibition wall-space for broadsides, posters, and the like. The current exhibition, he observes, features old Gore Hall in its full life-cycle, and a photographic record of the building of Lamont Library itself. He notes with approval a scattering of watercolors, one Hopper and one Marin among them, in a smoking-room, and a trial picture or two in the Farnsworth Room.

Unfortunately he is not disillusioned enough to fear that some or all of the wall space might easily become the refuge for castoff oils and inferior art in general. A fireproof building such as this is a natural subsidiary to a great museum like the Fogg. It will be more than a pity if well-chosen watercolors (oils are too heavy) and prints of particular appropriateness are not offered to the Library on permanent loan. Quite apart from efficiency of arrangement and availability of books to the instant need of undergraduates, the underlying philosophy of Lamont is to give the student the run of the stacks, make him walk through them on the way to his special alcove or favorite cubicle or particular chair, and expose him thereby to books and areas of books outside his present interest. It is only a step, as our undergraduate remarks, from Social Relations to shelves of books about books, books on sport, books on stamp-collecting, and a thousand other things. If not overdone, here is a great opportunity also to cultivate the undergraduate taste in prints, etchings, and watercolors which may some day find tangible reflection in his own dwelling.

IV

On the fourth floor our fourth undergraduate pauses to inspect the Forum Room designed to seat, at capacity, 160 persons. It is equipped with blackboard, with space for a projection screen, and a projection platform.

At the west end of the Forum Room a door leads directly into the office of the Curator of the Woodberry Poetry Room. The Poetry Room is the only room as yet unfinished and unfurnished. Endowed as a memorial to Professor George Edward Woodberry of Columbia, it too has been moved from Widener where it was first opened in 1931. What our last undergraduate sees, as he pokes his head inside, is a spate of unmounted bookcases of uncommon design. The wood is maple and elm; the architect is Alvar Aalto, the distinguished Finn. The cabinet work for this room was done in Sweden. Some of the handsome dowel screens were damaged in transit, and the room is therefore behind schedule. The Farnsworth Room has about 4,000 books; the Woodberry Poetry Room perhaps 3,000. Added to this, a collection of 775 poetry records, from Frost and Eliot to Auden, recorded readings of Shakespeare, Chaucer, Virgil, and the Bible by great teachers of the past, and a learned Curator in Mr. John L. Sweeney combine to give complete articulation to a room already famous.

Two levels up, our fourth man enters one of the Library's ten large Conference Rooms for a discussion period.

1949

"And the Injury of None"

IT is perhaps not without some point, on the tenth anniversary of the collapse of the boom days of 1929, to assemble the figures, facts, and epistolary quotations bearing upon the uncelebrated centennial of a unique organization contributive to a part of undergraduate existence at Harvard, and in that part responsible for furthering the education of an astonishing number among ten generations of Harvard's more notable sons. There is little in its name to suggest that such a history, however brief, can fire the imagination, for there is small poetic overtone to the Fund For Assisting Students at Harvard College, or the more common variants of the Harvard or Lowell Fund of Boston. But for a hundred years this Fund has operated, in the impassioned phrase of its founder, to "the benefit of many and the injury of none," and its story [1] is none the less remarkable for the apparent anonymity under which it has admirably functioned.

To give it definition in figures: The Fund For Assisting Students at Harvard College was conceived in 1838, in which year the original subscription of $11,350 was completed. From that date to this, not one cent of outside capital has been added; yet the Fund, through investment and interest on notes, has grown to a book value of $485,882.28 as of 30 April 1939. In that century of geometric progression it has loaned $450,457 to 6,350 Harvard men, or an average of

[1] Being the study of the familiar Harvard Loan Fund: the so-called Lowell Fund of Boston. The indulgent reader may skip through the two too-long letters, already scissored by the editor; but they are essential to the story for flavor as well as for fact. In 1959, with permission from the Supreme Judicial Court of Massachusetts, the Fund was turned over to Harvard College with a value exceeding $2 million!

154

nearly $71 to an equivalent of approximately one-fifth of the living number of Harvard College alumni. The Trustees' policy has been consistent from the beginning. Most of the loans have been granted to upper classmen; the invariable rate of simple interest charged has been five per cent, beginning from the day of graduation and not from the date of contract, as is the case with other loan funds at Harvard. For the span of one hundred years, tens of thousands of dollars have not, for one reason or another, been repaid; and in general no attempt has been made to press for repayment beyond the ordinary notification of date and subsequent letters of reminder. Yet the Fund has never ceased to grow, and today its beneficiaries (187 in 1939) depend upon it entirely for the April term bills.

That astonishing pyramid was built on a solid base. In 1838 (the administration of Martin Van Buren and the second year of the long reign of Queen Victoria) Josiah Quincy, class of 1790, was President of Harvard. He had seen the College through the Jubilee Year of 1836, "the birthday of the genial mother of our spirits," as the then future President Edward Everett,[2] class of 1811, had called it. Genius was abroad. Thoreau had been graduated inconspicuously in 1837, with Richard Henry Dana at the head of his class; James Russell Lowell and William Wetmore Story were new-fledged alumni (class of 1838), Edward Everett Hale was to graduate in 1839; the Faculty shone with the lights of Channing, Felton, Joseph Story, and Longfellow, among others; the Yard contained the College, and the first Gore Hall was beginning to lift its fourteenth-century Gothic head to become the precursor of Widener Library. Beyond the Yard sounded reverberations of the panic of 1837. The Independent Treasury Bill suffered opposition of the conservative Democrats in Congress, the Canadian Rebellion rolled

[2] In that same speech at Harvard's Bicentennial (8 September 1836) Overseer Everett had said: "Yes brethren, but little less than five thousand four hundred alumni have received the honors of Harvard College." In other words, the Loan Fund has helped in 100 years nearly one thousand more men than were graduated from Harvard in the first 200 years.

up the misty ingredients of a war cloud, and the citizen's eye in America turned hopefully to the west. Concerned with expansion of her own, New England Harvard felt more acutely the limitations of her $703,000 endowment. Among her many problems not the least was how "to aid need & merit, struggling for an education."

On 29 August 1838, President Quincy had a long talk with Samuel A. Eliot,[3] of the class of 1817, whether by prearrangement or chance it is not quite clear — though almost certainly at the President's call. In a fifteen-page letter [4] under date of August 30, Quincy refers to "the kind and liberal spirit" which Mr. Eliot displayed during this conversation, declaring that he feels justified "in the belief that you will give a ready attention to suggestions of an individual like myself." After reminding Mr. Eliot that Harvard could not ask such men as Samuel Appleton, Ebenezer Francis, or Jonathan Phillips [5] for aid to needy students, since they and others "are at this moment aiding & some supporting more than one student at the University," the President enters with vigor upon his fluently punctuated theme (the italics his):

"It is now nearly ten years, since I have been President of the institution. At every commencement great things are talked of, — glorious visions are hung in the clouds; — *100,000 dollars* are to be raised to give a lift to the University, — great debates are had — Committees are raised — a question arises how shall this great sum be appropriated — some are for reducing the expenses of the College generally — some would not have them reduced at all — some want to increase the numbers of ye College — others think there are enough already — the Committee report — the subject is post-

---

[3] Samuel A. Eliot, 1798–1862, a graduate of the Divinity School in 1820, Treasurer of Harvard College 1842–1853, was a Member of Congress, a public servant, and a man of whom Daniel Webster said: "He is considered the impersonation of Boston; ever-intelligent, ever-patriotic, ever-glorious Boston." He was the father of Charles William Eliot.

[4] *Archives*, Widener Library; my debt to Kimball C. Elkins is beyond payment.

[5] Of these three non-Harvard graduates, Phillips had received an honorary A.M. in 1818, and Francis (Treasurer of Harvard College, 1827–1830) was to receive one in 1843.

poned — they report again — nothing is done. — 'The bear is lost' while the hunters are disputing, how they shall divide the skin after he is taken.

"I have connected myself with none of these questions, nor have I appeared as the advocate or opponent of any one proposition. . . . But repeated disappointment has reduced my mind almost to a state of dispair. I literally feel that sickness of the heart, which arises from hope deferred.

"The conversation I had with you, yesterday, has determined my mind to the course, I am now about to adopt; — a course which I have hitherto from delicacy, or prudence scrupulously avoided. I have determined to spread out to you, and through you to any individuals, to whom you may see fit to communicate them, my views of the pressing wants of the College; — the result of the uninterrupted experience of ten years. . .

"The want of the College is not so much to furnish means for those actually members as it is *to enable those, who wish to become members of it, to do so, with a certainty that they can go through it, without being oppressed every term, with the fear of being compelled to leave before the next.*[6] A fear, which I know often interferes with their improvement, as well as their happiness. . . Great numbers, *are deterred from entering*, from the uncertainty in respect of the aid they are to receive.

"I have no doubt that within the two last years, I have had *forty* inquiries of this kind — 'Mr President, what is the degree of assistance a young man of merit can rely upon, in case he joins Harvard' — I have but one answer I can give 'the Corporation have a fund amounting to about fifteen hundred dollars, income, which they

[6] Apposite to this are the words of President Conant, as quoted by a Los Angeles newspaper reporting his talk before the Harvard Club of Southern California in the early autumn of 1937: "We cannot afford to let the accident of birth cripple the educational opportunities of youths of promise." He was, of course, referring to the recently established National Scholarships. One of the first principles underlying these scholarships, founded nearly one hundred years after Josiah Quincy's letter, is freedom for the recipient to study without fear — financial or academic.

equally distribute according to need, with some reference to merit
— the amount each individual can receive is uncertain — it however
never exceeds *fifty* dollars for the year, and is never less than *twenty
five* — The specific amount depends upon the number of applicants;
— and the degree of need & merit' —

"This answer I have usually found sufficiently chilling & I soon
see their names on the Catalogues of other institutions. I have no
doubt Harvard has lost within two years *twenty*, possibly, *thirty*,
of excellent young men, desirous to avail of its advantages, but deterred from the uncertainty and the amount of assistance they can
possibly receive at Harvard.

"At this point there are two classes of men, whom I wish to address. —

"These first are those, who say — 'we do not wish to increase the
numbers in that seminary. We wish a few to be educated & that
thoroughly. Let the best scholars be there educated; — and those
come, who are able to pay for it' — This language I know to be used
— & how shortsighted is this policy! How false to the true interests
of men of property!

"The Class of young men, who are thus excluded from the education which they desire, are the very men, which the wealthy
ought to desire and *earnestly seek to be associated with their sons.*
They are generally somewhat advanced in years — staid in their
habits — fixed in their principles — right in their views, — the good
order & the good spirit of the College is essentially modified by their
influences. If every man of property, who sends a son to College
would pay the whole expense of the education of a young man of
this description, he would do, probably, as much for his son as
though he gave him Five Thousand dollars. This in an individual
case, might be thought extravagant — but I refer to the effect, were
the principle generally adopted.

"It is a great misfortune to a College to have for its inmates, a
very great proportion of the sons of men [of] wealth.

"Nature has provided a compensation for their prosperity in *the certain deterioration of their sons, unless some strong counteracting influences are provided by themselves to destroy the corrupting effect of the expectation of property.*

"If they want their sons to avail as they ought, of all the advantages of the College, they can do nothing having a more direct or happier tendency to this end, than to *promote the increase of young men disposed to set a good example and to exert good influences in the Seminary.*

"The other Class of men, I would address, are those, who have correct views on this subject and who wish to see the numbers increased at Harvard, but who are perpetually lamenting that other institutions should so increase & Harvard remain stationary; and who are constantly looking for reasons in the inefficiency of instruction & of the immediate government, when there is, in fact, no reasonable cause of complaint on that subject, and when the real cause is as plain as 'the way to parish church.' Gentlemen ask 'why do other seminaries increase & Harvard not?' . . .

"The American Education Society [7] has for many years adopted a system of *loaning monies to young men entering certain colleges, on their note, payable* (with or without interest I do not know which) *within a certain number of years, after they have graduated.*

"The effect of this system I wish the friends of Harvard to observe — If you look at the American Quarterly Register vol. X. No. 1. for August 1837, you will find that this single society has supported 595 young men in 39 Colleges at an expenditure, in *one year* of $31,904 dollars! that of these 595 — while it supports *Ninety eight* at Amherst — *sixty* at Yale *Twenty six* at Bowdoin *Twenty eight* at Williams College — it supported *One* at Harvard.

"Now I make no complaint of that Society. They have a right to

[7] A Society for educating Pious Youth for the Gospel Ministry, founded 1815, chartered 1816. At one point in its history (1874) it joined the Society for Promotion of Collegiate and Theological Education, under the name of the American College and Education Society.

distribute their money on their own conditions & in the places they prefer — The cause of this extraordinary division I do not pretend to state — I only say *it is not because the instruction of Harvard is inferior, nor yet because its morals are worse than other Colleges.* . . .

"I have had four applications, within three days — all making inquiries such as I have above stated — to all the same answer has been given — & I suppose all are now on their way to another College.

"Having stated facts & my experiences, I now state my view of the remedy, and I ask you, Sir, as a friend to the University to show this letter & my proposition to such friends of the College as you please — stating at the same time that one gentleman has authorized me to say that he will give *One Thousand dollars, provided a sum not less than Ten Thousand dollars be raised* — on these principles I add — *I will give Five Hundred* [8]."

It is commensurable with the academic outlook of the times that Mr. Quincy is spontaneous to observe: "The whole sum will not be raised." And to draw the sting from this observation, he half-heartedly suggests that "it will not be immediately wanted." But the letter concludes on a hopeful note, diluted with resignation and sound, gratuitous advice on the administration of the Fund ("in the hands of men designated by some general relation to society"); and a note "on the Note of the student so receiving promising to pay the amount, within Five years after he shall have graduated to said Trustees, with interest." A further recommendation of life insurance "and assigning the said insurance to said Trustees" has never obtained. "Asking your pardon for this intrusion, which has alone resulted from the confidence your language has inspired" is lofty language today; but with those words the destiny of some 6,350 Harvard men — and thousands more to come — appears to have been auspiciously sealed. A momentous adjuration, when all is said.

[8] And so he did.

"AND THE INJURY OF NONE"

"Promise large and do nothing" is the negative philosophy which the President killed. One month and a half later (October 16) a letter of appeal was addressed to a selected list of Boston's wealthier citizens, asking them to subscribe to a fund to aid worthy students in Harvard College. The signatories, in this order, were:

> Samuel A. Eliot, class of 1817.
> George Hayward, class of 1809.
> Charles P. Curtis, class of 1811.
> John A. Lowell, class of 1815.
> John G. Palfrey, class of 1815.
> William H. Gardiner, class of 1816.
> Stephen C. Phillips, class of 1819.

All but one of these men, we observe, had graduated ahead of Mr. Eliot, the spokesman. If the President's sense of economy did not apply to paper and ink, the Committee edged, however imperceptibly, a little nearer to the terse:

Sir,

Notwithstanding the great number of applications which we are aware are constantly made to you for aid to benevolent objects, we feel no hesitation in presenting another in the hope of its meeting with your favorable regard. . . We persuade ourselves you will not esteem this language too strong, when we state to you that our object is to extend the benefits of education and that we hope to do this by increasing the number of deserving young men who may enjoy the advantages that are to be found at Harvard College and there alone in this country.

It cannot be necessary to dwell on or even to enumerate these peculiar advantages, as we believe it is generally admitted that the education which may be obtained at Harvard is, as a whole, superior to that which is offered at any other seminary in the United States. Nor will we enlarge on the importance of a good education to individuals or the community, nor on the desirableness of seeing Harvard College extending her usefulness to all who wish to avail themselves of the privileges she offers. . .

We are informed that a considerable number of young men of good characters and indigent circumstances are, every year, induced to go to other institutions for a collegiate education, though they would prefer

Harvard, from the greater facility of procuring the pecuniary aid which is indispensable to them. Numerous inquiries are made of the President what assistance the college can give and when it is discovered that it is both trifling and uncertain, the inquirer seeks elsewhere for that which it would be better for him and the public if he could obtain at Cambridge. The funds which support in great part those who need assistance in other colleges are derived from the American Education Society, who devote something like $30,000 . . . a year to the support of about 600 young men. Of these scarcely any are to be found at Cambridge. The last year but one of their numerous beneficiaries entered Harvard. It is not a favorite institution with those who contribute to the funds of that Society; and it cannot be expected that its beneficiaries should ever be found at Cambridge in great numbers. But there are others, and we trust you, Sir, are among the number, who believe Harvard College to be the best institution of the kind in the country, and who are willing to give something of their abundance for the purpose of assisting those who are unable to procure for themselves the education they covet, and for whose education it is unquestionably the interest of the richer portion of the community to provide. Anxious to promote at once the essential interests of the country and of the college of which we are Alumni, we present to you the following scheme for raising and using a fund for the education of young men at Cambridge. From $100 to $150 according to circumstances would probably be necessary for each individual per annum, amounting to $400 or $600, say on an average to $500, for the whole collegiate course. Let this sum be loaned on interest and with the security of an insurance on the life to be repaid at the expiration of four years after receiving a degree. If the principal of a fund of $30,000 could be invested under the care of an independent board of Trustees, fourteen young men could be assisted by the interest alone every year; and as it would unquestionably be repaid in great part, the use of a portion of the capital itself would be safe in similar loans. It is obvious therefore that more than has been mentioned may be effected with this sum and proportionate good with a larger or smaller one. Should such a fund be raised, it is proposed to place it in the hands of a Board of Trustees, consisting of three gentlemen disconnected with the College, but holding offices which would render it a fair presumption that they would be men of good judgment and unimpeachable integrity. The Actuary [9] of

[9] Mass. Hospital Life Insurance Co., founded 1818. Joseph Tilden, A.M. (Hon.) 1837, was Actuary 1838–1845, having been preceded by Nathaniel Bowditch, A.M.

the Hospital Life Insurance Company, the President [10] of the American Academy, and the President [11] of the Board of Investments of the Savings Bank have been suggested as suitable persons to be the first trustees, with power to fill vacancies from any portion of the community not directly connected with the College.

The Board should furnish such an amount as they might think proper to young men, recommended by the Faculty of the College but in no case should the loan to an individual exceed the amount of his quarter bill. . . Two gentlemen have proposed to give, the one $1,000, and the other $500, towards raising such a fund, and we know that others stand ready to contribute to it.

Does the plan meet your approbation so far as to induce you to aid us? We appeal merely to your judgment of its practical utility and to your disposition to encourage everything which has for its object the benefit of many and the injury of none.

P.S. A subscription paper for the object will be handed to you in a few days.

The subscription papers were duly handed, and the total of $11,350 was subscribed by October 29. In the following year, 1 August 1839, there was a meeting of subscribers, with His Excellency, Governor Everett,[12] in the Chair. Francis C. Gray, class of 1809, was made secretary of the meeting. The subscribers appointed a committee of three: Josiah Quincy, Charles P. Curtis, and John A. Lowell, to "name and recommend Five Persons to be the first

---

(Hon.) 1802, LL.D. 1816 (corrector and editor of J. H. Moore's *The Practical Navigator*), 1823–1838. Bowditch died in office, March 17; Tilden was appointed March 19.

[10] American Academy of Arts and Sciences, founded 1780. James Jackson, 1796, A.M. 1799, M.B. 1802, M.D. 1809, LL.D. 1854, was president 1838–1839. Nathaniel Bowditch had also preceded him in office, 1829–1838.

[11] Provident Institution for Savings in the Town of Boston, founded 1816. James Savage, 1803, A.M. 1806, LL.D. 1841, was president 1838–1856; he was also apparently chairman (or president) of the Board of Investment, of which John A. Lowell, fourth signer of the Appeal, was a member.

[12] Edward Everett, 1811, A.M. 1814, LL.D. 1835, President of Harvard, 1846–1849. In his letter of 30 August 1838, President Quincy had suggested for Trustees (*not* "subject to elections — if possible") the Chief Justice of the State, and the presidents of the Boston Athenaeum and the Agricultural Society, in addition to the presidents of the American Academy and the Hospital Life Insurance Co.

Trustees." The committee retired and promptly reported the following:

Ebenezer Francis, A.M. (Hon.) 1843.
James Savage, class of 1803.
William H. Gardiner, class of 1816.
Samuel A. Eliot, class of 1817.
Edward Wigglesworth, class of 1822.

On August 5 a Trustees' meeting was held and Edward Wigglesworth was elected treasurer and clerk. At the next meeting, September 5, a letter (unobtainable) from President Quincy was presented, recommending certain students in the College as suitable to be assisted by the Fund, as yet unnamed. The Trustees, with continued zeal to see the business through, again met, September 19, and adopted regulations for the Fund under the title (which is virtually the title today) of "Trustees for Assisting Students at Harvard College." Certain investments were decided upon; and it may be noted that *all* investments for the first few years were in bank and insurance stocks. On the books for 1857 appears the purchase of a railroad stock (Boston & Worcester).[13] The earliest bonds bought were railroad bonds (Cincinnati & Indiana), in 1867, with a book value of $2,586.17. Until recently, investments since 1867 have been almost entirely in bonds, with a few remainders from original bank stocks. During the last ten years the Trustees have diversified: roughly 60% in bonds and 40% in equities. On 22 November 1839 they granted their first loans, totalling $540, to five students. The growth of the Fund in the years that have followed may best be considered briefly in tabular form:

[13] Consolidated with the Western Railroad in 1867 (the year in which the Fund bought its first RR bonds!) to become the Boston & Albany. The early roads did not prove as stable as the Fund. The Cincinnati & Indiana was leased in 1866 to the Indianapolis, Cincinnati & Lafayette; in 1880 reorganized into the Cincinnati, Indianapolis, St. Louis, & Chicago; in 1889 incorporated in Ohio as the Cleveland, Cincinnati, Chicago & St. Louis. Three bonds of the latter, as a matter of record, are currently on the Fund's books.

Year	Amt. Loaned	No. Loans	Assets
1849	$795	28	$19,764
1859	$1,400	30	$29,763
1869	$0	0	$55,808
1889	$2,450	29	$87,269
1939	$16,075	187	$485,882

In 1889, the Fund's fiftieth year, the total assets of $87,269 included $39,117 in students' notes. The remaining investments were divided approximately into $12,000 (bonds) and $36,000 (railroad and bank stocks). In recent years there has been a rising curve in loan collections, although there has always been some loss. In 1939, for example, collections amount to $16,877 as against approximately $15,760 for 1938, $10,021 in 1937, and $5,545 in 1936. In spite of Josiah Quincy's early injunction, a due date has never been set for loans, and no collateral is required. The total expenses for the Fund are clerk hire and attorney fees.

The present Trustees, it is significant, are all descendants of the founders. The complete list is a roll of honor in the service of the College:

Trustees	Terms of Office
Samuel A. Eliot	1839–1842
Ebenezer Francis	1839–1855
William H. Gardiner	1839–1854
James Savage	1839–1871
*Edward Wigglesworth	1839–1864
Francis C. Gray	1842–1856
Nathaniel I. Bowditch	1854–1861
Samuel Eliot	1855–1856
*John Lowell	1856–1897
George S. Hillard	1856–1880
Charles R. Codman	1861–1918
Henry Austin Whitney	1864–1889
Theodore Lyman	1871–1889
*George Wigglesworth	1880–1930

Roger Wolcott	1889–1900
Harcourt Amory	1889–1920
*John Lowell	1897–1922
Arthur Lyman	1900–1933
Russell S. Codman	1918–1934
R. H. Gardiner, Jr.	1920–1959
*Ralph Lowell	1922–1959
Norton Wigglesworth	1932–1950
Arthur T. Lyman	1933–1959
Francis C. Gray	1938–1959

"The result," said Josiah Quincy in that first persuasive letter, "would soon be felt in its number." But it is clearly in perfection as well as in numbers that the centennial result is felt. In that list of 6,350 Harvard men who have benefited are concealed the names of many who achieved and are achieving distinction in life. The casual turning of the leaves of the old day book will show a Harvard President (Thomas Hill, class of 1843); two famous Harvard Professors of Law (Christopher C. Langdell and James B. Thayer); a writer (Horatio Alger); two Governors of the Commonwealth (Robinson and Brackett); a president of the University of California (William T. Reid); a Major General, U.S.V. (Francis C. Barlow); six other college presidents, eight deans, fifty or sixty distinguished professors of Harvard, Columbia, Cornell, Chicago, Vassar, Yale, Stanford, Maine, Syracuse, Brown, the Imperial University of Tokyo, McGill, and elsewhere; four judges and justices, including the Chief Justice of the Hawaii Supreme Court, nine or ten Overseers, a college librarian, a Senator, a Commissioner of the Chinese Imperial Maritime Customs, a Harvard Fellow, a past president of the Associated Clubs, a nationally known poet, one of the best known and best loved scholars of our time, countless Fellows of the American Academy of Arts and Sciences, and members of other learned societies. These are the men that a glance will recog-

* Treasurer & Clerk: Edward Wigglesworth, 1839–1864; John Lowell, 1864–1880; Geo. Wigglesworth, 1880–1898; John Lowell, 1898–1922; Ralph Lowell, 1922–1959.

nize. Behind them are the names of hundreds of others who have given, and are giving, useful and honorable careers to the benefit of the Nation — "and the injury of none."

1939

In History 5b

ONE personal undergraduate event of Friday morning must not pass unrecorded. History 5b — The Making of Modern America, 1865 to the Present — met as usual in Harvard Hall at 9 A.M. Professor Paul H. Buck, Dean of the Faculty of Arts and Sciences, the present lecturer in the course, was rounding into the first World War. The class had reached to about this point: out of the nineteenth Century emerged two dominant questions. Summarized, they were (first) how to solve in a democratic way the economic problems to effect an equable society, and (second) how to secure a peaceful world. This morning Professor Buck was to talk on Woodrow Wilson.

In the class were Navy students, returned veterans, civilian undergraduates. This was no peacetime class; this was no ordinary morning. Reflecting on the swift tragedy, still uppermost in the minds of students and teacher alike, Professor Buck faced his class, thought a moment, and yielded to inspiration and improvisation. Most of these young men were seven, eight, or nine years old when Mr. Roosevelt had first entered the White House. He was the only President of their time and generation. He belonged to the world, but in many ways he belonged most particularly to youth. What could one say? Abraham Lincoln died on 15 April 1865; Franklin D. Roosevelt on 12 April 1945. The similarity of circumstances needed no argument. But it made a beginning. The lecturer commenced:

> Hush'd be the camps today,
> And soldiers let us drape our war-worn weapons,

168

And each with musing soul retire to celebrate,
Our dear commander's death. . .

"As one studies history," said Professor Buck, "the stature of a man is judged by what he does to build or destroy the faith by which men live . . . Mr. Roosevelt was great because he, like Lincoln, restored men's faith . . ." That wanted to be said anyway.

So he continued, explaining to his students the peculiar poignancy of the situation to one like himself — a member of a generation which has seen two wars and the failure which followed so hard on the first. The class was absorbed, transfixed — hearing their own thought made articulate, finding their own ideas come suddenly clear. It was a strong and steadily moving talk, one of those rare intimate flashes for which all teachers wait and on which all students utterly attend, oblivious of the passage of time. There was more Walt Whitman, and Professor Buck stopped speaking.

But the silence spoke.

1945

Quinquennial

EVERY five years, on the hour, my favorite university issues a catalogue of its graduates stretching back to the days of the Indian. It grows fatter as time goes on. It contains names, degrees, honors, but no addresses. More generally it contains merely names and degrees. If there was no degree there is no name. John S. Jumpup, A.B., is included, but plain James Jumpup, Esq., who was a good lad, though not of the fellowship of scholars, is absent. You will find him more modestly with his kind in that other compendium, the College Directory. Thus a good many important people are successfully ignored.

To those on the inside the questionnaire for the Catalogue is flattering. It informs you that in addition to your degree (or degrees) it is anxious to include "certain academic distinctions." This is very pleasant. Glancing over pages two and three, it rapidly appears that the range of "certain academic distinctions" is wider, and somewhat higher, than you fancied. Why not? Life must not only be honorable; it must be honored. Let us begin with the highest.

"Have you ever held any of the offices usually recorded in the CATALOGUE, lists of which are given in paragraphs (a) and (b) under this question? If so, please state them, giving the information for which blanks are provided.

"(a) Offices under the United States Government; President; Vice President; President of the Senate (when not the Vice President); Member of the Cabinet; Senator; Speaker and Member of the House of Representatives; Ambassador; Minister; Chief Justice and Justice of the Supreme Court; Chief Justice and Judge of the Court of Claims; Judge of a Circuit or District Court; Major-

General and higher ranks not by brevet; Rear Admiral and higher ranks; and, since 1900, Assistant Secretary of State; Assistant Secretary of the Treasury; Solicitor General of the United States."

This calls for a pretty memory.

Have you ever been President?

No, you think not.

Vice President?

Ah, that's a different matter. Very likely you have. We'd better ask.

"Darling, have I ever been Vice President?"

"Vice President of what?"

"The United States."

"What a silly question. Are you crazy?"

"*They* didn't think it was silly. They're asking me right here."

"Who is?"

"The College Catalogue. 'Have you ever been Vice President?' it says."

"No, you haven't."

"It seems to me I remember it one summer — wasn't it in 1925?"

"That was the year we went to Rye Beach."

"So it was. How about Speaker?"

"After dinner?"

"Of the House."

"Whose house?"

"Never mind. Minister?"

"You've preached enough."

"Not that kind."

"Ask me another."

"Well, then, a Senator. Surely I've been a Senator? Everybody has."

"You *are* crazy."

"Or a Rear Admiral?"

No answer.

"Or a 'Major-General and higher ranks not by brevet'? There's something. We've got to be careful. If any brevets come round here offering higher ranks, don't let them in."

"Were you ever taken for Napoleon?"

"No, I'm serious. I *must* amount to something. You can't return all the blanks blank."

"Why the blank blank not?"

"Here's one: Assistant Secretary of State. When I was in Washington that time — you remember? — I assisted someone. Maybe it was the Secretary of State. It was an old man with a beard. He was getting on the street car."

"Go to bed."

"And then the Societies. 'Are you a member of any of the foreign societies, a list of which is printed on the next page?' Let's see. 'Finland: Finska Vetenskaps Societaten (Helsingfors).' I guess not. 'Hungary: Magyar Tudományos Akadémia (Budapest).' It seems to me I've eaten some of that. 'Denmark: Kongelige Danske Videnskabernes-Selskabet (Copenhagen).' Wasn't that the name of the boat we sailed on? We went second kabernes, didn't we?"

"Third."

"I'm sorry about this one: 'Have you received any honorary appointments under foreign governments? This does *not* include *decorations* such as Victoria Cross, Iron Cross, D.S.O., etc.' That's too bad. All those medals gone to waste. Are they still in my bureau drawer?"

And so after you have decided that you are not a member of the Académie Française, the Royal College of Surgeons, not Chief Justice, Ambassador to the Court of St. James, or a modern Leonardo, you remember that you did at least receive your degree (not degrees) though it came a year late, because you failed in you forget what, and is now lost in the attic. Write it down. They'll print that anyway.

If your name is Alexander Aab you may even head the list.

1932

Seminary

An Acre for Education

Very few people will be bold enough now to argue that the advance of women was not right or that it has gone too far.
— Arnold Bennett

ACROSS the Cambridge Common from Harvard, at the upper end where the shadow of the Washington Elm used to fall, is the center of Radcliffe College. The group of part Colonial, part Georgian, buildings closing in a semicircle which turns back hopefully toward Brattle Street forms what president and deans would call the academic group. The dormitories are in a separate cluster, several blocks to the north. All day long, in the college year, the stream of girls on foot or bicycle between the two refutes the tercentenary fact that Cambridge is a Harvard city. The red-brick wall on the Common side shelters a quiet campus, which in Harvard's vernacular becomes a Yard. To the east and south rise the older towers and the newer spires of the university of Emerson and Eliot; and the sharper winds of doctrine blowing west of north cut across the path of professors with green bags of books, and still more girls on foot or bicycle, hurrying between classes of two college communities as distinct as Minneapolis and St. Paul, now mutually dedicated to the pragmatic idea of joint instruction.

The familiar sight confirms the traditional reputation of Radcliffe industry, but gives no hint of what lies behind it.[1] The outward look is very much like the façade of an American college almost anywhere; and the encroachment of a modern city has not made the bricks more eloquent or the grass more green. That Rad-

---

[1] "Moral education is impossible without the habitual vision of greatness." — Alfred North Whitehead.

175

cliffe is New England and next door to Harvard sometimes leads
to confusion of the proper understanding of her aims and being. To
what extent New England, and how identified with Harvard? Yet
"the main question for the public interest in a college," said the
wise Dean Briggs in 1929, "is not 'How is it organized?' but 'What
does it accomplish?' "

It is a well known fact that Radcliffe women all over the United
States and in many foreign countries are actively engaged as educators, scientists, doctors, editors, artists, lawyers, scholars, actresses,
architects, journalists, curators, authors, and in many other branches
of human endeavor. No other American college for women maintains a graduate school in size or importance approaching hers. The
training at Radcliffe is the development of the finer qualities of
character and mind. But accomplishment and the opportunity to
accomplish are more than the skillful blend of teachers, books, and
bricks and motar. There is a definite reason for what Radcliffe has
been able to do, and a need for a more general understanding of
this reason if the circle of her friends is to be widened and sustained.

I

The principle that higher education for women [2] is a good and desirable thing enjoys almost complete acceptance today. So complete,
indeed, that it is easy to lose sight of the primitive fact that the cause
was won well within the lifetime of pioneers still uninclined to die.
Apart from coeducation in America, we have for active proof of
this acceptance an increasing group of women's colleges whose
names are almost as familiar as those of Harvard and Yale. Seven
of these are Barnard, Bryn Mawr, Mount Holyoke, Radcliffe, Smith,
Vassar, and Wellesley. They are situated, roughly, along the Atlantic seaboard, from the fringe of Boston to the fringe of Phila-

---

[2] About 400,000 American college students in 1937 were women. By 1952 the
figure had increased to 761,190. In 1900 the ratio of women students to men was
one to three; today the ratio is slightly more than one to two.

delphia. Massachusetts claims four, New York two, Pennsylvania one. Of the seven, Mount Holyoke is the oldest (1837); Barnard the youngest (1889); Smith the largest (2,279 students); Bryn Mawr the smallest (815 students); Wellesley the wealthiest ($33,535,746 endowment). Each grants the Bachelor's degree; Bryn Mawr and Radcliffe offer the Ph.D. In these relations Radcliffe (1879) was the fifth to be founded, is third (after Smith and Wellesley) in the number of students (1,531) and fifth (after Wellesley, Vassar, Smith, and Bryn Mawr) in endowment with $13,067,941. One should understand that it is both convenient and easy to speak of these colleges in such numerically comparative terms, for unlike any similar group of masculine institutions in this country, they have long since published jointly a sustaining program for women's colleges;[3] and as early as 1927 (*Atlantic Monthly*, November) the seven presidents signed an important article on "The Question of the Women's Colleges" — significant to the present paragraphs.

Comparison ends with these figures; but there is one respect in which Radcliffe College differs essentially from her sisters, and this should be made clear. Although she divides with Barnard, Bryn Mawr, and Wellesley all advantages offered by an available large city, and enjoys the further privilege of being front-fence neighbor to Harvard University, Radcliffe alone has had from the first the strength of a university faculty. Her teachers are Harvard's teachers and her springs are the springs of Dunster and Mather; the same which gave life to Emerson and Thoreau, to Agassiz, Eliot, James, and Holmes. "In everything but name," wrote President Le Baron

[3] From a movement which began in Indiana in 1948 — four years after the United Negro College Fund was established — some 391 non-tax-supported colleges and universities in 36 states are now members of one or another of the 32 state or regional associations or foundations organized to solicit gifts primarily from business and industry. Most of them have established central offices, with paid executives, to coördinate the program. Gifts are usually divided among the participating colleges under a formula based on the size of the institutions. One of the two regional groups is the New England Colleges Fund, Inc., established in 1952. Its 24 member institutions range alphabetically from Amherst to Williams, including Mount Holyoke, Radcliffe, Smith, Wellesley, and Wheaton.

R. Briggs of the Radcliffe before the second World War, "a Radcliffe degree *is* a Harvard degree. Radcliffe exists to give women a Harvard education by opening to them . . . as much as possible of what is best in Harvard. . . . Thus, from the beginning, Radcliffe has been a woman's Harvard. It is still a separate institution, with its own corporation, receiving from Harvard no direct financial aid. A Harvard Endowment Fund is not a Radcliffe Endowment Fund; and all that makes education more costly at Harvard makes it more costly at Radcliffe. . . . Its light is not all borrowed light; its individuality is as plainly marked as that of Vassar, or Smith, or Mount Holyoke, or Bryn Mawr. . . . Yet out of the tradition of Harvard comes Radcliffe's abiding strength, and the inspiration of that work which has brought distinction to so many of its graduates." That basic word comes up again: This in essence is "the *distinctive* thing for which we have aimed," said Elizabeth Cary Agassiz in 1883, one year after she had been elected first president of Radcliffe — then the Society for the Collegiate Instruction of Women. And that conception the years have not altered. The College is still "anchored against the whole teaching force of Harvard."

Three centuries of Harvard tradition have given to the University in Cambridge something of the look of everlastingness. In the near end of this long shadow lie the seventy-nine years of Radcliffe history that begins with an experiment in what the great Mrs. Agassiz herself called "such bare and meagre surroundings." It was furthermore a peculiar experiment which many predicted would end with equal misfortune in failure or complete coeducation. But it has ended in neither. The light of Radcliffe is today less borrowed than President Briggs implied. The College stands on her own soil, with her own buildings, her own endowment, her own direction, her own will. If not yet the look of everlastingness, she wears the look of permanence. And that permanence, wrote Christina Hopkinson Baker [4] in 1929, "has precedent behind it."

[4] *The Story of Fay House* by Christina Hopkinson (Mrs. George P.) Baker. (Cambridge: Harvard University Press, 1929).

II

It is not the year 1879, but the autumn or winter of 1876. Rad-cliffe College, "born of no man's or woman's ambition and wealth" is an idea as yet cloudy in the minds of two people. Mr. Arthur Gilman, an historian and literary man of note in his day, director of the Cambridge School for Girls, and a familiar Cambridge figure from 1870 until his death in 1909, discussed with his wife Stella Scott ("she urged upon me," rather) the need in Cambridge for an institution for the higher education of women. Discussion ripened to resolve. For two years a plan for such an institution was con-sidered and developed; but before it could be openly proposed, an event of great significance occurred. A Miss Abby Leach ("healthy, studious, capable, and well trained," said Dean Briggs of her many years later when she had become Professor Leach of Vassar) asked three Harvard professors to give her private instruction in Greek, Latin, and English. The men she asked were William W. Good-win, James B. Greenough, and Francis J. Child. Miss Leach suc-ceeded in her request, and by the excellence of her work convinced at least three important men that a young woman of college age may be as capable of advanced study as the young men in their Harvard classes. Miss Leach, outpioneering the pioneers, unaware of the importance of her venture in the impending creation of a college, lived to be known variously as "the nucleus" and "the en-tering wedge."

The moment for action had arrived. In 1878, Mr. Gilman has re-corded in a letter, "At last . . . I concluded to approach Professor Greenough. . . . I told him that I had made out a list of instructors in the different departments, and wished that he could do the same, and that then we would compare them. He expressed much interest in the plan and entered into it with warmth. He made out a list of professors, and it proved very much like mine. He told me of Miss Leach, whose presence, he thought, would lead the instructors to look favorably on the plan. . . . Meanwhile I had laid the plan before President Eliot, asking if there was any objection to carrying it out. He called on me and told me there was no objection. In January, 1879, we began to form the committee of ladies, taking pains to choose such as did not represent any 'cause,' or who would be looked upon as 'advanced,' or in favor of coeducation."

The plan, in brief, was to secure the immediate consent of a number of professors and instructors in Harvard College "to give private tuition to properly qualified young women who desire to pursue advanced studies in Cambridge. . . . No instruction will be provided of a lower grade than that given in Harvard College." It was estimated that while the expense of instruction would depend directly upon the number of students in the courses arranged, it would probably not exceed $400 a year, and might be as low as $250. The plan was not then so ambitious as to foster hope of the Bachelor's degree; but it was provided that "pupils who show upon examination that they have satisfactorily pursued any courses of study under this scheme will receive certificates to that effect, signed by their instructors." In the event that a pupil pursued four years of study, the signed certificate was to certify to the whole. The circular which conveyed this information over the signatures of a committee of seven ladies, including Mrs. Agassiz and Miss Alice M. Longfellow, and with the assent of President Charles W. Eliot of Harvard, was dated 22 February 1879. It was worded with care to avoid two possible major misconceptions: that the plan in any way tended to coeducation, and that Harvard College was in any way responsible for it. Thirty-eight Harvard teachers immediately offered courses; and it is encouraging to remember that among these volunteers were such men as Le Baron R. Briggs, James B. Greenough, William James, Charles Eliot Norton, and George Herbert Palmer. Fortified by the prestige of the committee of seven — "to give the public confidence that if young women were sent to Cambridge they would be cared for" — a community believed hostile to the cause of advanced education for women reacted well. Those who felt that the dignity of Harvard was threatened subsided after a satisfying outburst of "remonstrance and expostulation."

> A lesson all of us may take to heart,
> That if we would escape the serpent's tooth,
> We best leave Adam to his books apart.

The next few recorded events draw the threads together. In March, 1879, an advisory board of five professors was appointed to act with the ladies; and in August, Mr. Joseph B. Warner, a lawyer of Boston, was appointed treasurer, with a charter fund of nearly $16,000 in subscriptions to administer. In September came examinations for the "Harvard girls," as Mrs. Agassiz tentatively called them; and twenty-seven began their college studies in rented rooms of the Carret House, 6 Appian Way, adjacent to the present site of Radcliffe, wherein Mrs. Agassiz hung the muslin curtains of her own making. Of the year 1880 we know little outside the fact of continued existence. In 1881 Mrs. Agassiz was appointed a committee to interview President Eliot on the use of books from the Harvard Library, but particularly on "the feeling about our future." The future indeed was by no means yet secure.

Officially nameless until April, 1822, when inadequately christened "The Society for the Collegiate Instruction of Women," the organization was nicknamed almost at once the "Harvard Annex," and generally and popularly referred to as such for the next fifteen years. In May the committee for the Society agreed to constitute itself a corporation. On July 6 — the first meeting held after the articles of association were signed — administrative boards were established and Mrs. Agassiz elected president; and on August 16 the association was formally incorporated under the laws of the Commonwealth of Massachusetts. The skeptics' fears for the worst in the experiment were never realized: "We have had as yet no flighty students," Mrs. Agassiz was able and glad to write after the proper lapse of time; and there appears to have been in the same interval every evidence of "ladylike behavior in all respects." Her pride was perhaps pardonable, for the average age of the young women was less than that of the undergraduates at Harvard.

III

From 1880 to 1884 the Annex was busy at the healthy task of outgrowing itself. Forty to fifty students annually were dedicated to their studies; some $70,000 toward an endowment of $100,000 was publicly subscribed; a working library listed over 800 books; the ladies of the original committee "opened their houses," in the words of Le Baron R. Briggs, "to the eagerly studious girls . . . stirred by the triumphant optimism of pioneers"; and — quite as important as anything — the pleasant rooms in 6 Appian Way grew wretchedly too small. Prior to the founding of the Annex, the Gilmans had frequently eyed with almost hopeless desire a "noble red-brick house" at the corner of Garden and Mason Streets, almost under the shadow of the then magnificent Washington Elm. "It embodied," says Mrs. Baker in her charming history of it, "the post-revolutionary taste and the ideas of Charles Bulfinch." This was the Fay House, built in 1807, standing (and still standing) on the identical "i ackr" which a certain Guy Bambrige had been allotted in 1634 in what was called West End, as "up the river from Boston or down through the forest from Watertown." The house had roots. The soil underneath it, the Gilmans knew, meant something before even Harvard was founded: it had lain originally behind the protecting *pallysadoe* near the ancient path to Charlestown — the Indians walled out and history let in.

> Guy Bambrige
> Of Cambridge —
> Like *Ham*bridge
> Or *Aim*bridge?

'Twas lost on
Old Boston —
Still, over the same bridge,
The dam, or the tram bridge,
In stout "pallysadoe"
And not in a glade-o
Of Cambridge
Adumbrage
Guy Bambrige
Took umbrage
From bear, wolf, and Injun,
And scalpin' and singein'.

Allotted "i ackr,"
That old history-maker
Back there in the shade-o
Of strong "pallysadoe" —
That cotter,
That squatter —
Guy Bambrige
(Say *Ham*bridge)
Of Cambridge
(That's *Aim*bridge:
A dim ridge
Of timberage
Called "Westend")
Was destined
To die without knowledge
His land made a College.

In 1885 the Society purchased the noble red-brick house for $20,000 from Miss Maria Fay, daughter of Judge Samuel Phillips Prescott Fay, a Harvard graduate and overseer, who had died in 1856. Miss Fay had offered it to the Society unaware that it was the established choice of the Executive Committee. Money was raised again to meet both purchase and alteration, and classes opened there in September of that year. The house became at once what it has never ceased to be: the heart of Radcliffe College. It brought to the fledgling Society an atmosphere and history as delightful and charming as anything that had ever existed in Cambridge. And what is more, its humane and literary associations and lived-in air made it ideally suited to a college of women.

The man who built it in 1807 was one Nathaniel Ireland, a prosperous artisan who had died in poverty incurred after Jefferson's embargo proclamation, his estate passing at auction to the Reverend Joseph McKean, for about $4,000, in 1814. But his beautiful house remained: haunted by Bulfinch — in tradition if not on evidence — in oval room, bays, circular stairway, and mantelpieces.

Dr. McKean was a teacher, preacher, scholar, and second holder of the Boylston Professorship of Rhetoric and Oratory at Harvard — the sixth being Le Baron Russell Briggs. The McKean purchase is laid to the fact that the Boylston Professor (who enjoyed the still-existing right of pasturing a cow in the Harvard Yard) was officially obliged — although for no vaccine reason — to live near the College. The second incumbent had a reputation for "sincere and extensive hospitality," and with him begins the long tradition of generosity and open house, infectious to the final Fay. In the case of Dr. McKean it was peculiarly blended by a quarter cask of wine and a corresponding secretaryship of the Society for the Suppression of Intemperance.

The exchange of ownership continued, and the house began to befriend the literary. In 1819 Edward Everett, "whose influence on young people," said Emerson ". . . was almost comparable to that of Pericles in Athens," established himself in residence while teaching, lecturing, and commencing in 1820 his ardent editorship of *The North American Review*. A variously distinguished man he was: daringly appointed to a Greek Professorship at Harvard when he was scarcely four years out of College; later a member of Congress, Senator, Secretary of State, Minister to the Court of St. James's, four-term Governor of the Commonwealth, Harvard Overseer, and finally an unhappy Harvard President.[5] His presence of course lent luster to his hearth, albeit he wrote of his life at the time: "I die daily of a cramped spirit, fluttering and beating from side to side of a cage." He tarried there but briefly, though his mother and his sister, with her two sons, stayed on until 1824. Then Mrs. Francis Dana moved in. She was the daughter of President Willard of Harvard; and her father-in-law, the Honorable Francis Dana, made a name for himself as Chief Justice of the Supreme Judicial Court of Massachusetts and as Ambassador to Russia. His brother, in turn, was Richard Henry Dana, largely remembered for his son who was the author of *Two Years Before the Mast*. Mrs. Dana's daughter Sophia introduced "the brick house with a bow window" to the formal world of education when she opened the handsome door to a school for girls. "Two exceptions were made to the femininity of the classes," says Mrs. Baker. "Young Edmund P. Dana came as one of the family and little James Russell Lowell was permitted to come with his sister, riding down from Elmwood on his pony. The little boys sat on stools at either side of Sophia at the head of the table, James in an embroidered ruffled shirt with cuffs." But young Sophia was not long at teaching school. In 1827, "tall, graceful, and elegant in the oval room," she was married to George Ripley, a Brook Farmer, a founder of the Transcendental Club and, with Emerson and Margaret Fuller, of the famous *Dial*. In 1829 the house was occupied by Mrs. Francis Channing, sister-in-law of William Ellery Channing, a Fellow of Harvard College. In 1831 it passed into the hands of Stephen Higginson, Steward of Harvard, who never lived in it. But Stephen was the father of Thomas Wentworth Higginson, the author, who brought to the house at one remove

[5] Last of the nine Harvard Presidents, incidentally, to live in Wadsworth House, still facing into Harvard Square, and some 81 years older than Fay.

another important literary association. Then in 1832 came Daniel Davis, retired solicitor-general of Massachusetts. He was 70 years old and had thirteen children, and his was for that reason a lively household. The place was now named Castle Corner, and it figured even more in the gay society of the time. Daniel's daughter Helen, as a singer, began a Fay House musical tradition unbroken down to 1885.

Judge Fay bought the property for $4,500 in 1835. It had lost in the Higginson regime the circular stairway, acquired a new entrance and grey paint on the bricks.[6] The Judge, his wife, and two little girls brought it "a merry and vivid life"; but of the girls it is Maria particularly who is remembered. She was kindly, intelligent, cultivated, beloved. The first Radcliffe Scholarship (1890) was named for her. The Fays were not a year in the house (now known as the Fay Homestead) before Harvard celebrated the 200th Anniversary of her founding with a College Jubilee; and the Reverend Samuel Gilman — visiting them for the occasion — wrote "Fair Harvard" in the northeast bedroom. The last resident not a Fay (1866–70) was the handsome and most distinguished scientist Wolcott Gibbs, Rumford Professor of Chemistry at Harvard. "It was Gibbs's merit," wrote Frank Wigglesworth Clarke, "that he, more than any other one man, introduced into the United States the German conception of research as a means of chemical instruction."

So the years slipped by and the house wore well. When Professor Gibbs departed, Maria returned — for fifteen useful years. Lowell, Longfellow (he stayed once to shell peas), the Norwegian violinist Ole Bull, and William James in the residential days were frequent visitors. And not the least of this company, and by all odds the most picturesque: Evangelinus Apostolides Sophocles, University

---

[6] The house had at least a tenuous connection with tragedy, for it was to Judge Fay (according to family tradition as reported by Mrs. Baker) after a game of whist with him and Maria, that Dr. Webster confessed to killing Dr. Parkman. Dr. Webster's last letter before his execution — "a beautiful letter, calm and resigned" — was addressed to Judge Fay.

AN ACRE FOR EDUCATION

Professor of Ancient, Byzantine, and Modern Greek — as strange a character as Harvard has ever tethered in the Yard, and one whose history must some day be better known. He lived alone in Holworthy Hall, kept chickens in his room and in Maria's cellar, buried the dead ones in the Bambrige "ackr," received, consumed and dispensed each winter a cask of wine from a special vineyard on the heights of Corinth, and was himself once nursed in Fay House (in the room to the right of the front door) during an illness of over a year. It was of him with "his blue cloak and wild grey beard, his learning and his silence" that Professor Longfellow said: "He makes Diogenes a possibility."

But it was Maria who upheld the reality. "It was because she was such a lovely and cultivated woman," wrote one of her nieces, "that I gave the first scholarship to Fay House, that her name might be perpetuated. It was for the same reason that Mrs. Agassiz had the name Fay kept on the house. It seemed as if her spirit might in some way influence the following generation in quietness and gentleness. . . ." [7]

Of such are the ghosts of what is now Fay House. They were friendly ghosts to the students of 1885. No amount of architectural alteration changed their grateful presence. The corner castle now became a cornerstone. A house which had known teaching, music, the literary instinct, brilliant and cultivated people, all the fine texture of association, and was "one of the most pleasant and eligible situations in Cambridge," perhaps only came into its own. By 1890 the Annex was not merely indwelling, but already planning further expansion. Adjoining land was purchased and two small laboratories erected. Students increased from two or three score to one hundred and fifty; fifty to sixty of the Harvard Faculty were annually engaged in teaching the girls; $20,000 to $25,000 was publicly asked for and raised by Mrs. Agassiz. By 1892 Fay House had doubled in size, with the inclusion of an auditorium. Affairs of the Society

[7] Christina Hopkinson Baker, *The Story of Fay House.*

187

at last seemed visibly more secure. "Whatever be its attitude in the future — whatever its relation to the University — whatever name it may bear," said Mrs. Agassiz in her Commencement address of that year, "I hope it will always be respected for the genuineness of its work, for the quiet dignity of its bearing, for its adherence to the noblest ends of scholarship."

IV

If Fay House became the heart, Mrs. Louis (Elizabeth Cary) Agassiz was the soul of the burgeoning College. Her diaries and letters in the Lucy Allen Paton biography reflect a life that Charles Eliot Norton praised doubly for its "sweet and steady consistency of excellence." She had, he said, simplicity of heart. To the Annex her contribution "consisted in giving it, simply by being herself, an impetus, a dignity, and an unwavering standard that it could not have had without her."

She had married Louis Agassiz, Professor of Zoölogy and Geology at Harvard from 1847 until his death in 1873. Not living to see his wife's titanic share in the Radcliffe venture, it was nevertheless the School for Girls which she had founded in 1856 to assist him financially which led her, "according to her own testimony, to associate herself with the plan that resulted in Radcliffe College." From the beginning of that connection until her death in 1907 in her eighty-fifth year she held the esteem and confidence of President Eliot. In his commemorative address he said of her: "She believed that the connection of Harvard University with Radcliffe College was essential to the progress of Radcliffe. She believed that I had something to do with securing that connection. I had had something to do with it, but very little compared with what she had."

So it was Mrs. Agassiz who, early in 1893, began a series of almost daily interviews with him concerning a closer union of the Society and Harvard. The negotiations were involved and lasted into May;

but out of them came an historic agreement between the President and Fellows of Harvard College and the Society for the Collegiate Instruction of Women. The Society was to have a name, be self-governing, award diplomas for the Bachelor's degree — counter-signed by the President of Harvard and its seal affixed. The President and Fellows were to be the visitors of "X College" and to approve all teachers or examiners appointed. Thus the Annex in fact became an X; and where it had enjoyed two names — neither suitable — it must now cast about for a third. Emmanuel College was first suggested, whence had hailed John Harvard. But a coincident discovery at the University revived the name of Lady Mowlson who had given Harvard £100 in 1643 "for a scholarship, the revenue of it to be employed that way forever." Lady Mowlson was born Ann Radcliffe. Mrs. Agassiz suggested her name as appropriate with "a certain picturesqueness" for the College; and in October 1893 it was formally voted to take the proper legal steps to do her will.

However, the way was still not clear: objections, even petitions to the Harvard Board of Overseers, occluded all direct procedure. "The howl grew louder against Radcliffe," wrote Mrs. Agassiz in her diary. But the Society pushed on; the bill for a college charter was drawn, and a hearing before the Committee on Education of the Massachusetts Legislature at the State House in Boston set for 28 February 1894. The organized objection [8] at that hearing was based primarily on the fact that the proposed college was without adequate endowment to insure a guarantee of high character maintained. It was Mrs. Agassiz who won the cause. She argued her point cheerfully and with confidence. "She did not speak more than ten minutes," said President Eliot who disclaimed any personal credit for the bill's success, "but the effect could not have been more striking. I never saw anything like it in any legislative committee room, and I have been in a good many committee rooms in the course of my official life." The chairman came down from the platform and said:

[8] Committee on Endowment of Colleges of the Association of Collegiate Alumnæ.

"I'd like to do anything that lady wants me to do. . . . She must be the head of this proposed Radcliffe College." The bill of charter was passed. The Governor signed the act for the incorporation of Radcliffe College on 23 March 1894:

. . . The said Radcliffe College is hereby authorized to confer on women all honors and degrees as fully as any university or college in this Commonwealth is now so empowered respecting men or women: provided, however, that no degree shall be conferred by the said Radcliffe College except with the approval of the President and Fellows of Harvard College, given on satisfactory evidence of such qualification as is accepted for the same degree when conferred by Harvard University.

V

The command changed but little. Mrs. Agassiz continued president, Mr. Warner, treasurer; Mr. Gilman became regent, the Corporation and the Academic Board were enlarged. Miss Mary Coes, a Radcliffe graduate, was made secretary. Miss Agnes Irwin, a descendant of Benjamin Franklin and principal of a well known girls' school in Philadelphia, became dean. Mrs. Agassiz's relation to the students remained "one of affectionate personal intercourse rather than any immediate direction of their studies." But the College itself, having made the preliminary run, was like a ship passing out of the narrows into the open sea. Her position was definite, her profile unmistakable. We begin to sense both the quality of undergraduate life and the outward influence of many graduates. We begin to see results.

We begin to hear the ceaseless lament of all endowed institutions: the cry for endowment and unrestricted income. Radcliffe needed what Mrs. Agassiz called "better academic accommodations and opportunities for physical culture." President Eliot boiled it down to laboratories, departmental libraries, a gymnasium and lecture halls, and dormitories. "Now all these things [he said] cost money;

therefore Radcliffe needs great endowments, and needs them at once." Radcliffe got them — not *great* endowments, but sufficient for her first period of brick and mortar growth: the gymnasium (gift of Mrs. Augustus Hemenway); the land between Shepard, Linnæan, Garden, and Walker Streets; Bertram Hall — the first dormitory (gift of Mrs. David P. Kimball, and named in memory of her son). Bertram Hall was opened early in 1902; in December Mrs. Agassiz celebrated her eightieth birthday, with a Boston Symphony concert in her honor — and (far greater!) a multiple gift from her children, grandchildren, and many others of $116,000 for a students' house. The building was named the Elizabeth Cary Agassiz House, which the gentle octogenarian recorded in her diary as "quite a mouthful."

But the gift delighted her: "A long cherished wish of mine for Radcliffe College. . . . By virtue of this gift we hope that the more gracious and sympathetic side of life, without which no education is perfect, may accompany our academic instruction." A seven-league stride from that almost bleak beginning! She had said herself, rather sadly, at the 1886 Commencement: "We had nothing to offer you except the education which Harvard provides." . . . Did she not forget the one who was speaking?

Three new buildings added weight to evidence that an educational experiment had turned into an institution of learning. The fourth building was the Library, founded on Mr. Andrew Carnegie's gift of $75,000 and an equal amount contributed by alumnæ and friends of the College, but not erected in the great lady's lifetime. Indeed, with Agassiz House assured, and her fourscore milestone passed, Radcliffe's Victoria [9] — for such she was — relinquished her long reign. She had resigned as president in 1899, but accepted the post of honorary president — her active duties assumed largely by Dean Irwin. Now in 1903 she withdrew altogether, and Le Baron Russell Briggs, LL.D., Dean of Harvard College, was elected presi-

[9] "Who is herself an alma mater," said Le Baron Russell Briggs in June of 1904.

dent. We may observe that to her, most happily, "this means that Radcliffe is affiliated more closely than ever with the educational force of the University of Harvard." To President Eliot in farewell she confided (again in nautical terms): "How could our little craft be moored more safely than she now is?" Mr. Eliot said: "The College has got on fast."

That was sixty years ago. Far more than a wistful report of those days — of teacher and the taught — is compressed in a fine, witty, and badly neglected essay [10] by Grace Hollingsworth Tucker '03. To have had one Titan at a time, as Edwin Arlington Robinson would say, was obviously then impossible. There was Copey (Professor Charles Townsend Copeland), "the great teacher of English writers and written English," who refused to teach Argument at Radcliffe. " 'How deplorable,' he explained, 'for women to become apt in argument. We can't obliterate a natural tendency, but why cultivate it?' " There was Professor William Allan Neilson of the same Department (later President of Smith College) — "charming, gay, courtly, debonair. Where, you queried, had he left his sedan chair? Why had he discarded his short sword?" And Professor John Knowles Paine: "All through the severity of Cambridge winter he played and lectured in his overcoat, his collar turned up, a scarf muffling his throat, a black derby pulled down tight over his very bald head. He called out above a crashing *Allegro Vivace* the fundamentals of musical surgery" . . . There was the Titan Josiah Royce who produced "a philosophical hunger that should not be appeased"; and George Herbert Palmer, on whom the disciple turns her pen with skill: "But gently, surely, inevitably, by his vision of eternal verities, we wrote our own course, and with it molded our own lives." It was then, as Emerson said of something else, "the day of day." Indeed, the gods served Hebe — to shift Miss Tucker's title into the past tense: a mythical past which enjoyed its not altogether

---

[10] "The Gods Serve Hebe," *Radcliffe Quarterly*, October 1933; also *The Harvard Graduates' Magazine*, June 1933.

too sheltered Olympus and the olive grove, and "the moral stability we gained from gymnasium bloomers."

"Others will see the islands large and small," said Walt Whitman in what William James called "a divinely beautiful poem." One of the large islands in the Radcliffe sea was the great American philosopher himself; and a few years older than Miss Tucker's bright vignette is this recollection of him in *The Autobiography of Alice B. Toklas*:

> And so Gertrude Stein having been in Baltimore for a winter and having become more humanised and less adolescent and less lonesome went to Radcliffe. There she had a very good time. . . . The important person in Gertrude Stein's Radcliffe life was William James. She enjoyed her life and herself. She was the secretary of the philosophical club and amused herself with all sorts of people. She liked making sport of question asking and she liked equally answering them. She liked it all. But the really lasting impression of her Radcliffe life came through William James.

VI

The gods continued to serve. Only the names of the gods began to change or to grow; and in three decades we hear increasingly more of George Lyman Kittredge, Charles Townsend Copeland, Chester Noyes Greenough, and John Livingston Lowes in English; [11] of Edward Channing, Charles H. Haskins, and Samuel Eliot Morison in History; E. K. Rand in the Classics; Charles H. Grandgent, Irving Babbitt, J. D. M. Ford, and André Morize in Romance Languages; Frank W. Taussig and Edwin F. Gay in Economics; Charles H. McIlwain in Government; G. H. Edgell and Paul J. Sachs in Fine Arts; Archibald T. ("Doc") Davison in Music; Alfred North Whitehead in Philosophy; Theodore W. Richards and James B. Conant in Chemistry; George D. Birkhoff in Mathematics;

---

[11] Conspicuous by his absence is the great and beloved teacher, the late Bliss Perry. He gladly taught, but not at Radcliffe. "There were always more Harvard applicants for work in English than we could handle effectively."

George Washington Pierce in Physics; George H. Parker in Zoölogy; Earnest A. Hooton and Alfred M. Tozzer in Anthropology; Harlow Shapley in Astronomy. The gods never die. . . . And while these Harvard scholars continued to teach or (like Lowes and Shapley) began to teach at Radcliffe, the graduate began to take her place in the forefront of national life.

Helen Keller, the best known and perhaps the most remarkable living Radcliffe graduate [12] received her A.B. in 1904. In four years, while her college education was literally spelled into her hand ("my hands are busy listening"), under sympathetic but impartial gods

---

[12] Space forbids inclusion of a representative list of Radcliffe alumnæ who have won distinction in many fields. Mention of Miss Keller, however, suggests the names of a few (by no means all) who have achieved national or international recognition. The names of those who have died are in italics. These alumnæ are: *Grace H. Macurdy* '88, former Professor of Greek, and Chairman of the Department, Vassar College; *Sophie Chantal Hart* '92, formerly head of the English Department, Wellesley College; *Christina Hopkinson Baker* '93, writer and educator; *Eleanor Hallowell Abbott* '91–'93, '09–'11, author; *Annie Jump Cannon*, Gr. '95–'97, astronomer; *Gertrude Stein* '97, author; *Maud Wood Park* '98, first President of the National League of Women Voters, first donor to the Radcliffe Archives; Cornelia James Cannon '99, author; *Josephine Sherwood Hull* '99, actress; Mabel Wheeler Daniels '00, composer, *Katharine Fullerton Gerould* '00, author; *Lucy Ward Stebbins* '02, former Dean of Women of the University of California; *Sarah Wambaugh* '02, international authority on plebiscites; *Sara Murray Jordan* '05, gastroenterologist, Lahey Clinic, Boston; Margaret Harwood '07, astronomer; *Elsie Singmaster* '07, author; *Lucia Russell Briggs* '09, former President of Milwaukee-Downer College; Hetty Goldman, A.M. '10, Ph.D. '16, archæologist; Martha M. Eliot '13, former Chief, United States Children's Bureau; Marion Sharkey Doyle '14, national education, public service; Anne C. Bezanson '15, economist; Dorothy Sands '15, actress; Helen C. White '17, Professor of English, University of Wisconsin; Susanne Knauth Langer '20, philosopher; Agnes Rindge Claflin '21, Professor of Art, Vassar College; Dorothy Adlow '22, art critic; Mary W. Lasker '22, philanthropist; *Janet Fairbank* '23, opera singer; Vera Micheles Dean '25, Professor of International Development, New York University; Cecilia Payne-Gaposchkin, Ph.D. '25, astronomer; Muriel V. Roscoe, A.M. '25, Ph.D. '26, former Warden, Royal Victoria College, and now Chairman, Department of Botany, McGill University; Victoria Lincoln '26, author; A. Elizabeth Chase '27, Docent, Yale Art Gallery, Yale University; Helen H. Howe '27, monologuist, novelist; Elinor Hughes '27, critic; Ruth Elizabeth Bacon '28, Chargé d'Affaires, American Embassy, New Zealand; Rosemary Park '28, President, Barnard College; Doris Zemurray Stone '30, anthropologist; Sylvia L. Berkman, A.M. '37, Ph.D. '42, author, and lecturer in English, Wellesley College; Maxine Kumin '46, poet; Adrienne C. Rich '51, poet.

she successfully tried her strength "by the standards of those who see and hear." She has spoken of her professors as though she had seen and heard them. To whom were they ever more real? Mr. Charles Townsend Copeland, she said, "more than any one else I have had until this junior year, brings before you literature in all its original freshness and power. . . . When a great scholar like Professor Kittredge interprets what the master said, it is 'as if new sight were given the blind.'" As if new sight! "I sat at her right in Economics 1," said Miss Tucker, "her able teacher and companion, Miss Sullivan, on her left. In Helen's upturned palm Miss Sullivan's fingers rested lightly, and seemed hardly to move during the lecture. But Helen's laugh at Mr. [A. Piatt] Andrew's sallies rang out only a second after ours, so swiftly was communication made. . . . The finest story about her came to me, I think, from Professor Fred Norris Robinson. . . . Professor Robinson planned to set down on the examination paper the first line of a mighty passage [line 80] from *Samson Agonistes*, asking the class to finish the quotation. Remembering Helen, he put down instead, 'Write from memory the passage in *Samson Agonistes* that you like best.' Only Helen Keller set down the lines he originally had in mind:

> Oh dark, dark, dark, amid the blaze of noon,
> Irrecoverably dark, total eclipse
> Without all hope of day!"

Dean Briggs of Harvard was Radcliffe's part-time president for twenty years, from 1903 to 1923. In 1900 he had unwittingly anticipated the office by making an address at the quarter-centenary of Smith College, quoting from Dr. Thomas Fuller's *The Church History of Britain* on the "Conveniency of She-Colleges." Much later it was President Neilson of the same she-college who said that the Dean's chief contribution to Radcliffe was to make it respectable. "Radcliffe," echoed Professor K. G. T. Webster, head of her Academic Board, "would have been grateful enough to have him simply as a beneficent figurehead, a protecting personage, a wise and experienced chairman of her various boards. She got all of this and something more which was of greater value; namely, a man of unbounded humanity who put all his abilities unreservedly at the service of the institution." As a young tutor in Greek, the Dean had been one of Mr. Gilman's volunteers; and during his long and devoted service he never lost sight of the fact that Radcliffe had been founded in a quicksand, and that "gradually, steadily, miraculously, with no convulsion of Nature, the quicksand . . . hardened into a rock." He had seen the Radcliffe campus composed, as he put it, "chiefly of a few back yards and an undersized apple-tree." He came to Radcliffe with a conviction, already implicit in that Smith address, from which he never diverged: that colleges for women should be "training-schools for the appreciation of high aims," and that they should not teach women to compete with men. His was a chivalrous credo: "For purity of thought and heart, for patient courage, for recklessly unselfish devotion, for the love that rests and strengthens and inspires, we look to women. These are the best things in women; these are the best things in life: in them men cannot compete with women, and women lose them if they compete with men." Mrs. Agassiz in 1899 had worried less: "I am confident of one thing, however, which is that the largest liberty of instruction cannot in itself impair true womanhood." If there was wit in Professor Neilson's remark about respectability, there is truth in the fact that Mr. Briggs "helped to fuse a loose student sentiment into a great loyalty." And, continues the Dean's biographer,[13] "he made it possible to add many important new courses to the curriculum; and he did his share and more in bringing the modest resources of the institution up to the substantial sum — according to the treasurer's report of 1923 — of a little more than four millions of dollars." He championed in Radcliffe "the honest liberty of free speech," and inveighed against the college-woman snob, the anti-domestic, believing that her business "is not to scorn the cabbage, but invest it

[13] Rollo Walter Brown, *Dean Briggs* (New York: Harpers, 1926).

with a rose motive." He was lovable and kind, of homely grace and infinite warmth. He could be strict, was unwavering in decision — particularly when adverse; and Mrs. Agassiz's record of no flighty students is reflected in the President's report of 1910: "Throughout the year no serious case of discipline occurred." He became endeared to generations of Radcliffe women as he had early become endeared to generations of Harvard men. He is caught full-face in Robert Hillyer's poem:

> His head thrown back, his amiable walk
> Timed equally to progress or to talk . . .
> These I remember, and remembering, see
> The Dean walk home toward immortality.

VII

That expanding curriculum affected not only the undergraduate but the graduate students in Radcliffe. The first A.M. had been awarded in 1890; and the Ph.D. in 1902. These called for a surer longitude and a wider latitude. It became more and more possible for the student at Radcliffe to approximate the course-ranging of the student at Harvard.

Five deans held office under President Briggs. Miss Irwin retired in 1909, receiving "unmistakable testimony to the affection of friends and colleagues." [14] Miss Coes '87, A.M. '97, the Secretary — "Keeper of Marks, exponent of optimism" — succeeded her. "Not a man or a woman in the world loves Radcliffe College as she loves it," said her President. She died in 1913. After Miss Coes came Caroline L. Humphrey '98, Acting Dean (1913–1914); Bertha M. Boody '99 (1914–1920); Mrs. George P. (Christina Hopkinson) Baker '93, Acting Dean (1920–1921); Marion E. Park (1921–1922) — who re-

---

[14] The words of President Briggs in his Report of 1908–1909. He also said of Miss Irwin: "She brought to her office long experience with girls, exceptional culture, and brilliant personal distinction. Her services to the College were many. She helped to shape and steady its policy. She raised money in its behalf. She represented it admirably in public."

signed to become President of Bryn Mawr; and Mrs. Baker again Acting Dean (1922–1923). Miss Alice M. Longfellow [15] had succeeded Joseph Warner as treasurer in 1883; Mrs. William G. (Lilian Horsford) Farlow was the next to assume the office (1891–1894); and Major Henry Lee Higginson who followed her (1894–1905) was succeeded in turn by Ezra H. Baker.

Building activity continued. A second dormitory, the Grace Hopkinson Eliot Hall (named in honor of President Eliot's second wife, and also a gift of Mrs. Kimball), was opened in 1907. The library saw completion the following year; Sarah Wyman Whitman Hall (a dormitory) in 1912; James and Augusta Barnard Hall in 1913. One by one the integers in the vision of Mrs. Agassiz emerged.

It became clear also that undergraduate life in the new century was taking on new patterns. Agassiz House with its theatre, living room, informal lecture hall, restaurant, and many smaller rooms was at once the center which its donors designed it to be. It housed the plays of the Idler Club and the plays of the departed 47 Work Shop which Professor George P. Baker directed. As they came into being, the English, Debating, Poetry, Liberal, and Music Clubs each met there, as did such later additions as the Salon Radcliffien, and the International Club. Other enterprises flourished. *The Radcliffe News* and the Year Book were founded. The Choral Society, under Professor Davison, began its notable career which early included excellent performances of Gilbert and Sullivan, of student compositions, and offered the superb experience of participation with the Harvard Glee Club in Christmas Carols and with the Glee Club and the Boston Symphony Orchestra in the production of "Parsifal," "King David," the Brahms "Requiem," the Bach Mass, Beethoven's "Ninth Symphony" and "Missa Solemnis," and work of like dimension, under the late Dr. Serge Koussevitsky. The Radcliffe Orchestra opened another valuable outlet. Student Government and the Athletic Association organized and lasted. Athletics widened to include

[15] Radcliffe '79–'81, '84–'90. Mrs. Farlow was Radcliffe '79–'80, '84–'85, '87–'88.

swimming, tennis, archery, fencing, hockey, riding, and the dance. In 1914 a Radcliffe chapter of Phi Beta Kappa offered its key to the ranking scholars; but the College has had no connection with national sororities. Each college generation found some new and vigorous activity. In the classroom the free elective system of Eliot's Harvard narrowed definitely toward the tutorial of Mr. Lowell. When President Briggs retired, divisional examinations were already established in the fields of history, government, and economics, and loomed imminent in neighboring areas.

VIII

In 1923 the command changed again. Miss Ada Louise Comstock, dean of Smith College and former Dean of Women at the University of Minnesota, became Radcliffe's first full-time president; and Bernice Veazey Brown '16, Ph.D. '20, assumed the offices of dean and vice-president. John Wilber Lowes (the son of Professor Lowes) was elected business manager. Mr. Baker resigned as treasurer in 1924; Mr. T. Jefferson Coolidge was appointed acting treasurer until 1927, when he was succeeded by Mr. Lowes. Mr. Lowes in turn was followed by Mr. Francis C. Gray in 1930. Bernice Brown became Dean of the newly-organized Graduate School in 1934, and Mrs. Wilbur K. Jordan, Dean of the College.

There was physical change as well — even in the depression years. Le Baron Russell Briggs Hall (largest dormitory of the College, accommodating seventy-nine students) was dedicated in 1924; and the Dean himself laid the cornerstone, shoving it under the building, as he said, "with all the people living in it." The Alice Mary Longfellow Lecture Hall followed in 1930. In 1932 the William Elwood Byerly Hall, next door to Fay House, was dedicated to science. It offered twenty-three laboratories as well as lecture rooms and the most modern equipment for work in chemistry, physics, and astronomy. In 1928, with the universal adoption of the tutorial system, a house suitable for tutorial conference was opened on Appian Way not far from where the College had begun. The Ella Lyman Cabot Hall (dormitory for seventy-two, opening in the autumn of 1937) completed the second building cycle. But there was a single codicil: one full of color.

Visitors at Harvard from the English universities sometimes observe the lack of flower beds in the Yard and in the vast extension of academic acreage to the north and south of the original province now within the iron fence. Euclid and the founding fathers were more concerned with geometry and the soul than with nature; and Harvard has preserved throughout the centuries a kind of New England austerity with respect to trees, shrubs, and plants. But her sister to the northwest has a greener thumb; and down at the southeastern corner of the Radcliffe Yard, secluded from the passerby, is a lovely little cloistered garden with fountain, ornamental shrubs, flowers, and half-hidden fragments of a wall. It is astonishing to come on as you step out of Alice Longfellow Hall: enchantment you would expect to find in a coign of Smith or Wellesley. Yews and paper birch contrast in green and white and preserve the New England flavor. A little plaque tells the visitor that it was "given in memory of Roberta A. Barron of the Class of 1928, by her mother, Mrs. Etta Barron, who wishes to provide a living spot of greenery rather than a bookplate or some other inanimate object." At dusk it is like the background of one of the English oils by John Fulley-love that brighten Edward Thomas's *Oxford*, with something of the particular solitude of the garden of the Master in University College. New, it contrives to look old and gently stubborn — as it should: perhaps the vestigial border of Maria Fay's own garden, or gardens even earlier than hers. It reminds one new inspector of what Walter Pater said in tribute to Michelangelo: "And on the crown of the head of the *David* there still remains a morsel of uncut stone, as if by one touch to maintain its connexion with the place from which it was hewn."

IX

Between the geographic centers of her academic and dormitory groups, the student life at Radcliffe even before the darkness of the Second World War was richer and fuller than the Gilmans or Mrs. Agassiz could possibly have dreamed for the girls of the future who

> Could grasp as well
> What a theorem means
> As a recipe
> For a pot of beans.[16]

By 1943 — which turned out to be the end of an era — about half the undergraduates were living in dormitories and college houses; and they enjoyed the atmosphere and charm of a private dwelling. Their daily activities had become as diverse, exciting, and interesting as they cared to make them. They worked hard. Their plan of study and general reading was already referable to individual tutors and subject to sympathetic direction. Advice did not end in the lecture hall. Beyond work itself lay a world of special interests and congenial pursuits unidentified with what the seven heads of seven colleges were unanimously condemning as "flickering momentary interests." Music, writing, editing, producing, acting, athletics, social intercourse, all the outward delight connected with a modern college, organized and colored by tradition, was opening to every girl. Like and unlike had in 1943 — as they have today — equal opportunity to measure abilities, link ambitions; to judge and appraise, to experience and attain; to find fresh and lasting friendships.

It was a pleasant, rewarding world for the student riding out the end of the depression years. The Library, of over 90,000 volumes and more than 2,000 music records, was used to the limit of seating capacity; and the great collection of the Widener in Harvard became available with a card. Sites and buildings of historic significance in

[16] Mount Holyoke Centennial Poem, by Roberta Teale Swartz, A.M. '26.

Cambridge, Boston, Concord, and Lexington colored the imagination and rewarded the youthful visitor. The lives of Longfellow, Hawthorne, Alcott, Emerson, Thoreau, and Holmes were neither so far away nor so long ago that their testament and influence could fail to touch the perceiver along the local path. The rustic gods were never all in Vergil: Walden still found its own way of remaining young. In city direction, the enriching life and hospitality of a great university, the music, theatres, and museums of Boston were (as they are today) surprisingly close to Fay House.

It was a not too difficult world for the student after Pearl Harbor. The College, like Harvard, changed to a three-term, twelve-month year, and the normal four-year course was telescoped to three. In January 1943, a contingent of WAVES moved in (with considerable shuffling about and doubling of quarters on the part of undergraduates). These were trainees in the Supply Corps. "The Waves," reported Assistant Dean Mildred P. Sherman, "fitted easily into the Radcliffe picture." As to the undergraduates: "The general feeling among the students is that being in college is a privilege which must be justified by serious work." She further notes "an unusually large group of married students in residence," and "twenty-one others married during two semesters. . . . Almost without exception these marriages have been well-considered, and not at all the hasty war marriage that is to be deplored. Radcliffe students [Mrs. Agassiz would have liked this] do not yet seem to have lost their heads." Miss Comstock (paying tribute to Miss Sherman) noted "a sense of greater responsibility for the tone and quality of college life."

Radcliffe under her third president was proud of her scholarship. In 1943, 43 per cent of the graduating class of the College took honors — slightly less than the percentage in the two previous years — and 51 per cent cared enough to try. New teachers were constantly new attractions. About 149 courses were given in 1942–1943 — the great majority by full professors and associate professors. The graduate degrees (79) awarded in the academic year outnumbered those of the other six in the seven-college group combined. By the end of that decade, of all degrees together (Bachelor to Doctor) 6,354 had been awarded by Radcliffe since the charter was granted in 1894. And of the 1,057 students enrolled in 1942–1943, 796 were undergraduates, 253 of graduate standing, five were research fellows, and three (normally ten or so) travelling fellows. Obscured in these numbers is the significant range in the regional sources which they represent. The student body of the early years was largely of local origin. In 1897 only 24 per cent of the 424 students in Radcliffe came from beyond the State of Massachusetts, and this 24 per cent was divided by numerical coincidence between 24 states and one foreign country. In 1943, of a total of 1,057 Radcliffe students, 570 came from outside of Massachusetts, including 74 from the other five New England states, 132 from New York, 247 from 35 of the remaining states; and 33 from twelve foreign countries.

X

The twenty devoted years of inspired leadership which Ada Louise Comstock, Litt.D., LL.D., L.H.D., had given to Radcliffe College came to a close with her retirement after Commencement in 1943. Honored by many colleges and universities, including the Oxford University M.A. in 1949, she herself had honored Radcliffe in countless ways. Aristocratic, with imperial dignity and genuine charm, she left a bright impression on everyone who met her, whether informally, on errands of administration and discipline, or on state occasions. She had wit and grace in speaking, and the ability to hold an audience. She was loyal to her staff. She brought the world's horizons right to Fay House, and her office somehow had the look of inherited responsibility and *noblesse oblige*. She was indeed a great lady from the beginning, and at a meeting of the Radcliffe Trustees on 24 May 1943, a resolution composed by Mr. John F.

Moors was gratefully spread upon the minutes. It would have pleased Mrs. Agassiz and Maria Fay. In spite of five *whereases*, so tedious an ornament of all such pronouncements, it remains a very touching and adroitly-worded testimony. *Whereas*, it begins:

Whereas Ada Louise Comstock became President of Radcliffe College twenty years ago; and whereas since then her personal influence has in many good ways become nationwide and the College has grown mightily in usefulness and the respect of mankind; and whereas this growth has been primarily due to her wisdom and to her unfaltering courage amid many perplexities, culminating in the tragedy of the second World War; and whereas her labors have in the end been crowned by a new and mutually helpful relationship with Harvard, Radcliffe's best friend; and whereas she is about to retire as President,

Be it resolved that there be spread upon the minutes of Radcliffe College this expression of the gratitude, admiration and affection felt by the trustees and of their confident hope that for many fruitful years she will continue, as in the past, to be a great citizen of a great Republic.

Miss Comstock in her last annual report to the Trustees (30 June 1943) expressed her own gratitude in these words:

There is a certain loneliness in an administrative position such as the one I have held. Criticism must be borne and responsibility accepted which no one else can share. The great off-set is the knowledge that in the governing boards are wisdom and courage and generosity — which can be called upon in any crisis. It is for that consciousness of always having strength and support at hand that I am most deeply grateful.

Her successor was Wilbur Kitchener Jordan,[17] Ph.D., then 41 years old, an historian who had taught at Harvard, in Missouri, in California, and finally at the University of Chicago where he had also been general editor of the University Press. As a former tutor and history instructor, he was not new to Radcliffe and the distaff side of education, and Dean Cronkhite in her 1943 Christmas letter to former members of the Graduate School rightly praised him in

---

[17] Since 1946 he has been listed in the Harvard catalogue as Ph.D., L.H.D., Litt.D., LL.D., Professor of History.

particular for fifteen important words drawn from his inaugural address: "The minds of women, quite as truly as their legal personalities, are at last enfranchised." Under the April, 1943, contractual arrangement with Harvard which had thereby assumed responsibility for supplying Radcliffe with instruction, the College itself in a sense had widened its franchise. Miss Comstock was quick to reassure the Trustees of her complete satisfaction with the change, and of her personal confidence in the new President's ability to cope with any problems which, at any time, might arise out of it.

I shall not attempt in this report [her last] to go into detail regarding the contractual arrangement with Harvard, which is, from the point of view of Radcliffe organization, the most significant event since our charter was granted by the legislature in 1894. To students in the College it will probably seem that little change has taken place. As before, our instruction will be given by members of the Harvard faculty; as before, our standards and requirements will be those of Harvard. The difference will be most evident in the Business Office, where a single check to Harvard University now replaces the hundreds of checks drawn for individual members of the Harvard faculty. The inward change of which this alteration in mode of payment is an expression lies in the assumption by the University of responsibility for supplying Radcliffe with instruction. In the past, though Radcliffe's ability to grant degrees depended upon their certification by the President and Fellows as equivalent to Harvard degrees, Harvard as an institution was under no obligation to supply us with the means of attaining to that equivalence. Our dealings, in procuring instruction, were with individual members of the faculty; and faculty and departments as such had no official sanction for devotion of time and thought to Radcliffe problems. Under the new arrangement departments are charged with the duty of providing Radcliffe with instruction adequate for the attainment of degrees and of the same quality and standard as that provided for Harvard College and for the Graduate School of Arts and Sciences; and the faculty as a whole must frame Radcliffe educational policy. An anomalous relationship becomes under the contract one of specific rights and obligations.

By the terms of the contract, it may be ended with due notice at the will of either party. I believe, however, that it will never give place to the old loose association. It brings about an adjustment of fundamental importance in the development of Radcliffe; and President Conant and Dean Buck should always be counted with President Eliot as layers of foundations in the service which, through Radcliffe, Harvard gives to the education of women.

Though the new plan is simple in its outlines and has been carefully worked out, unforeseen problems are sure to rise out of it. The College is fortunate in having President Jordan at the helm while these problems are being met. His acquaintance with Harvard and Radcliffe organization and personnel and his experience in other institutions fit him well to serve the College at a time when ignorance of the local scene or too complete an identification with it would be a disadvantage. But this is a minor reason for looking forward with confidence to President Jordan's administration. His scholarship, his character, the warmth and largeness of his personality give everyone who loves Radcliffe happy assurance for the future.

In 1939 Mrs. Wilbur K. Jordan, the President's wife, had resigned as Dean of the College, and Mildred P. Sherman became acting Dean for the following year. From 1940 to 1942 Miss Katharine E. McBride was Dean. Like Miss Park, she too resigned to become President of Bryn Mawr, her Alma Mater from which she was graduated in 1925. Miss Sherman replaced her in office and remained Dean of the College for seven years when she accepted appointment as the first Dean of College Relations. The office of Dean of the College was abolished, but Wilma A. Kerby-Miller continued as Dean of Instruction, to which post she had been appointed in 1946, and Mary Small Moser '40 likewise remained as Dean of Residence, to which office she had been appointed in 1949. Of all these Deans, Miss Sherman [18] had the longest connection with Radcliffe. A graduate of the University of Michigan in 1921 (her A.M. is Radcliffe 1932), she began her administrative pilgrimage as Mistress of Le Baron Russell Briggs Hall when she was a graduate student. She also became a trustee of the College — a board which numbered 40 in 1957. As to that, the dean *emerita* of trustees is Anna Wellington

[18] Mildred P. Sherman died in 1961.

206

(Mrs. S. Burt) Wolbach '04, who served from 1911 to 1957 with devotion and distinction.

From 1937 to 1949 no new buildings were added to Radcliffe; but in the fall of the latter year Mary Buckminster Moors Hall, the gift of John Farwell Moors — a member of the Radcliffe governing boards for over 50 years — in memory of his mother, was opened as a dormitory with a capacity of 104 students. In 1950–1951 the library was remodeled and modernized. From 90,000 volumes and 1,500 music records in 1937, it has now increased to the point of 130,000 bound volumes, about 7,960 music records, and 6,520 music books and scores. In 1952 the Daniel Henry Holmes Hall — made possible by the Georgine Holmes Thomas bequest — became the residence of 102 students in carefully designed double rooms. It differs from the other existing dormitories in providing ample and attractive quarters for a musical center, the heart of which is the Susan Alice Ensign Morse Music Library, to which has been transferred the large collection of records and scores above referred to. Adequate listening and practice rooms and the latest development in modern sound equipment have opened to the College a sonic world for curricular and much extracurricular activity. The living room is designed with a raised platform large enough for two pianos and provides the appropriate setting for informal concerts. Holmes Hall is the northernmost point of Radcliffe proper. It looks down the athletic field in a southeasterly direction toward Bertram and Eliot Halls on Shepard Street. It is partly hidden by Moors Hall at the northern end of the field, and runs back (or northwest) almost to Linnæan Street. As to that, Radcliffe to the north is now no longer outnumbered (ratio of 19 to 14) by the buildings of the academic group opposite Cambridge Common. All these structures are comfortable in leaf or vine, the grass improves from year to year, and recent decades of construction and landscaping have added greatly to the symmetry of the Radcliffe scene. The hurricanes of 1954 did some damage — more to the northern area than to the southern:

one hard-to-spare willow, as well as one large and one small elm, went down before the wind. Smaller trees fell in the old and somewhat sheltered Yard of the academic group, *ex mero motu*.

XI

When Bernice Brown (now Mrs. Leonard Wolsey Cronkhite, L.H.D., LL.D.) assumed the office of Dean of the Graduate School in 1934, she entered into a responsibility in Radcliffe second only to the office of President. She brought to her work both a width of administrative experience, a double background of Law School training and research in the Humanities, as well as a natural capacity for understanding human relations. Dean Cronkhite would be the first to deny her hand in a project which today provides the one community graduate house expressly created for the use of women graduate students in any college wherever; yet the *Christian Science Monitor* was simply recording the fact when it observed (before ground was first broken) that "the center has been Mrs. Cronkhite's pet dream for many years. Year after year in the problems and experiences of Radcliffe girls she has seen the need for it."

Of all the Ph.D.'s awarded to women by institutions in the United States in the year 1955–1956, Radcliffe was first with 36. In the more than half-century stretch from 1902 (when the first Ph.D. was conferred) Radcliffe has granted 794 doctorates and 4,245 degrees of Master of Arts. In 1957–1958 there were 400 graduate students from the United States and 24 foreign countries, representing 139 institutions. The growth of Radcliffe as a national institution is more clearly reflected in the College itself, for in this same academic year the College enrollment of 1,046 undergraduates was drawn from 44 of the 49 states and from sixteen foreign countries. It is almost axiomatic that there will always be more foreign students in the Graduate School than in the College.

"Research for a Ph.D. can be a rather lonely, isolated sort of existence [said the *Monitor*, quoting the Dean]. Our girls spend days in library cells, and when they get through in the evening, they have no place to gather informally with their fellows. The Graduate Center across the street from the Radcliffe Yard can completely change this. It will not be just a dormitory: it will be a way of life, an environment."

The Graduate Center — the first and largest unit of the Quadrangle, on the corner of Ash and Brattle Streets — was completed and dedicated on 3 November 1956. Dean Cronkhite said in her report of June 1957, that it "serves as a symbol of the community of scholars, the fellowship of students and faculty, which we have hitherto lacked." The dedication itself was a brilliant event, all bright with academic costume, and bustling with a throng of representatives of neighboring institutions, learned societies, and of the fifty countries "from which our foreign graduate students have come in the last five years." Mabel Daniels, '00 wrote a *Canticle of Wisdom* for the occasion, sung by the Radcliffe Choral Society under the direction of Professor G. Wallace Woodworth. Of the several addresses, perhaps that of Cecilia Payne-Gaposchkin, Professor of Astronomy, most aptly expressed the commitment of the graduate mind to scholarly pursuit. Her title was "No Wine So Wonderful As Thirst" — six words which came from Vassar and the late Edna St. Vincent Millay.

This first unit of the Center houses 49 graduate students, with rooms for a succession of guests, and has drawn together under its roof a great variety of social and semi-academic activities. It is no cloister in this secular world, for three Radcliffe ladies have elected to be married there. Like all useful and needed additions to any college or university, it was a popular building even on the drawing board; and Radcliffe is proud of the fact that nearly 6,000 donors contributed to its construction. As the result of additional gifts, the Residence Wing, adjoining the western end of the Center, was opened in the autumn of 1958.

With the completion of the Refectory — the Coffee House in the basement had served temporarily as a dining room — the landscape of the Graduate Center was engagingly enlarged with a quiet garden enclosed by three sides of the building: "a garden planted with sweet-smelling flowers like lemon verbena, rose geranium, mignonette, and heliotrope. For the garden is named for Helen Keller [*Radcliffe Quarterly*: August 1954] and it is right that *her* garden should be especially full of fragrance." The little fountain at the center — and what fountain in any garden was ever more appropriate? — bears the inscription:

In memory of Anne Sullivan, teacher extraordinary, who, starting with the word Water, opened to the girl Helen Keller the priceless world of sight and sound through touch; devoted mentor and beloved companion through Radcliffe College, 1900–1904.

Even before the foundation of the Center was laid, President Jordan, Dean Cronkhite, and Mrs. Charles W. Phinney '21 paid tribute to Miss Keller — "the gold I have found in the darkness"— standing in sunshine and shade on the unseeded spot where the garden was to be planted. Her response (for greatness is a kind of simplicity) is worth remembrance:

What a heart-warming experience it is for me to come back to Radcliffe. It seems but yesterday that I was walking with my teacher through these halls of learning, absorbing from her faithful fingers streams of knowledge from the mighty ocean of the ages.

You could not have thrilled me with a more precious sense of understanding than by holding up my teacher's name and mine for remembrance in a bond of love and accomplishment. The world owes an unpayable debt of gratitude to its teachers, and it was because Anne Sullivan gave herself to me that as a human being I was able to convert my handicaps into channels of service to others. Now I feel her very near as I contemplate the tribute garden — a symbol of my joyous pupilage — and the fountain that shall sparkle with the radiant significance of Anne Sullivan's act of creation. My belief is that we have not really been apart these many years, but the immortal glow of her spirit shines bright at this moment. And it is you, dear friends, who have wrought this climax to the story of her faith in me and whatever service I have rendered.

It is wonderful to be thus enveloped in the memory of her who labored that I might see life exalted in all its aspects and share in its endeavors. Even so may Radcliffe continue along its glorious journey of education, finding new ways to enlarge, strengthen and better humanity!

XII

If one were to write a thesis on the Radcliffe Graduate School, the author would turn not only to the annual reports of the Dean but to a series of Christmas letters to former graduate students which Mrs. Cronkhite began in 1935 and has continued ever since. Informal, and no longer than three small pages each, they projected in advance of the Graduate Center a communal spirit which is now a reality. From year to year she has written of such minor and major matters as various foreign-language-speaking tables in Bertram Hall; of trips and excursions to Concord, Salem, and the Wayside Inn; of graduate students admitted to courses for credit in Harvard's Littauer Center (Public Administration); of the first Radcliffe diplomas (1939) for the Master of Arts in Teaching; of refugees arriving from many countries; the comfort taken, in a world of so little peace, in "the picture of stability and vigor which the Graduate School continues to present"; analysis of the occupation and distribution of recent Ph.D.'s; of the granting of Radcliffe membership in the honor society Sigma Xi in 1942; a note on the Christmas Carol Service in the Harvard Memorial Church — one of the most gracious of all Radcliffe-Harvard enterprises and one of the several living monuments to Professor Archibald T. Davison who founded it. The list continues with the announcement of the Harvard Medical School "after many years of hesitation," voting to admit women as candidates for the degree of M.D. (1945); arrival of Helen Maud Cam from Cambridge University (first holder of the Samuel Zemurray Jr. and Doris Zemurray Stone Radcliffe Professorship in Harvard University) who taught English constitutional history; and of the second holder, Cora Alice DuBois, in the field of anthropology; announcement of the first women admitted to the Harvard Law School (1950); mention of the medallion to be awarded on occasion by the Radcliffe Graduate Chapter of the Alumnæ Association to distinguished former members of the Graduate School, the first recipient being Vera Micheles Dean; talk of the coming Diamond Jubilee (1953); of the new red academic gown for the Ph.D. (1955). In 1957 Mrs. Cronkhite reports on being welcomed by alumnæ in Rome (social worker), Delhi (civil servant), Bangkok (professor), Manila (journalist), Tokyo (biologist), and on through 18 cities — "all carrying out what they had learned at Radcliffe."

Parallel to the Christmas letter of the Dean of the Graduate School is the *Radcliffe Newsletter* addressed — as such college publications are at Dartmouth, Yale, and Harvard, for example — to the parents of undergraduates. In the issue of March 1958 (number 14 in the series) Miss Sherman as Dean of College Relations, talks about Radcliffe health; about the new Harvard-Radcliffe theatre [19] to be built on the site on Brattle Street originally reserved for the Radcliffe Health Center; about a meeting of parents of students from the Greater Boston area who discussed "Radcliffe Education and your Daughter"; about the latest raise in tuition and its ancient corollary (faithful as a following dog) of increased scholarship stipends; a word on the opening, scheduled for September, 1958, of Ada Louise Comstock Hall, Radcliffe's newest dormitory; and a summary of the astonishing range of Radcliffe's concern for an insistence on athletics for all. "Bicycle riding," Dean Sherman observed in conclusion, ". . . is indulged in by about half the College."

XIII

Other considerations reflect the experimental urge at Radcliffe. In 1937, for example, the Director of the Appointment Bureau, Miss

---

[19] The Loeb Drama Center was formally opened in 1960.

AN ACRE FOR EDUCATION

Edith G. Stedman '10, organized a Management Training Program — popularly known as MTP until 1956, when the title became the Harvard-Radcliffe Program in Business Administration — contracted, of course, to PBA. This program was a one-year graduate course, "for a limited number of young women of superior ability and character," offering basic training for administration in both line and staff departments of organizations and industries such as the U. S. Rubber Company, Sylvania Electric Products, Inc., William Filene's Sons Company, Jordan Marsh Company, the John Hancock Mutual Life Insurance Company, the Massachusetts General Hospital, and Stop & Shop, Inc. The electing student discovered that her work was divided into three academic sessions separated by two periods of field work of four and six weeks, respectively. The familiar case method was used, and during each field work period the student was placed as a full-time employee in an organization appropriate to her needs. Applicants for PBA were required to have a degree from an accredited college. No academic credit was granted, but a certificate was conferred on those who successfully completed the requirements of the course. Beginning in February 1954 the program was strengthened by the emergence of the Harvard School of Business Administration as co-sponsor. Commenting in his Report to the Trustees for 1954–1955, President Jordan cited Mr. T. North Whitehead, then concluding his eleven years as Director of MTP, by saying that under him, "the philosophical aims of the curriculum of the MTP [now PBA] were well and maturely developed, the prestige and the curriculum steadily enhanced, and it was during the closing year of his tenure that an eminently satisfactory constitution was developed under which the responsibility for this important educational venture will be jointly shared by Radcliffe and the Business School." In 1963 this program became obsolete when the Business School opened its doors to women as candidates for the M.B.A. degree.

Then in 1946 Radcliffe College and the Massachusetts General

Hospital instituted a coördinated plan to provide a combined liberal arts and professional training in the field of nursing. Candidates under the Liberal Arts and Nursing Education program were obliged to satisfy the normal requirements for the Radcliffe A.B. degree. The dual course ran for six years, the successful candidate receiving both the A.B. degree and the coveted R.N. from the School of Nursing. A joint committee from both institutions acted on the requests for scholarships and loans. The program was recently discontinued at the undergraduate level.

"God keep me from ever completing anything," wrote Herman Melville in *Moby Dick*. One thing likely never to be completed — for such is the fascination of the endless task involved — is the College's venture (1944) with what is called the Radcliffe Women's Archives. In 1943 the College received a valuable Woman's Rights Collection from Maud Wood Park '98, and her friends. This assembly of the records of the National Suffrage Movement from Colonial times down to 1920 was amplified by other important manuscripts and papers concerning the workers for women's suffrage (1890–1920) in Massachusetts, and consequent data concerning the gains for women since 1920. Additional gifts followed almost immediately, with the result that Radcliffe is now in control of a steadily growing collection of primary and secondary sources relating to historical contributions to the welfare of mankind made by American women. The range has extended from political books, manuscripts, papers, records (and so on) relating to such women as Julia Ward Howe, Mary Coggeshall, Maud Nathan, and others, to material on the growth and influence of women's professions.

This special library has defined its purposes: the search for undeposited source material dealing with women's lives, activities, interests, and ideas; preservation by microfilm of deteriorated papers, providing service to researchers in a centralized location, collaborating with other libraries — again and so on. The first Director of the Archives was Mrs. Richard Borden; she was followed in 1959 by

Mrs. Peter Solomon, whose address is Byerly Hall, Radcliffe: Too little information, unfortunately, of this important Radcliffe venture has yet found its way to the general public.

Reaching beyond her undergraduate and graduate boundaries, Radcliffe in 1951 instituted a series of courses in the area of adult learning. These were the *Radcliffe Seminars* "designed for mature women who wish part-time study of college caliber in small groups, under the guidance of outstanding teachers." There were seven such seminars offered in 1951–1952. They were taught by the discussion method, met for two consecutive hours each week for a period of sixteen weeks, enjoyed the instructive merit of reading and writing as well as discussion, concluded with no examinations or credit toward a degree, but were attested by a proper certificate of work completed. These seminars were extremely popular and successful, attended by 240 women — with the expected age differential. The subjects ran from "The Causes and Prevention of War," "Ancient Greek with Readings," and "Cicero and the Religious Problems of His Age," to "The Spirit of Protest in Nineteenth Century American Literature" and the inevitable (though by no means the most popular) course called "The Role of Women in American Society." Seminars involving languages such as Latin, Greek, and French did not require of the participants a specific knowledge of the language involved. Such well-known scholars and experts as instructors included Professor Albert Guérard, Professor A. S. Pease (former President of Amherst), Louis M. Lyons, journalist and Curator of the Nieman Foundation at Harvard, and the late Langdon Warner. The charge for these seminars (only one to an applicant) was $60.

XIV

President Jordan, at mid-point in his second decade of office, shared with his colleagues in sister (*really* sister) institutions the full and almost overwhelming knowledge that higher education for women is entering a new and intensely self-critical period. The day of sending young ladies to college to give them a kind of finishing-off — a trip round the world without ever leaving the campus — is a day departed. "I think that a man should compare advantageously with a river, with an oak, with a mountain, endless flow, expansion, and grit," wrote Emerson in his *Journal* about 100 years ago. He failed to say with what a woman should compare,[20] but it is not impossible that a female Emerson will emerge in our time and will say it; and it is more than possible that she will emerge from Radcliffe, just as Emerson emerged from Harvard. One thing at any rate is certain: the great woman philosopher, doctor, teacher, biologist, or humanist is just as likely to emerge from north of the River Platte, south of the Amazon, or east-west of the Irrawaddy as she is to appear from Concord. The national role of Radcliffe has been steadily expanding. "While resolved to fulfill its moral obligation to all gifted young women in the metropolitan region of Boston who desire to attend Radcliffe," said President Jordan in 1945, "the College has felt strongly that the resources of faculty, libraries, and laboratories which its possesses are held as a trust for the benefit of able and ambitious young women throughout the nation. The changing complexion of our student body is rapidly making us a truly national college and is, simultaneously, imposing on us the obligation of a quick adaptation to meet the future."

All this time the administration continued to be a vigorous champion of the cause of adaptation to the times. In 1946, reflected President Jordan: "The University has considered most carefully the needs of youth in the present age and has made extensive and significant changes in the structure of the curriculum designed better to equip them for moral and intellectual franchise in the free society." Thus

---

[20] He did say a month earlier: "I think that as long as [women] have not equal rights of property and right of voting, they are not on the right footing." But *dux femina facti* was never on the Radcliffe shield.

begins his enthusiastic support of the courses in General Education — the logical outgrowth of the objectives of that famous University Committee of which he was an active member. In 1947 we find the President expressing delight in the Zemurray Professorship (already mentioned) as symbolizing "the closeness and the harmony of the relationship between Harvard and Radcliffe." And yet (he goes on) "it must be remembered that Radcliffe is a college for women and should devote its resources and energies to attacking those problems which are found in our society by educated women who should be amongst its leaders." It is toward the end of his 1947 report to the Trustees that he speaks of adding in the summer "a number of intensive, practical, and concentrated courses in the techniques of selected occupations in which women may find a fruitful whole- or part-time career." In the long and warm days following that statement, the College initiated a course on publishing techniques. It should also be noted that several summers earlier a six-weeks Secretarial School had come into a still flourishing existence.

In 1948 the President noted that "fewer than 0.8 per cent [of the student body] were last year dropped for academic reasons, and only 2.0 per cent were at the end of the year on academic probation. This is by far the best academic record in the history of the College." A few paragraphs later he is praising Miss Cam, adding what perhaps had needed to be said before: "It is, I think, of the first importance that Radcliffe students should have in their midst a woman teacher and scholar of such greatness."

From time to time the problem of the married student — particularly her chances of staying on to graduate — is reflected in the President's reports. In 1949 we find him suggesting that the Trustees might give consideration "to a possible housing development which would offer to these [married] students a better standard of living and fairer opportunities for group solidarity." By 1951 the applications for admission to Radcliffe had risen by another 8 per cent, and the total was almost twice the number who applied for entrance in 1944. Most cheering of all, perhaps, was the fact that in 1951 Radcliffe's donors — "careful and considered in their benefactions," as the President describes them — had designated almost half of all that they gave for *unrestricted* capital or endowment.

The healthy state of the College is further reflected in the still widening interest and responsibility of the undergraduate herself. If she woos "the spontaneous art," as Radcliffe's most recent poet, Adrienne C. Rich '51, has called her little Radcliffe pamphlet on music, she has also rolled up her sleeves and worked to help earn her tuition (more than 1,600 paid jobs in 1957). The century of self-service finds her, for three to five hours each week, cleaning dormitory rooms, waiting on tables, drying dishes, operating switchboards — "all gratis," Mr. Hal Clancy reported cheerfully, writing in 1951 in *Coronet* — meaning that the reward is not in cash but in useful discipline. Or, as Dean Kerby-Miller observes, "Although it was an economy measure, it also develops self-discipline, teaches the importance of doing cheerfully things one doesn't especially enjoy." Well, "if youth has its troubles," as Thomas W. Lamont reflected in writing of his own day in Exeter and Harvard at the close of the nineteenth century, "the chief of them is that youth cannot last."

Though it likely has not been said to her, the average Radcliffe student today might well have heard the admonition which Henry James gave to Rupert Brooke on the one occasion when they met. He told him "not to be afraid of being happy."

XV

The older gods of whom Miss Tucker was writing in 1933, and many others of the first three decades of the present century, have largely vanished from the scene. New names have taken their places *pari passu* — some of them the names of men who were teaching more than two decades ago, but most of them of men who have come forward since 1933: Raphael Demos in Philosophy; Crane Brinton, Charles H. Taylor, and Arthur Schlesinger, Jr., in History; Kenneth B. Murdock, Howard Mumford Jones, Perry Miller, I. A. Richards, Theodore Morrison, Archibald MacLeish, Douglas Bush, Harry Levin, and Albert Guérard in English;[21] Walter Piston, G. Wallace Woodworth,[22] and Randall Thompson in Music; John H. Finley, Jr., Mason Hammond, Werner W. Jaeger, and Sterling Dow in the Classics; Arthur D. Nock in the History and Philosophy of Religion; Merle Fainsod, Carl J. Friedrich, McGeorge Bundy, and Samuel H. Beer in Government; Sumner H. Slichter and John Kenneth Galbraith in Economics; Bart J. Bok in Astronomy; Kenneth J. Conant, Jakob Rosenberg, and Benjamin Rowland in Fine Arts; Louis F. Fieser and George B. Kistiakowsky in Chemistry; Philippe E. LeCorbeiller in the Physical Sciences; Gordon W. Allport in Social Relations. The list — any such list — is arbitrary and could easily be extended, even as this one has already been shortened by the deaths of Professors Slichter, Jaeger, and Nock, and by the retirement or resignation of others.

XVI

On the second and third of December, 1954, Radcliffe celebrated her 75th anniversary with a simple yet gay and impressive program. Dr. Godfrey L. Cabot, of the Harvard College Class of 1882, served as Honorary Chairman, Dean Mildred P. Sherman as Chairman. The celebration opened with a formal reception for alumnæ, trustees, and special guests. Some 1,200 were present, most of them visibly im-

---

[21] Death had taken two others within recent years: F. O. Matthiessen and Theodore Spencer.

[22] Who has brilliantly carried forward the work of the late Archibald T. Davison with the Radcliffe Choral Society, which continues to give annual concerts with the Harvard Glee Club and the Boston Symphony Orchestra under BSO direction. His retirement as conductor of these two groups (RCS and HGC) was announced in June 1958. Professor Woodworth was succeeded by Professor Elliot Forbes.

pressed by the historical display of Radcliviana in the library, featuring (among other things) alumnæ achievements in many fields — art, music, theatre, writing, and business. On the second day there were two important lectures: one in science by Professor Philippe LeCorbeiller, and one in the humanities by Professor David E. Owen. Professor Owen chose to give his most celebrated classroom lecture, "The Crystal Palace," as representative of his course on Victorian England. A buffet lunch, served simultaneously in all the dormitory dining rooms, was followed by formal exercises in Sanders Theatre at which seven distinguished alumnæ of Radcliffe, and President *Emerita* Ada Comstock Notestein, were honored with citations. Alumnæ who received this tribute were Cornelia James Cannon '99, author; Mabel Wheeler Daniels '00, composer; Marion Sharkey Doyle '14, national education; Josephine Sherwood Hull '99, actress; Dr. Martha May Eliot '13, physician, teacher, and public servant; Cecilia Payne-Gaposchkin, Ph.D. '25, astronomer; Doris Zemurray Stone '30, archæologist and humanitarian. The citation to President *Emerita* Comstock provided the fitting climax:

A daughter of the Middle Border who has given a long and fruitful life to the whole of her country. Wise in her counsels, inexhaustible in her labours, steadfast in her devotion to principles, she stands as chief architect of the greatness of this college.

After Miss Comstock, surely the late Josephine Hull was the best known person present:

An actress of spirit, whose private genius has created in the American theatre a succession of cheerfully improbable characters impossible to forget. A paradox of innocence and cunning, familiar as old lace itself, by her wit she has added a new dimension to the actor's art.

The Radcliffe Choral Society, the Harvard Glee Club, and the Harvard-Radcliffe Orchestra under the direction of Professor G. Wallace Woodworth and Mr. Attilio Poto performed the "Psalm of Praise," an exciting and brilliant modern choral work composed for the occasion by Miss Daniels.

XVII

Each autumn the academic spring returns and the college comes to life. The conditions of that life are deceptive: so easy in anticipation — and even in retrospect. "And so you morrowed on," wrote Walter de la Mare. Such a pretty phrase, poetically congenial to the special quality of each young swift-slow journey down the days of books and youth. "A genuinely liberal education is an education in attitudes, and a way of refining the sensibilities and the powers of discrimination and independent thought." The voice of the analyst breaks in,[23] and there is no disputing the sanction of these words. But what touchstone is there? The *social* attitudes are important: *sartor resartus*, for one thing. A non-parent, non-teacher may know next to nothing of the intellectual outlook of the Radcliffe undergraduate — either instinctive or imposed — save that her single attitude toward dress is agreeable rather than spectacular. This is well worth noting. In five years the fading national wardrobe of blue jeans may be as obsolete as the Empress Eugénie hat is obsolete today. But blue jeans have at no time been standard equipment at Radcliffe where the education in one attitude, at any rate, is above criticism: the young girls on foot or bicycle earlier referred to rarely if ever suggested that they were leaving the corral for the chuck wagon.

Basic, however, to women's education in general are these more elemental words, not of the analyst but of the philosopher: "Female education, when you come to consider it, is fundamentally complicated because it has to provide simultaneously for two completely different modes of life. From the beginning of Vanity, whenever that may be, till well into her middle age, a woman requires accomplishments different from — indeed, almost opposite to — those which will make her old age happy." This is the observation of Freya Stark whose orderly and civilized mind is on a plane with the

[23] Harold Taylor, Former President of Sarah Lawrence College.

oriental texture of her superior prose. It is useless to quarrel with that definition. If it were written as a codicil to the Radcliffe diploma, it would serve to attest the fidelity with which this College has increasingly sought to provide an education for young women which will shield them from the deadly absorption of inert ideas — of which Professor Whitehead has warned us — and give them in equal measure the confidence and vision to acquire at least some of these dual accomplishments which they will separately develop in the years ahead. It is "the richness and freedom of life at Radcliffe," as a popular article in *Mademoiselle* some years ago described it, which make an inevitable mark on the student body. It is precisely the impetus toward that richness and freedom of life which, from the presidency of Dean Briggs through that of Miss Comstock, was renewed and renewable from class to class. Only the dynamic could have brought the once-sheltered Annex to a present position of enviable power. Nothing can be learned in isolation. Life is not a cross section of the hexagon compartments in a human beehive. Just as the Radcliffe student today will cross the street to a Harvard classroom, to enter a world of teaching and communicated thought as reasonably good as the Nation today can offer, so she continually crosses and recrosses the contiguous areas of language and music, art and architecture, history and science, archæology and astronomy, poetry and sociology, journalism and the classics, biochemistry and creative writing. Her Cambridge world is now as complete a microcosm as she may find.

All this was no accident. General Education in the Humanities, the Social Sciences, and the Natural Sciences has extended the whole concept of higher education. A Humanities concentrator, for example, instead of adding an old-fashioned elementary course in physics or chemistry or biology designed for the future physicist, chemist, or biologist, may now, within the space of a single academic year, survey the whole of man's most significant achievements in any of these sciences, and study them in relation to terrestrial life itself.

The persistence and development of general examinations, the popular swing toward going out for Honors, the increasing student respect for and benefit derived from the reading periods, are all inclined to develop the kinetic idea of the correlation of knowledge and the obliteration of an earlier scholastic tendency to sudy A or B or C in antiseptic isolation. The Radcliffe student today has a much clearer notion of Mr. E. M. Forster's sharp distinction between the great books which simply extend the reader and the great books which are of immediate influence. *War and Peace*, the author of *Two Cheers for Democracy* has said, "made me feel small in the right way, and to make us feel small in the right way is the function of art; men can only make us feel small in the wrong way." It is a healthy sign when higher education at last begins to make the student "feel small in the right way." The continuing fluidity of not only the General Education courses but the course which education in general is taking, as President Jordan pointed out, is one assurance that the paradox of intellectual growth and the essential rightness of feeling small in the right way are as important in the academic scheme of things as the very diversity of the curriculum itself.

Now that diversity, so appalling to the novice who opens almost any college catalogue, is at last a controlled diversity; and the controls have developed quite naturally from the vast grab bag of President Eliot's free elective system to the sensible patterns of legitimate choice which the student has today. One comes to the Radcliffe curriculum as through the small end of a cornucopia. A little pamphlet called "Studies in the Freshman Year" has reduced to eight pages the selection of courses open to first year students: alphabetically from Anthropology to Social Relations. Nothing essential is forbidden or overlooked. The true range is almost as wide as the Emersonian conception of poetry — "the eternity it inherits." Anthropology, the classics, engineering sciences; Chinese, Classics of the Far East, Slavic, and Romance languages; mathematics, astronomy, philosophy, music, fine arts, and the physical sciences divide the intellectual spectrum. The eye falls on courses designated Slavic Aab and Bab.

> Should one eschew the Physics lab.,
> There's always Slavic Aab and Bab.
> Are you a hab-not or a hab?

But they are all Habs, under the gift of fortune, though they may not know it.

XVIII

Coördinate education is — or was — the Fay House phrase for the joint instruction which the Harvard faculty (since the 1943 agreement) offers to the young women of what the *Harvard Alumni Bulletin* has called Sister Radcliffe. It is well known that certain Harvard alumni viewed the step taken by President Comstock of the College, President James B. Conant and Provost Paul H. Buck of Harvard and their respective governing boards, somewhat as approval of an act of infiltration.[24] On the lighter side, whoever said that "Harvard is not coeducational in any respect except in point of fact" drew repeated and re-echoed laughter for nearly a decade. Perhaps what Santayana said of William James might comfort those who feel that Radcliffe's coördinate education is Harvard's coeduca-

---

[24] Anonymous lines in "The College Pump" of 25 September 1948, a column established by the editor in *The Harvard Alumni Bulletin* in 1940:

> I hate the fact that Harvard's now a School;
> It grieves me that the Yard as such is dead.
> From Grampa's campus to the swimming pool
> What is this rumor that we've turned coed?
>
> The goody's gone; the biddy has her place;
> A spread is now another high school dance.
> Fair Harvard, why this fall from ancient grace?
> A good swift kick — but in the slacks or pants?

tion: "A philosopher who is a teacher of youth is more concerned to give people a right start than a right conclusion."

Be this conclusion as it may, a boundary has been crossed, and Radcliffe girls today (including freshmen since 1950) are not only admitted to the Harvard classrooms, but certain Harvard undergraduate classes also meet at the College across the Common. A Radcliffe student is not permitted entrance to Lamont Library, but most other library, archival, museum, and observatory facilities are at her disposal. She may also be active in certain Harvard extracurricular activities through a Radcliffe membership in the *Crimson*, the Year Book, Radio WHRB, the *Advocate*, the Harvard Dramatic Club, and the like. The Final Clubs, the Signet Society, the Harvard *Lampoon*, and other undergraduate organizations are still reckoned among the unyielding. Of course — as a member of the Choral Society — she has long since sung in public with the Glee Club. People forget that early observation by Dean Briggs (*v.* p. 178). Co-ordinate education in reality is no more than the shift of joint study from the "small advanced classes" to classes large and small, advanced and elementary.[25] It has been that way for more than a decade. It seems unlikely that, on the teaching policy level, there will ever be any further change — or exchange — in the Radcliffe-Harvard relationship.

XIX

Along in the 1950's, just before Harvard squared away toward the gigantic (and successful) task of raising $82.5 million, Radcliffe took stock of her own house and larder and announced a ten-year plan

---

[25] *The Report of the Committee to visit Harvard College* in 1952, of which Dr. W. Barry Wood, Jr., was Chairman, had this to say: "The change has meant, of course, closer contact between Radcliffe and Harvard students in many ways. . . . It has created new problems, or altered old ones, such as the relationship between student organizations, entertainment of women guests in Harvard dormitories, etc., but on the whole the relationship is healthy and satisfactory, and there has been little complaint or criticism from either side."

with a goal of $10 million. After seven years and $7 million in hand to show for them, the Program was satisfactorily terminated in July 1961, leaving the College materially strengthened by the generosity of its alumnae, parents, and friends who had provided essential money for both new endowment and new buildings, including the Coöperative Houses, Comstock Hall (newest of the dormitories), and the Graduate Refectory.

In 1961 the Governing Boards decided to conduct all of Radcliffe's future fund-raising activities through an organization to be called the Radcliffe College Fund, responsible for both capital gifts and for the alumnae annual-giving program for unrestricted funds. Basic objectives of the present capital program are:

1) A new House Center, composed of seven residential units for 300 students and resident faculty members or faculty families; including common rooms, recreation, and dining facilities.

2) A Library Center in the residential quadrangle north of Walker Street, to contain the central undergraduate collection of 150,000 volumes and room-space for seminars and tutorial as well as for faculty offices.

3) Remodelling of the three existing House Centers: adding dining halls, common rooms, and faculty residences comparable to facilities in the new House.

At this point a glance at some comparative Radcliffe statistics for 1944–1945 and 1962–1963 are pertinent. Mentioning the earlier year first, we observe that the number of undergraduates in the College has increased from 843 to 1,163; of graduates, 335 to 504.[26] Tuition has risen for undergraduates from $450 to $1,520; for graduate students from $450 to $1,520. Radcliffe's endowment has grown (book value) from $6,200,000 to $17,431,229, and (market value) from $6,600,000 to $22,071,362; academic plant assets, from $3,338,000 to $8,611,195. Administrative and operating expenses are up from

---

[26] Beginning with the academic year 1962–1963, the conferring of all degrees — at the undergraduate as well as the graduate level — is done by Harvard.

$597,000 to $5,130,476; scholarship awards have grown from $75,500 to $290,000. In 1962–63, 300 scholarships (30 per cent of undergraduates) averaged $1,200. In the Graduate School, 135 fellowships (26 per cent of the graduate students) averaged $1,300.

XX

Radcliffe continues to strengthen further her national ties. A college with her present reputation has not only the right but the obligation to invite the consideration of America's distributed youth. In competition with sister institutions better endowed and better equipped, it is still clear that she has certain unique advantages to offer which should be available to the young women who seek them out. Unfortunately many of these young women are turned away because they need the help which only scholarships can give.

XXI

The end of every history is the day it goes to press; and the present story of Radcliffe was last enlarged and revised in 1958. Much has happened to the College in the lustrum just over — in five regenerative years, that is: three of them the first three of the College's fifth president. A summary is called for, though not officially; and the following paragraphs are timbered with foursquare words as befit a time of action. For these three years of accelerated revolution, affecting and altering the life of both graduate student and undergraduate, have equally broadened their opportunities and shaped a new Radcliffe, even more intimate and intrarelated than in the past.

The third woman to direct the College is President Mary I. Bunting, Ph.D., L.H.D., LL.D., S.D. Hon., who succeeded Wilbur K. Jordan when he resigned his office in 1960 to resume the teaching of history. Widowed mother of four children, distinguished microbiologist, gold medalist of the National Institute of Social Scientists,

Mrs. Bunting has described herself as "a geneticist with nest building experience." Dynamic and incisive, she has warmly applied cool scientific methods to the academic assembly, and has done it with notable and rapid success. Most notable of all, she has fully meshed the gears of Radcliffe and Harvard, and the College now functions more easily than ever within the larger structure of the University. Radcliffe no longer maintains her separate graduate school, for example. Her graduate students since 1962–1963, though automatically enrolled in Radcliffe College, have been fully qualified members of the Graduate School of Arts and Sciences at Harvard, aimed toward a Harvard degree and Harvard diploma. In short, the Radcliffe graduate student still lives in, and is a part of the Radcliffe College community but her training is in a University.

Believing that "education has to be a part of adult life in a new way," Mrs. Bunting announced in November of her first year in office the establishment of the Radcliffe Institute for Independent Study, an experimental program in women's education "to encourage professional excellence in highly qualified individuals for whom the usual educational grants are not ordinarily available; to enable such women to keep their talents vigorous and their training meaningful during periods of their lives when time for their own creative or scholarly work is essential but difficult to obtain." The Institute grants no degrees, is not a graduate school but a community of scholars and artists. It has three classes of membership. The Associate Scholars — twenty at present — are women concerned with *independent* scholarly or creative work on a part-time basis. Their annual grants vary, with a maximum of $3,000. Associates usually live within commuting distance of Cambridge. The Affiliate Scholars are women who hold appropriate advanced degrees in their professions and wish to undertake additional course and clinical training. A few full-time scholarships of no set stipend go to special applicants who have achieved a certain distinction in scholarship or the creative arts.

AN ACRE FOR EDUCATION

Beyond and above all Associates and Affiliates are the Institute Fellows: "women who have achieved great distinction in a professional career in any field." The Fellows are selected through nomination; they may come from anywhere in the world. If they have much to gain at Radcliffe through freedom for their own work, it is clearly implicit that by their presence and occasional lecturing they will also give much in turn. The Institute is flexible enough to declare itself concerned with "problems peculiar to the education of women and the fullest utilization of their educated talent.[27] Not since the founding of the Society of Fellows at Harvard by President Lowell has any similar organization approached the potential of the Institute in its daring concept.

President Bunting's wide background as teacher, dean, and scientist — Douglass, Bennington, Goucher, Yale and Wellesley — as well as her continuing service on commissions and committees in the educational field, enabled her to design and initiate Radcliffe's House Plan economically by adapting dormitories and off-campus buildings to form (as of now) a trinity of Houses on the points of the compass — South, East, and North: each House headed by a distinguished Harvard faculty member and his wife, and benefited (as at Harvard) by Faculty Associates. These three existing House Centers will soon be requited by a fourth; and all three (to conform with the new one) will be remodeled to include dining halls, common rooms, and Faculty residences. Each Center already has its own Dean, so that henceforth the undergraduate will enjoy continual benefit of counsel and direction from one who will come to know and understand her need and problems.

An acre for education? The Indian ground allotted to Guy Bambrige more than three hundred years ago has gradually spread across both state and nation, and its golden dust blown out beyond the shores of his own land. Time has strengthened the long chain of

[27] See p. 221.

association; enriched some literary, social, and human traditions; surrendered the house in which much of it is blended; granted pioneers and leaders, the fellowship of a few great men and a few far-seeing and purposeful women. The living proof of these and them is lodged in a college contagious with the ambition of youth. And Radcliffe, still a college, is the perfect example of Professor Whitehead's definition of the true function of the university: "To preserve the zest of life by uniting the young and the old in the imaginative consideration of learning."

Nine years beyond her Diamond Jubilee, Radcliffe is determined to continue to give the best possible education to the best possible selection of students. She recognizes that education is the vague amorphous word which none can define or weigh but all can recognize. Whatever it means, youth is looking for it. Perhaps the definition that Robert Frost once gave to something else will help: Youth is looking for it

book-like on a shelf,
Or even better god-like in yourself.

1938–1963

Luminary

It is after midnight toward the end of May, and the atmospherics are moist but fragrant. Outside my window in Wadsworth House a sudden rallying cry for Rinehart, like an impromptu Hyla chorus, has subsided. Examinations begin tomorrow: lights burn late, and all the books of Lamont and Widener are piled together hopefully on the scale of justice. But nothing has changed, of course; and one little blue book still outweighs them all. In the morning the double smoke bush between my window and the south side of Grays will be infested with honey bees and Eight-spotted Foresters — the sunshine moth that feeds on our Boston ivy. The pair of oven birds and the redpolls of last year did not return this spring. The brown thrasher paused in transit as in the past, and now father robin has taken over. The Yard has a good supply of worms, but a few weeks ago he was making nothing but dry runs. For robins every day is examination day.

The Lights Come On

YOU never know just when, for there are not in all the buildings together filaments enough to make the Yard a brilliant place, even by any city back-street standard. Murky Cambridge dusk — how damp, how murky! — and then of a sudden you turn a corner and there is the familiar outdoor bracket beacon, like the carriage lamp of another age, brightening a segment of brick and showing a pool of amber on the rotting snow beneath. Now half a dozen other lights are winking from the windows of Weld, Grays, and the rest. Back of tall pillars the curtain of Widener slowly rises and inward illumination comes up as on a vast but silent stage. A voice calls far across from the steps of Hollis. Figures about the Yard grow shadowy and soft and moist. A match flares to a cigarette. Evening becomes official, and the gloom is gradually filtered everywhere with the innocent pin-points of sixty-cycle sunlight.

Down in the Basin, half the Harvard Bridge — the Boston half, perhaps — has already responded to the throwing of a giant switch. From shore to center the dwindling silhouette is brilliant with little bulbs: an accusing finger in the direction of Cambridge, warning her to forget the budget and mounting taxes and turn on the juice of the other half. This (in good time) the servants of the City Fathers will surely do.

Up the river sweep the beams and half-beams of homeward suburban cars against the slower-moving glitter of inbound Boston traffic. The Weeks Bridge, a pretty Georgian fragment thrown across the Charles, and her less beautiful elder sister to the west, flank the batteries of increasing window light from the Houses and

233

the Business School. It is Monday evening — high table, that means, at Lowell House — and the graceful Lowell tower emerges in the gloom, touched off by your modern reflectors, cunningly concealed. Cambridge is a city of spires now, even by night, and at other times there are three of them ablaze at once. In the river, where the ice is going out in jigsaw-puzzle fragments, float these images of phosphorous. A pretty sight, with spring so faintly stirring in the night air: a moment of security, almost, in a world so pitifully insecure.

The lights of Harvard's Cambridge come on with a greater front and a steadier shine than they did for our more somnolent ancestors. Even the now old-fashioned arc of hotly sputtering carbon, still casting weird tree-shadows on a wall in Plympton Street, has probably more candle-power within one cracked globe than half the Yard could muster in the rosy days of *The Rebelliad*. And what would the ancients say to the milk-white Taj Mahal, the Good Gulf gas station on the site of dead Beck Hall, the dreary?

Light has always been one of the first symbols of colleges and learning. Centuries and electrons have not changed us there. The point is that at Harvard the lights *can* still come on — in fair weather or in rain, in a time of free thinking, or of the soul's own darkness, when man shall save his birthright only by a masterful resolve.

1941

Celestial

Stars used to shine in such a simple way,
But now with frightful telescopic scenes
The night is horrid. What would Pascal say?
I've read too much of Eddington and Jeans.

MATHEMATICS is the purest science, but astronomy has for the layman that quality of ascension which defines a stellar purity. Astronomy is visible and large — remote, yet remindful that man is but a squatter on the fell plains of the zodiac. There is something celestial, too, about the silent little domes which rise on the hilltops of our cities of learning or stand like symbols of hope on the unexpected mountains of the world. If we as people have now withdrawn from the night, as Henry Beston has suggested, and lost that Arabian familiarity, it is comforting to think that in almost every civilized land, in a world at peace or at war, reflective portholes open to the sky, and messengers who commenced their journeys centuries ago arrive with every tick of the clock to tell us something we did not know before.

Each of us at some period in our lives has looked for a moment through the small end of a telescope at the craters in our moon,[1] on those other moons of Jupiter, at binaries, at the disk-like rings of Saturn. Those brilliant, queer impressions of outer worlds once magnified remain with us the rest of our suburban lives. The cold November sky powdered with stars, occasional eclipses and the smoked glass through which we view them, or the colored festoon of Aurora Borealis remind us from time to time of the men who trade with aberrations, with refracted light. A remote race, for the most part: vigilant, hopeful, constructive. Dealing in orbits, gases,

[1] But just *whose* moon did not suggest itself in 1947.

spectra, and kiloparsecs, the astronomer has little smalltalk for the man in the crowd. Now and then he issues casual bulletins of reassurance on the passage of Earth through the tail of a comet, tells us that the Philharmonic's noisy competitor is a fleck on the face of the Sun, and gives us to understand that while man's anger is rising the galactic glass is falling. Occasionally the romanticist in him points out some curious cobwebs on a Mars or weighs the spectral lines of a new element not quite so precious as it is unobtainable. The misty vapors round a Venus reopen conjectures of planetary life. Beyond all this lie the secret things the astronomer does in alliance with his brothers in the less pure sciences, working as they are, shoulder to shoulder for the betterment and the erasure of mankind. He hands them his evidence and hastily returns his eye to the keyhole. Fission is nothing new to him. Clouds over Hiroshima and Bikini are but a tatter of fog compared with some nebular disturbances local to Orion. Lately he has allied himself with the weatherman, and from his igloo-aerie issues now a new conception of the lacteal content of the Milky Way and a word for the pilot over Pittsburgh. Above all, he knows better than most whence we came, and he has a somewhat unpleasant idea of where we are going.

He is a kindly person and minds his own business. Were the world filled with his image there would be no wars, and the good life would emerge a cut above party politics. On occasion he takes a holiday. The last six days of December witnessed a meeting in Cambridge of the American Astronomical Society. Big words are involved. Big things are afoot and aloft; but nothing bigger than the disinterested minds of these men who toil unheralded and for the most part alone. Let us distinguish this spatialist from the specialist. His cell is small and round; his roof revolves. He dwells and thinks high. But he is looking away from the world, not at it, and the darkness through which his thought is voyaging is brighter than Newton's day.

1947

Cambridge Sky

WHEN a deep snow has fallen, "hiding difference, making unevenness even," the sky itself lets down into Cambridge with the clear white flower of its realm; and time, as we walk abroad in the morning, has lost as much as fifty years. Wall and house and chimney, and the simple grill work of the fences, seem all as ancient in their mantle as the masoned arch of a stone bridge or an old well dreaming under lichen. The traffic, that on any other day streams loudly through the Square, moves haltingly with padded foot and wheel, and for once in the long year its flow is at a minimum. Streets which normally bear less of it (like Craigie and Linnæan) keep, long after the plows have passed, much of the quiet and unobtrusion I remember as a boy in the roads round Woodmere on Long Island. I thought then that a fall of snow in winter could still the living world. And as I went about the farm, twanging the taut chicken wire to see the flakes fly from its hundred hexagons, I never doubted that sublime delight in the crystal fields about me was intagliated in my heart forever, and that silence of the kind would drop again so often as the skies shook down their load.

It is so that on a winter's day, before the sun has ruined the delicate white web of every tree and bramble, or stolen from the unsheltered side of the rough oak the feathery pattern on its trunk, the intimations of antiquity are strong; and here, in a community grown suddenly old, I might be setting out across the Common with Mather or Jared Sparks. Such drifted quiet! I renew in it again and again the thoughts and associations of my boyhood, though I move and justle in the company of generations that knew, how long before me, the looping ribbon of the Charles and heard, like all Socinians, the toll of Harvard's bell. At the foot of Garden Street, hard against the old First Church, the headstones of the burial ground sprout and bristle in the sudden snow. On a slab of granite near the sidewalk is written in uncial: "8 miles to Boston." A legend, I take it, undefeated by the subway, and yet intact with interest: for once, on a warmer day, I came upon a child lost in the absorbing process of copying it down. A few years ago I heard an elderly lady ask, at a meeting of the Cambridge Historical Society, if anyone recalled the name of a gentleman who used to walk, in brass buttons and a cocked hat, down this very street — it might have been in '55. I do not remember him; but surely he must be lying here, like others of his period, and more of an earlier time when Holden Chapel was a barrack and lads of the College first went blithely out to war.

Occasionally now the sky has in it, of all the swollen year, the clearest chisel of marble and the deepest vent of blood. On such a day it sharpens to the eye with the cold lustre of cold sharp steel; and when the wind has settled in the north, spreads out its fleece till a long reach of it discloses the blue-white mottle of the binding on my copy of John Keats. Or the great canvas tightens under the power of astringent; and here are heavens pulled like a drum, while we put about our business with troubled mind, fearful lest something between the poles of night and day should strike mightily the tympanum and rend us senseless in a flood of sound. But for the most part, though the sky is depended and physically near, there is about it, in the long middle months, an air of perpetual sadness and melancholy that touch on times and themes and places at an infinite remove. It is not a friendly sky, for desolation is its tenant. To look upon it from the frozen rim of Fresh Pond, where Henry James used to walk, or the crown of Belmont Hill, is to mirror in one's eyes the steep of solitude above Monadnock or Chocorua when the full fields breathed with life, but which we now can hardly bear because it leans beyond the last horizon and the world about us has gone bleak and naked as a dry bone in the desert.

On evenings, after the days have begun to grow longer, the lid will lift a fraction in the west, as if God were sniffing at the cauldron, and then dark hills begin to smoulder, and the long crack burns richly crimson at the passage of the sun. At such times I have seen a purple vapor rise for a moment in marvelous effect against the first dull stratum of cloud; blown, as it were, of great lungs or of enormous leathern bellows. And when this crimson deepens to an angry red, though leagues of stellar air stand insulate between, I feel the heat of it stir in the marrow as surely as the open bonfire giving of its blaze.

Feet that move across the Yard on academic errands have come, I find, to crackle the stiff, frozen boards that cover the diagonals of every path. Even there, in the shelter of so much brick and mortar and under the druidic arms of such elms as lived out their giant, pestilented fellows, winter has drifted in and sparkles like a diamond. Something quick and social has fallen with the snow, and the silence that lies in pools about me is laced with a crunching and the ring of many voices. It is as if the face of this foliate world were lifted from the drowse and murmur of scholarship and looked suddenly astonished upon the glitter of the sun. In its light is all renascence; in its courts one walks a king. Then late of a morning the heavy clouds come bellying over, and the surface turns to ice. The squirrel, out of the wind's way and asleep in his hidden basket, hears but the creak of great trees and the echo of a shout from the archway of Sever; but the blue pigeons that in summer revolve above an airy lattice, and whirl in company through the sacred wood, go prowling about the snow with hungry eyes and blustered plumage, and huddle into clefts and under eaves of the buildings least exposed. In the small delta by the site of old Dane Hall that burned [1] when I was in College, a pair or trio of copper beeches, conditioned in New

[1] I saw it burn. Lehman and Straus Halls were not yet built when this essay was first printed. The great low lateral branches of the beech trees — five by actual count — must have gone in the unsymmetrical 1930's. The naked glove-grey torsos give good shade, it is true; but does not an English diploma likewise give good

England soil, wear the deep burnish of their name. They are the last trees to put out their leaves in the spring. They were grown for winter, with a deep arboreal symmetry and great horizontal branches that sprawl upon the ground. What gales could buffet them as flay the cedars along the Jersey coast or the scraggly, flat-foot pines of Maine? Here in serenity they put down the roots that are their mouths, and scarcely tremble for a blizzard above them, howling the bitter north into the chimney pots of Grays and Matthews.

Over them, as over the blue-green dome of Hemenway, and the bulbs that lie buried with their Latin names in the rock gardens by the Herbarium, the cold figures of the constellations gather and emerge. When the clouds have blown off "from a high and frosty heaven," and the street lamps emit their frail, deliberate light, the tangle of bright stars in branches, and the pure stream of them broken loose across the meridian, fasten in the mind with a shock of sudden wonder or distrust. One cannot escape it. A student stumbling home from the library, his mind filled with vectors or Plotinus, drinks at the great fountain before he finally climbs the stairs, not knowing to remember that George Moore nightly did the same under the trees in King's Bench Walk. That grave and golden landscape, the pasture of a solitary in winter ways, amber with dead grass and vivid with the reddish pods of sumac, dies like a *miserere* when we contemplate the stars. I recall it was here in Jarvis Field that I first looked through a telescope and saw the rings of Saturn and the moons of Jupiter, and pilfered with the eye the shadowy, strong craters of the moon. Indeed, astronomy is cradled here, for it was in this very town that the Clark Brothers first ground the enormous lenses for which they were famous; and the curious, naked ruin of some large refractor, rusted and empty on its iron trunnions and still

---

service? Laterals or Latin: each is easily pruned. And so are essays: but I have let this one stand, twigs and deadwood and all, just out of sentiment. It was written earlier than the published date. "The sky," said Harvard's Emerson — and the words come back to me day after day — "the sky is the daily bread of the eyes."

pointing at the sky, may be seen on Henry Street, a stone's throw from the Charles.

Coming home on a winter night — for the leaves do not hide it then — my friendliest beacon is the light on Observatory Hill, winking out with pendulum precision each second of time. I look for it as for the light in Hollis. It burns mysteriously from dark to dawn, and marks how near the spring has come by the advancing hour at which the Pleiades and Gemini wheel down and westward to meet the swallowing earth.

1928

Ancillary

Summa is i-cumen in,
   Laude sing cuccu!
Laddes rede and classe lede,
Professor bemeth tu —
   Sing cuccu!

Scholour striveth after Aye,
   Bleteth after shepskin ewe;
Writë theseth, honoure seazeth,
   Murie sing cuccu!

Cuccu, cuccu, wel singes A·B cuccu;
   Ne flunke thu naver nu;
   Sing cuccu, nu, sing cuccu,
   Sing cuccu, Phye Betta Cappe, nu!

Blue Reflections on the
Merchants Limited

In Memory of A. Whitney Griswold

New Haven for the traveller is the station
At which he takes his watch out and reflects
That one more chapter and one more libation
Will prove the killer the man whom he suspects.

Or, if he's headed for the Northeast Corner,
He'll bid the waiter bring his apple pie;
And, with a scorn that well becomes the scorner,
Permit New Haven to invade his eye.

The curious traveller will, however, ponder
This change from Diesel to electric power,
Or vice versa; and then his mind may wander
Beyond the club car and the cocktail hour.

Is this the symbol of the arts and science:
Promethean engine and the magic flare
Of light? The happy conflict of two giants:
Pure physics and the voltage of Voltaire?

It needs no twentieth century scholar-gipsy,
Adrift between the Back Bay and the West,
Reported now at Berkeley or Poughkeepsie,
Chicago, Princeton, Texas, to attest

245

IN SIGHT OF SEVER

The inward spirit and the outer valence —
Unebbed of strength, unlikely to go stale —
Which in the face of friends, against assailants,
Is still two centuries and a half of Yale.

Yonder she rises! And the industrial city,
Industrious now to fence her safely in,
Is careful as a Faculty Committee:
No hoi-polloitering where the blues begin!

The gnathic index as a useful measure
Of cranial bones suggests the word we need:
The Gothic index to New Haven treasure
Reveals the flower of mediaeval seed.

Harvard is rich in architecture, richer
Than cream that tries to rise on powdered milk.
Our copious Gropius, than which none is whicher,
Is foil to Mem and Matthews and their ilk.

Yet what is this behind the blue façade there —
These colleges of ancient tower and court?
Was someone playing with a Georgian quad there,
And swept it all behind the Davenport?

No matter. Yale has wonders by the acre.
In this drab world, as everybody knows,
She built the Bowl of Bowls. But did its maker
Foresee these others: Cotton, Dust, and Rose?

Scions of Yale who gathered to their fathers
When still Manhattan was a rambling town
Were great in peace and war. The thing that bothers
The Cambridge crowd is that they won't stay down.

BLUE REFLECTIONS

We have your men of letters — and of liters:
Poet and chemist, and all those in between.
From Government to Forest we're competers —
Competing like two lovers on the screen.

At raising money, who's the Boola-Boola?
Your Fund is leader in this abstruse field.
We hear your horrid cry of Moola-Moola!
The crimson in our blood-bank is congealed.

Take Presidents. Ah, *there* we're still defending!
Two Adams and two Roosevelts. None laughed
That off. Three centuries! Is it ending?
Or *must* you cultivate the tribe of Taft?

The lithic lace of Harkness takes the rising
Rays of the Crimson dawn — a sporting touch.
On land and water we are still surprising
One or the other, but probably not much.

The old days hale us back to field and river:
New London, Brickley's toes, and those of Coy;
The coonskin coat, the mid-November shiver,
Mory's and more and more and more . . . O boy!

Wide is the land. And great beyond the greatness
Of name and years divisible by youth,
You've held your ground; and lasting well the lateness
Of this dark hour, held steady to the truth.

And you, Sir, as you honor us at table,
May we suggest that we would honor both
Yourself, your University, still able
To quoth New Haven, "Evermore!" Unquoth.

1952

Oxford Nearly Visited

For Philip Hofer and the C.O.V.

Come, for I need you, porter, and your heft
With all this duffle and these overcoats.
As I have stumbled through the Continent,
Equipped for catching trains and losing boats,
Your dear face was familiar where I went;
And if *rapides* had left
Perchance the *gare du nord*, the *gare de l'ouest*,
Alone in the vile station we would then
Check and recheck the blooming stuff again.
Come, porter, this is not an idle jest.

Here where the noise is virtually as bad
(Though English smells are different from the French)
I came with Bradshaw into Paddington,
And now upon a proper English bench
I weep, I weep! The Oxford train has gone
(No, leave them there, my lad).
So while the London trippers hurry by,
Each with his third-class ticket and his tea,
Resolved for Ifflington or near the sea,
Here will I dream on Oxford till I die.

Here will I dream on garth green shaven lawns
And last enchantments of a middle age:
Towers and Quads and Carfax, and the spires
That lit the souls of many an English sage;

Beauty uncrumbled out of English shires,
And the still smoky dawns,
With all that sweet integument of youth.
Grave Colleges who held within their walls
Whole centuries of Davids and of Sauls:
Shy traffickers investigating truth.

Here will I dream on Balliol more because
Of Arnold and young Swinburne than of Clough:
Swinburne the swimmer, Prince of Proserpine,
And Arnold who wrote poems on his cuff;
Magdalen, Brasenose, Trinity, benign
Old cloisters of our Laws,
Humanities, *Belles Lettres*, and the rest;
Shotover Hill, and Isis, the strange fuss
Of cricket unintelligible to us,
And the red sun delaying in the west.

The train is gone: the one Zuleika took
What time the Emperors broke into a sweat.
O solemn Trajan, replica'd in Rome,
The vaguest traveller you have never met
Sees but the flower rooted in thy dome,
And stops awhile to look;
And in that city of superior gloom
Shivers a little from so strange a sight,
And spends the livelong day and half the night
Wandering as a ghost beyond the tomb.

Addison's walk, the Mitre, what of these?
Faint passages descending from the High,
Quads unexplored, and flocks within their folds,
Or Magdalen Tower struck against the sky;

Bicycles (rented) pedaling past St. Aldate's? . . .
The fragrance of a cheese,
And a slow stoup of ale these many times,
Fade with the Don "in amply bellowing gown,"
The Gothic murmur of an ancient town,
And the still fading flower of Oxford chimes.

Gone, gone, like knowledge in the Warden's wake,
Or verses done by Calverley of Christ's;
A scholar-gipsy in the Cumnor hills —
He who revolted when the world enticed —
And haunts his silence that the moonlight fills;
For whose own gracious sake
I, too, shall garner but the ends of dream,
Fingering haply one or two small tricks —
Something I bought there once for three-and six —
And coin the silver of my Oxford theme.

The train has gone. No more the dusty leaves
Unrustled in some Bodleianic close.
Pater and Pusey, Addison and Swift,
I could not see your spectres if I chose:
But as a shipwrecked sailor shall I drift
Where the great storm-wind grieves;
Dreaming on Oxford under lateen sails
Until at last, abandoned by the crew,
I am that Casual, half indignant, who,
Like some old hero unrecorded, bails.

1927

Monetary

Sometimes in the routine of life — for even a University has its own patterns of routine — any one of us may lose sight of the real Harvard, the soul of the place: the ancient Harvard respected and honored throughout the civilized world. The Yard is here, and all the natural extensions of it; the buildings, the several Faculties, the Administration, and most of all the endless flow of students. And we are all here too: those of us who serve in other ways. But we are not, taken all together, like a great enterprise or company, a steel mill, an assembly plant, or a vast department store. We do not light up with neon signs at night, we are not on the billboards, we sponsor no comedian or Stop the Music on the air, we do not change our models or streamlines from year to year. We have no dynaflow, make no supersuds, offer no plastic innovations, have no circulation or readership to advertise, no warehouses or branch offices, no delivery trucks or private shiplanes to the sea. We split no stock, cut no melons. We are simply on the move. Our worldly business is up and down the mainstream of a tradition whose source is enduring.

A native Executive Sec
Of a Fund at Nahuatl Toltec
    Has denied that his needs
    Are for Mexican beads.
Huatl please him? Nahuatl? A chec!

Money from Where?

EVERY educated person in the United States today is reasonably well aware that the privately endowed colleges and universities are feverishly absorbed in the difficult task of raising money.[1] Yonder institution is out for one million and a half dollars, another is after seven million, and a third has a ten-year over-all expansion program calling for seventeen million. The liberal arts college or the great university, like the library of which Archibald MacLeish once wrote, "is never bought; it is always in process of purchase." But so endemic is the present dollar disease that the chorus of campaigns sounds something like the Hyla voices of a postponed spring, though less romantic. Complete success (please note) is here and there reported, but there is no doubt whatever that campaign anxiety is related to a lot of hypothecated checks signed with invisible ink. What truth is there in the notion that the weaker of our privately endowed institutions of learning will not long survive, that the stronger will be impaired as time and successive — and unsuccessful — campaigns advance? Modified disaster of this sort was predicted eighteen years ago, and the predictors were wrong. What lies ahead? Where is the money coming from — and is it coming?

It was once so different. It was even not unlike the picture of the Whirlwind Campaign which the late Stephen Leacock gave us in 1912 in perhaps his best book, *Sunshine Sketches of a Little Town*.

[1] The prophecy, guesswork, and didacticism which follow appeared originally as an editorial in the *Harvard Alumni Bulletin*. I have added the word *foundations* to the fourth paragraph from which it was accidentally omitted in 1948. This was the year in which the Harvard Fund completed a three-year campaign to endow the Lamont Library for undergraduates.

253

Educators will remember or recognize the Leacock slyness back of the unaffected humor.

He'd happened to be in one of the big cities when they were raising money by a Whirlwind Campaign for one of the universities, and he saw it all. He said he would never forget the scene on the last day of it, when the announcement was made that the total of the money raised was even more than what was needed. It was a splendid sight — the business men of the town all cheering and laughing and shaking hands, and the professors with the tears streaming down their faces, and the Deans of the Faculties, who had given money themselves, sobbing aloud. He said it was the most moving thing he ever saw.

Well, the Deans of the Faculties today, under the present economy, have even less money to contribute to their own cause, though they may have more reason to sob aloud. They and their presidents and treasurers are aware of certain unfavorable facts. Their institutions need money — not only to advance toward the meridian but to retain their ranking as of now. The sources to which they may turn for help are obviously these: their alumni, other private capital, the corporations, foundations, and the state. To most of us it is unthinkable, as one educator has written, that "only the state can resolve the dilemma now faced in financing the future of higher education." If that is a fact, then free enterprise indeed is dead. But with respect to the first three sources the following paragraphs, taken from the New England Trust Company's *Taxes and Estates* for September, are immediately pertinent.

With few exceptions, great wealth among individuals in this country is history. The multi-millionaire has become a colorful figure of the past and individuals who can claim a million dollars are becoming scarce. Wealth accumulated in the past is being divided and sub-divided, and new wealth is more difficult to acquire and retain. This trend is readily apparent from figures submitted by the United States government and by the Trust Division of the American Bankers Association.

According to the Bureau of Internal Revenue, estate tax returns show that estates of over $10,000,000 declined almost 50% in a ten year period. In the same period, estates of $1,000,000 declined 8.9% and estates of $500,000 to $1,000,000 declined 10.2%. On the other hand, the government returns show a small increase in estates under $200,000 and a substantial increase in estates up to but not exceeding $100,000.

From these figures two inferences may be drawn: First, that the income of the *average* alumnus in America is undoubtedly on the rise; and that in consequence the alumni fund, now generally accepted and cultivated by most colleges and universities as a reliable wellspring for unrestricted or deficit money, should continue to grow and flourish. Second, that the day of the large and generous individual benefactor is appreciably over, and that hope of large contributory endowment must lie in the direction of corporations and corporate business. "The fact that a great part of our national wealth is locked up in corporate form," as Laird Bell '04 said in an article called "If Corporations Will Give," published in the *Atlantic* for last May, led him to explore the whole subject of the future financing of our schools, colleges, and universities. Not overlooking the complex question of increasing competition from the state universities, Mr. Bell in his article established reasonable and reassuring arguments as to why corporations already are giving greater support to privately endowed institutions. "Forward-looking managements [he said] are . . . turning more and more to the widespread facilities of universities for light on their problems, and the field has been but scratched." We believe with Mr. Bell that "if corporations can be said to have an over-all faith, it is clearly in private enterprise." We are inclined to predict that in the area of science the tide of corporation gifts will show a marked (and publicized) increase over the next few years, some other things being equal. But most of all, we take heart over Mr. Bell's courageous challenge to corporations great and minor not to limit their support to the more obvious fields of science and industry, but "to recognize an obligation to promote both theoretical research at the university level and the production of good citizens at the college level." What national recognition, in turn, awaits the corporate authors of the first full step in this last direction!

In a country of abrupt changes we look for abrupt warnings. The extent and sporadic success of current endowment campaigns in colleges and universities from coast to coast may momentarily allay our fears. But the warning has definitely been sounded, and the first to hear it should be alumni everywhere. They alone, through the channels of their annual-giving funds have the opportunity and the basic income to pledge the enthusiastic and rounded support of their institutions which, in turn, will affect the rising tide of corporate giving. The college or the university supported to the limit by its own graduate body is the going concern a corporation will recognize and respect as such. *Finem respice.*

1948

The Language of Request

W RITING these words [1] long after midnight in an old frame
house at Harvard which has weathered 230 New England winters,
I suddenly discover the symbol I have been looking for. The house
is warm. The source of its uninterrupted heat lies three-quarters of
a mile away in a great power plant of the Cambridge Electric Light
Company down on the river. We are heated by a flow of excess
steam which has already done its work in a turbine or two and
might well be released as so much unwanted hot air save that someone has wisely channeled it through swaddled pipes in a long tun-
nel just to comfort my room and some hundreds of others like it
in adjacent college buildings. Communication with the mother
source — mother source to alma mater — is achieved at a very low
pressure, at a relatively low cost, and with a Fahrenheit finality
that is near perfection. George Washington and Emerson may
have shivered in this house in other days and other centuries, but
certainly not I.

I trust that my symbol by now is clear. Those of us involved in
raising money for college, university, institute, or school are vitally
concerned with communication. We are all trying to improve our
two-way circuit. We may fancy ourselves as experts on the dynaflow of hot air and steam; but too many of us, I think, are searching for perfection in high pressure and speed, and too few are
aware that there may yet be undiscovered rewards through low
pressure and condensation. If I may carry my symbol one step fur-

[1] Eventually read at a meeting of Alumni Fund Directors, District I, American
Alumni Council, held at Dartmouth College.

ther: in Cambridge we use a power house to heat a University. We do it quietly and efficiently. Why can't we, I ask myself, make use of our college, university, institute, or school not simply to warm the alumni before they surrender cold cash, but (in Wordsworth's approximate phrase) "to warm, to comfort, and command" — in other words, why can't we speak to them, not avidly, but vividly in the mother tongue?

What have we done to, what are we doing to, our lines of communication? I remember some words of Angus Og in James Stephens' miraculous book, *The Crock of Gold*: "I sing to the ears that are stopped, the eyes that are sealed, and the minds that do not labour." Is there anyone in this business of fund raising who has not at some time or other felt as did James Stephens' articulate god? Then let us ask ourselves, when we wonder why this year or next year our fund is running behind in numbers or dollars or percentage, whether the ears are stopped, the eyes are sealed, and the minds do not labor, or whether something is disagreeably wrong with our lyric.

I speak with apprehension at a time when things are going pretty well. Annual giving in America on the part of alumni has never stood at so high a peak. It is even better than that. We appear to be standing on the top of Wachusett or Monadnock with our eyes on some as yet unseen Katahdin. But I would sadly remind you that there is a long succession of valleys between Wachusett or Monadnock and Mt. Katahdin. And our song, it seems to me, has become pretty shrill and insistent. It has very few agreeable overtones, and, if more than 30 years of experience in fund raising has taught me anything, it is becoming by and large monotonous and of a single pattern: *We need, you give*. Furthermore we are singing, unlike James Stephens' character, in growing competition with an impressive new baritone and soprano whose serenades are directed at corporations, foundations and such of our alumni and alumnæ as occupy the orchestra seats just right and left of the center aisles.

A mighty wave of music is in the air, and the box office receipts are quite soundly predicted as very large.

> Seven wealthy towns contend for Homer dead,
> Through which the living Homer begged his bread.

Most fortunately, of course, we represent the *living* Homer and do his begging for him. Furthermore, it is our unwavering resolve that the whole country rather than seven wealthy towns shall contend for him at least tomorrow if not today, and that they will sustain him alive and forever.

We are charged with the responsibility of raising through annual giving that money which is for the most part unrestricted: the lifeblood of our institutions of higher learning. The need for this money will increase as time goes on, and to that idea we are surely committed. Yet however well we may have done our work, and however far we have come with respect to participation and dollar support, it strikes me that we are all on the road to perfecting techniques of pressure and repetition, parrot gab and gimmick language, the very opposite of those qualities of individual imagination and contagious delight which we find or seek ideally in our teachers, administrators, in our presidents and our governing boards in the academic world.

When we were graduated into that fellowship of educated men, we carried away a small but precious legacy of inspiration which the best of our instructors gave us. We honored them for reasons we did not then pause to define. But one of those reasons was surely their skill in honest persuasion. What I said once to the graduating class of a very small and very young New England college is pertinent to my present theme: English is the tool which you will have to use day in, day out. Our language is not only one of the most beautiful in the world, but it is one of the most difficult. It is an incredibly easy language to manhandle. It is rich in colloquialism, rich in slang, in vulgarities — if vulgarities can yield riches — and

259

already blighted by the terrible growth of jargons which have attached themselves to special disciplines such as the social sciences and some of the arts. No school or college as yet, I submit, is much more than halfway successful in teaching the average student to speak and write not only correctly but with imagination, color, and creative impulse. Furthermore — and here I turn to Henry Beston: "What has come over our age is an alienation from nature unexampled in human history. It has cost us our sense of reality and all but cost us our humanity. . . . We have become vagrants in space, desperate for the meaninglessness which has closed about us."

So I say to you that in our continual effort to enlist, for the continuing support of our institutions of higher learning, those who have benefited from their catholic as well as specialized training, we are somehow failing to communicate with them in the language and with the dignity and distinctive grace which, among other things, their money is given to uphold. I admire a fine split-level house, but I do not admire split-level education. Education is either on a high level or it is not. The alumnus or alumna who has satisfied his or her entrance requirements and proceeded to the bachelor's degree has a certain obligation to society; and if he or she has also an obligation to or a sustaining interest in the institution which granted that degree, then the lines of communication between them should be firm and secure and touched beyond doubt with the genius and quality of the institution itself. There is surely not an intelligent man or woman enriched by a college education who would not give anything to hear once again the voice of some favorite and respected teacher on his favorite theme. Winch of Wesleyan, Churchill of Amherst, Woodberry of Columbia, Strunk of Cornell, John McCook of Trinity, David Lambuth of Dartmouth, Bliss Perry and Copey and Dean Briggs of Harvard, were such teachers. What echoes of their private music do we awake or think that we awake in our instrumental capacity?

As I look over the selected quantity of our promotional material which, like all of you, I scan from month to month, how very few pieces seem really to suggest in tone or language or typography the image of a center of learning, and the enormously important and exciting message about it which they were designed to convey. For one thing, where is that liquid simplicity? Where, so often, is impeccable taste and judgment? You know the answer as well as I do: they come with a shock of recognition in the rare and unusual communication at low pressure. Within a few days one such has crossed my desk. It is President John Dickey's report addressed "To all who care greatly about Dartmouth," and it announces what many other colleges and universities are announcing this year or have already proclaimed: the opening of a large capital campaign "to build strength upon strength for the future." Just the sound of that phrase has the ring of an old Greek coin. These rare qualities were implicit in Bruce Barton's personal appeals of some years ago in behalf of Deerfield Academy; and again in that series of remarkable letters by Earle Ludgin and John J. McDonough from the University of Chicago. What therapy! Messrs. Ludgin and McDonough made you feel that their University was itself speaking out of a full heart and empty purse. But still, "We talk too much," says Howard W. Mort — since I mentioned Chicago. We do indeed; and we are too involved.

> Ay, but to die, and go we know not where.

These ten simple words from *Measure for Measure* are, you will observe, ten monosyllables. They are memorable in part *for that reason alone*, as are ten others from *King Richard the Third*:

> Or let me die, to look on death no more!

Or take the closing 15th line of Robert Frost in "Hyla Brook" — the line which prevented his poem from being a sonnet, but gave it nonetheless its final passport to remembrance:

> We love the things we love for what they are.

Again, ten words — all monosyllables — but the effect is sheer magic. Say it again, and we see that this one of Frost is at the heart of what we are trying to communicate in our composite way:

We love the things we love for what they are.

Sentiment, we must remember, has to be controlled. It is easy to slop over; and between sloppy sentiment and the regional tally sheet with the cold chorographic assistance of IBM, I instinctively prefer the latter. But my quarrel is not with *necessary* techniques or methods, but with the need for all of us to speak and act as though we were an extension of, and not simply a blunt instrument for, our alma mater. If, in your daily mail, you receive from anybody anywhere one remarkably written letter, with what delight do you read it. Well, that is the kind of a letter that ours should be *in every instance* — a letter for the top, not the bottom, of the pile.

For I maintain that in essence we are a department of the Humanities, and not a mechanical agency created to perform a mechanical operation. We are projecting institutions — we are *not* subjecting the alumni. "Dear every one," says a character at the beginning of one of E. M. Forster's novels; and in that salutation is the key to the fallacy of our position. "Dear every one" is preferable to "Dear John" when we don't know John from William or Jerry; but "Dear every one" is what we mean if we can truly speak *ex cathedra* and not *ex machina*. I am sorely troubled when a distinguished young graduate writes to my office and says that he wants in the future to hear only from his class agent and not to receive our general appeals and reminders which, he tells us, are emotion-laden and no better than the solicitation from his cleaner. Now it is true that we are ready and available to clean pockets; but the humor of the parallel is lost in the realization that in his mind we are pigeon-holed as a cold-blooded organization out for money and nothing else. We have failed, in our message, to project the concept of a college or a university.

How different is the letter in the same mail from Idaho, written by the mother of an undergraduate! She had told us why she couldn't give, and I had written her a long reply to say that I myself had come to New England from a high school in Oregon, and that I understood what family sacrifices can really mean. In one sentence she cleansed my mind of that crack about the cleaner. "I appreciate," she wrote, "your understanding of how we . . . people of the big West feel about the wonderful opportunity your efforts bring our eager sons." Let me repeat in other words: it is our function to make friends and to strengthen friendly ties. Our dollar return should be predicated on that and on that alone.

Quite by accident, I put this thesis to the test two years ago in a summer piece to the entire alumni body of Harvard College which I called "After Thirty Years." I was trying suddenly to explain why working for a university is, as I have written elsewhere, what Willa Cather said in another connection in *My Ántonia*: "That is happiness, to be dissolved into something complete and great." For once I found myself talking not about money or the need of it, but of my College and my University as I had known and loved it over more than three decades. There was nothing miraculous in what I did: it was simply that for once I was trying unconsciously to express myself about myself and to say something of gratitude to the thousands of my fellow alumni with whom I had had some correspondence at one time or another.

"This gift," one man wrote me recently, "is for the institution that represents one of the great achievements of American democracy." All our institutions represent one of the great achievements of democracy. In "the noble merchantry of civilization" — which is the late John Buchan's phrase [1] — let us remember that we are *of*, and not just *on the side of*, the Humanities.

1957

[1] See p. 18.

After Thirty Years

THIS is really a personal letter. It ought to be written with pen and ink, for it is the *only* personal letter that I have ever addressed, or am ever likely to address, to all the 44,000 alumni of Harvard College. I have my reason for diverging from tradition. In one year or another since 1926 I have thanked about 65 per cent of you for a gift or gifts or many gifts to the Harvard Fund; and since this is the thirtieth anniversary of its founding in 1925, and a similar milestone for the executive secretary, I am thanking 65 per cent of you again and thinking hard (yet leniently) of 35 per cent as I do so. *Milestone*, I might remind you, is a word which hasty printers convert quite easily into *millstone*. Not this one!

Many thousands of times in thirty years I have faced at odd hours, night and day, a blank sheet of paper, wondering what I should say to someone among you. Adequate or not, the noun always found its verb, and the paper its matching envelope. Alas, if only one of these letters out of Wadsworth House had been as apropos as this specimen [1] of bread and butter:

Dear Bob: Some parties deserve a letter, some don't. Yours does. Here's mine.

But a lifetime of outgoing Harvard correspondence at the rate of at least a million words a year provides me with a file of memories. Any individual foolish enough to spend twelve months or so rereading it would find the contents more exciting than the telephone directory but inferior to the sweep of *War and Peace* and the daedal wit of *Pickwick*; but he would surely learn how the

[1] C. F. Weed, LL.B. '98 to Robert B. Greenough '92, M.D. '96, both deceased.

Fund in some way managed to put down its roots and survive a depression, two wars, hot and cold, and several hurricanes. Above all, I like to think that the carbons would show — and this is most important — that the Harvard Fund [2] is first of all an instrument of good will. If Wadsworth House itself has come to symbolize the Fund in the minds of many, thirty years of excitement, enthusiasm, and occasional inspiration have been lost if it does not also signify the court of first appeal on Harvard matters of astonishing variety.

For we live on letters. They alone (or almost alone) over the signatures and out of the minds of our Class Agents have brought us this year as of mid-July more than $420,000 from 10,000 contributors — not noting the anniversary fact that many men have given twice. But I am thinking, rather, of the incoming letters accompanied or unaccompanied by checks: those of inquiry, commendation, delight in Harvard, censure of Harvard; those of creative suggestion, of understanding; those for tradition and against tradition; letters written in remembrance and with love, or in skepticism and rebuke; letters considerate of our own defective judgment and mistakes. Of late the vast majority have been on the side of encouragement. All of them of every kind, with amazingly few exceptions, have always been, in Henry Beston's great phrase, "on the side of life." Harvard herself has always been on the side of life. Let us never forget that.

Many of you must remember some of your letters, for by and large they have been far more memorable than ours. But if Wadsworth House has occasionally been helpful in turn, that help is still outweighed, as it should be, by the perceptibly widening circle of responsive interest in the College itself. All the unrestricted money in the world, as well as dollar leadership among all Alumni Funds wherever, cannot vie in importance with the instinctive spiritual bond between Harvard and Harvard men. Someone has given us a

[2] In the fiscal year 1962–1963 The Harvard Fund became — with becoming logic — the *Harvard College Fund*. When the Harvard Fund was founded in 1925 it was designed to raise unrestricted money annually for the College *and* the Graduate Schools. Since 1948 the Fund has raised money solely for the College.

phrase for this: *The aristocracy of those who care.* This is something very precious. Let us not forget that either.

Wit has never been wanting. Scrawled on the back of a subscription blank or set like a gem in the middle of distinguished and well-ventilated prose, it takes the eye at once to shine amid the clutter on the desk.

Who am I not to join so many?

There is genius in that sudden question as there was wit and ingenuity in the following lines from a classmate of President Pusey which revived us toward the close of the depression.

Halogens:

As I am an aluminum of two colleges besides Harvard, and can not, with my bismuth in its present state, pay antimony to all three, I hope you will not think me a cadmium if I do not caesium this opportunity of making a donation. So far this year I have metal current expenses, but in these troubled times when the future holds in store we know not phosphorous, I could not make a contribution without boron from the bank. It would nickel out of my savings. A manganese spend his dollars these days; a tin spot is gone in no time. One is lead to feel he is pouring them down the zinc. Much better to sodium up in a stocking. So don't be silicon not make any contribution this year unless a bromine helps me out.

Very unruly yours,

Fortunately our correspondent left us one metal which he did not use. So we wrote him simply: "Iron stand you."

To take the gift from the giver for so long is to realize how strained and rusty are such words as *grateful, appreciate,* and *thank you.* We need a new vocabulary, a fresh response, a handshake rather than a penshake. Sometimes in answering a critic of Harvard policy based on one offending action I am tempted to ask him if he will not weigh three centuries of teaching, training, and example against his split-second of displeasure. For perhaps the critic in his haste, like the giver in his impulse, need only to be reminded. Believing this to be so:

Harvard has given great men and great ideas and great citizens and great teachers to the nation; she has seen us through nearly a dozen wars. She has given us four presidents of our country; she has stood like a rock in our midst. She has weathered criticism just and unjust, and abuse which is never just; she has looked at her own faults, which have been not a few, and has striven to correct them. She is far from perfect, but she knows that perfection is nothing more than the perpetual will to seek it. If she was ever the rich man's college, she is just as much the poor man's college today; for her sole requirement of the entering student is that he have character, ambition, ability, and the capacity to learn to think for himself. She is not prejudiced with respect to race or creed or color. She is able and eager to help those who enter her gates. She is anxious to be one thing above all: a better Harvard tomorrow than she was yesterday. To that end, she is permanently for change, but always with an eye to the unchanging values of the human spirit. Lastly, and most important: she has faithfully stood for freedom of the mind and the dignity of the individual; and never more so than in the strange, abrasive period which has followed World War II. As one man recently wrote to my office: This gift is "for the institution that represents one of the great achievements of American democracy."

Over the next thirty years I trust and believe that the Harvard Fund will keep pace with the oldest College in the country, which it is dedicated to support. This letter ends with a note of gratitude — the old word again — to the 65 per cent, and couplet for the 35 per cent. My couplet was written as an Epitaph on a Waiter. Will it serve?

> By and by
> God caught his eye.

2 August 1955

Trout in the Milk

THE true Thoreauvian should never be at a loss for words. In the India-rubber knapsack, of which Channing speaks, there were partitions for books and papers; and in the minds of Henry's students there are similar partitions for the hazelnut phrase which has outlasted his hard bread and pork and offers the sustaining warmth of strong, hot tea. Unbuckle the flap to memory and what do we find?

The world is a cow that is hard to milk.

I am no more lonely than a single mullein or dandelion in a pasture.

A straight stick makes the best cane, and an upright man the best ruler.

Above all, we cannot afford not to live in the present.

I want nothing better than a good word.

We live thick and are in each other's way.

I have found that no exertion of the legs can bring two minds much nearer to one another.

It is time that villages were universities.

A man must find his occasions in himself.

I went to the woods because I wished to live deliberately.

I never found the companion that was so companionable as solitude.

Some circumstantial evidence is very strong, as when you find a trout in the milk.

I have several times shown the proprietor the shortest way out of his wood-lot.

Some few of these aphorisms are familiar, though none of them so famous as "The mass of men lead lives of quiet desperation," or so beautiful as "The bluebird carries the sky on his back." But in the folded knapsack there are still others envisioning the future which is now our own uncomfortable present. Miltown and atom and the commercial spirit:

What is the pill which will keep us well, serene, contented?

. . . When I build my next house, and have the roof 'all correct' for bombshells.

We glory in those very excesses which are a source of anxiety to the wise and good.

This last is taken from Thoreau's college Commencement part, 16 August 1837, delivered when he was but twenty years old.

Now it is well that we are not all of us Thoreaus. Genius that he has proved to be, and for all the light and luster he has shed upon the world beyond his Harvard, he was far from being, in fact or potentially, the tractable alumnus. One cannot imagine him as an Overseer. ("It is hard to have a Southern overseer; it is worse to have a Northern one.") He would never have become a reader of the *Bulletin*. ("I never read any memorable news in a newspaper.") Or a contributor to the Harvard Fund. ("Others have been curious to learn what portion of my income I devoted to charitable purposes.") Or a marcher in the Commencement procession. ("If a man does not keep pace with his companions, perhaps it is because he hears a different drummer.") Or even a member of the Committee on the Happy Observance of Commencement. ("I hear an irresistible voice which invites me away from all that.") Or in attendance at a football game. ("All memorable events, I should say, transpire in morning time and in a morning atmosphere.") Or an avid supporter of A Program for Harvard College. ("Beware of all enterprises that require new clothes.")

On the other hand, he revealed the instinctive qualities of a superb Class Agent. ("I naturally shouted again and again, but the Indian curtly remarked, 'He hears you,' as if once was enough.")

Yet scattered through his letters there is brief but delightful evidence that the man who once lived in Hollis was fully aware of the continuing existence of his College. In November 1847, ten years after he was graduated from Harvard and two months after concluding his compost-graduate studies at Walden, Thoreau wrote to Emerson (then in England):

It is true enough, Cambridge college is really beginning to wake up and redeem its character and overtake the age. I see by the catalogue that they are about establishing a scientific school in connection with the university, at which any one above eighteen, on paying one hundred dollars annually (Mr. Lawrence's fifty thousand dollars will probably diminish this sum), may be instructed in the highest branches of science, — in astronomy, "theoretical and practical, with the use of the instruments" (so the great Yankee astronomer may be born without delay), in mechanics and engineering to the last degree. Agassiz will ere long commence his lectures in the zoölogical department. A chemistry class has already been formed under the direction of Professor Horsford. A new and adequate building for the purpose is already being erected. They have been foolish enough to put at the end of all this earnest the old joke of a diploma. Let every sheep keep but his own skin, I say.

Such a wonderful waking, redeeming, and overtaking involved, we may suppose, a relatively small sum of money — certainly an insignificant sum of money compared with $82.5 million which is the present goal of A Program for Harvard College. Writing one month later to Emerson, who was still in England, Thoreau included a couplet which would be a dangerous motto for the Program:

> "Commence at one end and leave it half done,
> And let time finish what money's begun."

Nevertheless, Thoreau would heartily approve the independent character of his University, could he see it today. (*Heartily* is the precise adverb he would choose.) God knows "we live thick and are in each other's way"; but we shall live thinner and better in Cambridge for the new brick and mortar to come. And there will surely be no termites at our sills and foundations so long as we have the flow of annual unrestricted funds to replace and alter and improve. He would understand all this, for Walden in a sense was Thoreau's private college, though he actually lived there but two short years — not long enough for the termites to get at him. His Hollis Hall of brick survives, but his house of shanty boards — which stood him a cool $28.12½ — has long since vanished. What does Ogden Nash say?

> Some primal termite knocked on wood
> And tasted it, and found it good,
> And that is why your Cousin May
> Fell through the parlor floor today.

At the close of his essay called "Wild Apples" Thoreau is again prophetic: "I fear that he who walks over these fields a century hence will not know the pleasure of knocking off wild apples. Ah, poor man, there are many pleasures which he will not know!" Ah, we *are* that man; but here, my friend, in your old University there is one pleasure fortunately that has not changed. "The really diligent student in one of the crowded hives of Cambridge College [you said] is as solitary as a dervis in the desert." He still is and wants to be; and those most mindful of his need and jealous of his voluntary solitude are waiting and working for a windfall. It may not be of wild apples. Symbols change from century to century. Let us try another one, applicable to the Harvard Fund and Program givers from Concord to the Oregon toward which you once said you must walk. Richard Armour of California has put it into verse:

> Shake and shake
> The catsup bottle.
> None will come,
> And then a lott'll.

5 August 1957

Voices in the Yard

LATE at night in Wadsworth House is when I hear them best. Emerson, of course, spoke of Cambridge at any time as being full of ghosts — but he failed to mention the voices. Lacking Emerson's anointed eye, as he calls it, an ear is perhaps the next best thing. Sometimes the voices are single, sometimes antiphonal. Thoreau comes in well on warm spring nights, about the time when the snapping turtle begins to be restless out toward Walden. ("Surely, men love darkness rather than light.") But the voice for summer's end is the querying voice of Henry Adams. It is stronger this year, the one-hundredth anniversary of his graduation from the College. He speaks, you will remember, in the third person.

Far back in childhood, among its earliest memories, Henry Adams could recall his first visit to Harvard College. He must have been nine years old when on one of the singularly gloomy winter afternoons which beguiled Cambridgeport, his mother drove him out to visit his aunt, Mrs. Everett. Edward Everett was then President of the college and lived in the old President's House on Harvard Square. The boy remembered the drawing-room, on the left of the hall door, in which Mrs. Everett received them. He remembered a marble greyhound in the corner. The house had an air of colonial self-respect that impressed even a nine-year-old child.

[Years later, after an] interview with President Eliot, he asked the Bursar about his aunt's old drawing-room, for the house had been turned to base uses. The room and the deserted kitchen adjacent to it were to let. He took them.

The old President's House referred to is Wadsworth House, in which these lines are being written. The drawing-room on the left of the hall door is now the alumni reception room. In the room on the right hangs the Stuart portrait of Edward Everett. One of the base uses to which Wadsworth House was put just 54 years after Henry Adams saw Mr. Eliot was the installation of the Harvard Fund within a broom's length or so of that remembered marble greyhound. Henry makes an uneasy tenant. He is a pro and con man — mostly con. Some of the things he said about his College:

What he did not know, even after four years of education, was Harvard College.

The college offered chiefly advantages vulgarly called social, rather than mental.

Harvard College was a negative force, and negative forces have value.

The four years passed at college were, for his purposes, wasted.

Harvard College was a good school. [Do we owe the first degradation of the word *college* to Henry Adams? Today you will find nothing but schoolboys at Harvard, Dartmouth, Yale, Chicago, Cornell, Ohio State, or California. In some of them, of course, you will find schoolgirls.]

The Class of 1858 to which Henry Adams belonged was a typical collection of young New Englanders, quietly penetrating and aggressively common-place.

Four years of Harvard College, if successful, resulted in an autobiographical blank, a mind on which only a water-mark had been stamped.

The degree of Harvard College had been rather a drawback to a young man in Boston and Washington. [A student had told him: "The degree of Harvard College is worth money to me in Chicago."]

Henry Adams never professed the smallest faith in universities of any kind.

Harvard College remained a tie, indeed, but a tie a little stronger than Beacon Street and not so strong as State Street.

Socially or intellectually, the college was for him negative and in some ways mischievous.

The influence of Harvard College was beginning to have its effect.

Looking back on *The Education of Henry Adams* — and this is no essay in criticism — it seems clear that he was always pulling out his college measuring stick. But Henry was not alone in the family as a critic of Harvard. His brother Charles Francis Adams, Class of 1856 — for two years they roomed together — sums it up in this way:

> As it was, I was tumbled into the common hopper, to emerge therefrom as God willed. No instructor produced, or endeavored to produce, the slightest impression on me; no spark of enthusiasm was sought to be infused into me. In that line I owed far more to Charles Sumner than to all of the Harvard professors put together. *And it was exactly the same with my father before me.* From the recitation room I got as nearly as I can now see almost nothing at all; from the college atmosphere and the close contact with a generation of generous young fellows containing then, as the result showed, infinite possibilities I got much of all that I have ever had of quickening and good. So, after all, I owe a great debt to Harvard.

Inside and out, Harvard's remarkable achievement is that she has produced, over the centuries, so many powerful dissenters. When one looks into it, who at some time or another would not set a different sail? An Adams lurks in all of us. On the fourth of July the voice of Francis Parkman carries all the way from Concord's celebration:

> Students of Harvard do not on all occasions appear much better than their less favored countrymen, either in point of gentlemanly and *distingué* appearance or in conversation.

George Santayana, while still an undergraduate member of the Class of 1886, met Henry Adams in Washington. " 'So you are trying to teach philosophy at Harvard,' Mr. Adams said, somewhat in the gentle but sad tone we knew in Professor Norton. 'I once tried to teach history there, but it can't be done. It isn't really possible to teach anything.'" Nearly three-score years later (1944) Professor Santayana — quite possibly by then with the gentle but sad tone of Professor Norton — spoke with an Adams inflection: "While at Harvard a wealth of books and much generous intellectual sincerity went with such spiritual penury and moral confusion as to offer nothing but a lottery ticket or a chance at the grab-bag to the orphan mind."

In 1954, thinking back nearly half a century, not Henry Adams but Van Wyck Brooks is whispering (for the living voices don't come through so well): "I often wondered if I had learned anything at Harvard that I could not have learned equally well at home, reading, listening to music and looking at pictures. . . . It seemed to me later that I had never been touched by anyone's intellect until I met J. B. Yeats [the poet's father] in 1909."

There is someone else. It is John Marquand, I gather, speaking with such slyness through the class history of one of his characters in *H. M. Pulham, Esquire*.[1] Listen closely, though, until you recapture the undergraduate voice of Henry Adams in 1856:

But College has been very much abused; much more so than it deserves. . . . If the College is dangerous and hurtful, the store or the counting-room is as bad, or worse.

The counting-room — base use of Wadsworth House! In the year of the Program, this is the last reminder of the Harvard Fund. Awake! Awake! For what is the history of education? Who is not positive that a negative force has value?

> The decent docent doesn't doze:
> He teaches standing on his toes.
> His student dassn't doze — and does,
> And that's what teaching is and was.

15 August 1958

[1] For the text, see p. 134.

The Alewives Are Running

Anadromous, the common shad
Swims up the river just to add,
According to his golden rule,
A freshman class to that old school
Of which he is himself a grad.

ALL of us from childhood on have accepted the evidence of bird migration as we accept and expect the rhythmic sequence of night and day. Even the midtown dwellers, denied the sight of an early robin or the first uneasy bluebird, may wake to read with understanding sadness that a flight of warblers has crashed an Empire State Building that wasn't there in the foggy flyways of the birds of the Coolidge Administration. Far fewer — unless the Californians — are watchfully aware of the more delicate and astonishing migration of the butterflies — the monarchs in particular. On the other hand, to those of us along the Pacific and Atlantic littoral, the turn of the spring means equally the running of the salmon and the steelhead, or of the salmon and the shad — the bones and fins and flesh from the oceans' depth returning up their native spawning-rivers to complete the mysterious cycle of life. Yet better still for the lucky some of us: this strange wild choking tide of the homing alewives, flooding with life a handful of the little rivers of Massachusetts — as well as all hospitable inlets along our seaboard from the Maritimes to the Carolinas — in the weeks that follow on the vernal equinox. Stranger in human terms is a kind of local conspiracy to keep this bio-secret; and many a young man will survive four restless springs at Harvard, and not Plato, Pareto, Camus,

Joyce, nor Keynes, nor the language of nuclear fission will tell him when or where. Even a telephone operator down Middleboro way, when asked in good season if the great migration had begun, was obliged to call the neighboring towns for help. "Say," she said to her inquirer when the nature of the event was explained to her, "is this just weekends?"

Take the defining word itself. Most Bostonians adrift in Kansas City are puzzled to discover that *channel cat* is on the luncheon menu. Quite in reverse, the equivalent young man from Missouri, driving from Harvard Square to Arlington and the far-off winter paradise of Conway, is surely bemused by the crossroad sign proclaiming the desiccate course of the Alewife Brook Parkway. But if today he still does not know the meaning and history of *alewife*, have him to understand that it is a salt-water fish, a foot or less in length, averaging 300 to the barrel for a total of 200 pounds: a member of the herring family, related to sprats, shads, pilchards, and menhaden; a fish to be taken by hand, net, fork, spear, scoop, dredge, or vacuum suction. *Gaspereau* in Canada, *buckies* in Rhode Island, and *catthrashers* in Maine; but *alewives* in Massachusetts, plain *herrin'* on Cape Cod — a glut to the Indians who taught their use as fertilizer, a salty boon to the pioneer of the smoke house, when "children ate them on sticks like candy."

Unlike the salmon, the alewife cycle is quantitative rather than qualitative. Spawned in fresh-water ponds and streams, he enters the ocean as a fingerling. Deep in the Davy dark, which is Dylan Thomas's phrase, he ventures we know not where; but in the fourth year — sometimes in the third — he returns in bewildering numbers to precisely the same stream or pond to spawn and insure the future of the race. The alewives' advent is pure poetry. Listen!

An alewife's body is marvelously fitted to situation — peace or turbulence, light or dark, flood and ebb, ripple or rile. This inhabitant of the sea weaves up through the overhanging springtime and seems a part of it, experienced as to its flowering.[1]

The alewives are running! They come in the lap of the tide, over a spit of sand perhaps, up into a curving creek; they come in the stem and froth of waters, under the shadowing wings of hundreds of gulls. They come by the whispering thousands, over the lip of falls and the water-step of ladder, the vast quaking wake of them filling a small stream (as I have seen it) from bank to bank: tails, dorsals showing above the eddies, a living current of silver, blue, and gunmetal grey. "In terrible simplicity," writes Mr. Hay with intuitive perception,

the alewives were swimming toward the inland gauntlet they would have to run, having a title, by their common, wild, and ancient advent, to all great kindled things . . . I by an old and natural right felt a fierce water-deep wonder of the spirit. The beyondness in me went back to its beginnings. I thought of the nights on which children I have known were born, and of the voyages of war, leave-takings at railroad stations and at ports of embarkation, and of dreams in which I struggled toward new meetings and other lives. The wind blew through the arches of the stars, and the surfaces of the dipping earth, water, and sky in their lasting communion made me dizzy. I felt a cold inevitable grandeur, below consciousness, a swim and go in an uttermost wild world, past home or my life's memory.

Such is the moving and dramatic part of this "indefinite context of generation." At this point our theme becomes a symbol. Logging his spring observations by the waters of Stony Brook and the chain of three ponds above, down there at Brewster on the Cape, Mr. Hay gives a guess at vital statistics. Of one hundred million alewives hatched (in the three ponds) out of an original nine billion eggs, five per cent, or five million, have to reach salt water "to assure a normal spawning migration in three or four years' time" — allowing, of course, for inevitable mortality demanded by the sea.

[1] From *The Run* by John Hay '38 (New York: Doubleday, 1959).

THE ALEWIVES ARE RUNNING

A freshman class to that old school
Of which he is himself a grad?

I trust the academic parallel comes clear. The alewife cycle is four years. The smart ones would appear to make it in three. More efficient than their human counterpart, every commencement is also their reunion — a joint celebration. However they mix and mingle, wax or wane in the shoals and deeps of the sea, their loyalty to home and alma water remains inflexible. No bulletin or agent's letter reaches them; yet back they come, to suffer an income tax which is frequently death, and to pay such an inheritance and capital gains assessment that they must live (or navigate) next door to oblivion. Together they breast the current with the characteristic fortitude of a group that has benefited from adult education. And when at last they depart for their universal home, they are a spent crowd, for they have both replenished endowment and labored to re-establish the honor system. Nor can we fail to observe that their fervent interest in the old place parallels that of the alumnus who deplores the passing of the library or dormitory familiar in his time. For local evidence exists that returning alewives at the conclusion of the ceremony will circle about at the *exact* spot where an original outlet was sealed off a hundred years before!

Well, the alewives are running up the streams and little rivers of Massachusetts — and up the Charles itself as far as Watertown — pulsing to their death or destination even as this invertebrate piece of paper has fluttered through the mail to its address. Life goes on — and the College year, and the College itself, and the Harvard Fund. And the mystery of life remains. And so does the pleasure of fishing with a barbless hook.

1 April 1960

279

"Oo-too-koo"

NEAR enough now to the end of my journey through Wadsworth House — some 36 years of world-travel within four walls — I view with a twinge of sadness the inevitable conclusion of these essays written to a somewhat captive, though generously uncaptious, audience: a kind of writing that is not a task, but a venture in privilege. From the beginning it might have proved the one-way correspondence I had feared: 47,000 envelopes, 47,000 stamps, 47,000 wastebaskets. But it never has. On two occasions I wrote boldly as a naturalist, which I am at heart though not in fact. Will you believe that some people prefer a flyrod to a pen? Fishing last year with a barbless hook — a chancy matter at best — the net result beyond all hope and expectancy included 1,100 *second* checks for an additional $37,000.

It was Thoreau and his aphoristic trout in the milk which suggested that allegory of alewives running on the Cape. A queer conspectus to send in search of money! It appears, however, that the Fund went fishing off the Grand Banks in the fairest weather, under summer's cloud and in the balsam offshore breeze of middle-afternoon. So once again in the spring of the year (under Taurus, the bull market) I have dropped the lead and taken soundings. Having no helicopter, sonar equipment, much less the trawler instinct, I can not guess where the solvent schools are feeding at the moment. In size they may be running better than Dow-Jones average. Dow-Jones, that is, not Davy. We shall await reply.

Riding the crest of this deep-sea image is that starry word up yonder: *oo-too-koo*. You have observed its shape and symmetry and have remarked, perhaps, the balanced grace of a loaded kayak. Now *oo-too-koo* is the one word that makes me wish we might correspond in the language familiar to Unalakleet in Alaska — an impossibility, of course, since the Eskimo never got round to inventing an alphabet with which to write. He was too busy struggling to survive. He has never had any blubber to spare for Dear Old Permafrost, his universal alma mater. In fact, he would not even recognize his *oo-too-koo* if he saw this civilized reproduction of it. And who is civilized? Is it not he who is the master speaker, master of the art of condensation, possessor of a tough vocabulary far richer and far more inflected than is ours? "Most Eskimos, in their ordinary talk, use 10,000 words a day, while the average educated white man uses only about 3,500."[1] Where we take refuge in a juicy sentence, he uses one crisp word. Consider *paktok*, which means one "is not sure about something and goes to see how it is." Thirteen words for one! Many a graduate will return to Cambridge next month in the spirit of *paktok*:

> Back to the Square again,
> changed like the face of us;
> Back to the air that is
> ghostly with trace of us;
> Back to the haven of Hollis,
> the northernmost
> Part of the Yard and the
> things we love more than most.
> Back to the towers, Littauers,
> high Leveretts:
> Buildings all built since our
> day. But whatever its
> Purpose and name or its shape
> or its lack of one,
> Back to what's building in back
> of the back of one.

And so could I wish for *oo-too-koo* in certain letters of acknowledg-

[1] Sally Carrighar, *Moonlight at Midday* (New York: Knopf, 1958).

ment. It is much too soothing a word to be offensive, too appropriate not to make its point with the man who should, and might have, and really meant to measure his gift against the national urgency. For *oo-too-koo* means "small and I wish it were bigger." Conversely, there are other times when a Fund director would like to dictate simply: "Dear Mr. Stoughtonworthy: *Mick-shrok*. Sincerely yours. . ." *Mick-shrok*, Miss Carrighar tells me, means "little but satisfactory." Well, *mick-shrok* to me is the $5 or $10 from the young law student, the teacher in his first uneasy classroom, the lad with the faraway APO address, the expectant father of twenty-four (age not children), the weary intern.

On the other hand, who can supply the word of any kind, Eskimo or English, with which to invade the silence of the silent? Right this moment there are nearly 20,000 related men who *believe* in Harvard College, who *understand* her increasing dependence on free money, who *know* that the Program which they supported was largely for restricted money, who *are* proud to have given not once but five, ten, twenty, or thirty times in the past to the Harvard Fund, but who have *not* given this year — at least so far.

> You used to sing so awful well
> In former days gone by,
> But now you never sing at all;
> I wish you'd tell me why.

In all of a long and affectionate study of that lonely man who was Edward Lear, I have found no line for sadness equal to

> In former days gone by. . .

But the strength of the past-giver audience is fortunately resolved in Byron's reckless line:

> Who listens once will listen twice. . .

Five or six years ago I said that we live on letters. One could live for a long time on a recent letter from a non-Harvard parent who this year sent us a check for $5,000. "It is a wonderful feeling to me and my wife [writes another] to know that Harvard will take a very poor boy, as is ours, and make it possible for him to make a contribution to society." These are letters, mind you, from parents already burdened with the cost of tuition. But in the realm of the alumnus, this is current Exhibit No. 1:

The amount is at the same annual rate I pledged when the Program for Harvard College was inaugurated [an amount] which I have since tried to maintain.

It was not a Harvard but a Brown man, my old friend Chesley Worthington, L.H.D., exemplary editor of the *Brown Alumni Monthly* and a former president of the American Alumni Council, who wrote and published the following limerick in the early fifties:

> A Harvard alumnus named Swift
> By a head-hunting native was biffed.
>   The head was sent for'rd
>   To David McCor'rd.
> It upped the per capita gift.

5 May 1961

In Sight of Sever

What you seek in vain for, half your life, one day
you come full upon, all the family at dinner.
                                    — Thoreau

AN old friend and classmate,[1] an intuitive scholar speaking
Mandarin and honored still for a mind like a flawless piece of jade,
once explained to me in simple English that "A Buddha is what
you do to it." Since his death in 1960 these words have taken on
a wider meaning every time I say them over. For example, who can
fail to regret that a student *at* Harvard is not equally and always
a student *of* Harvard, since Harvard, like the Buddha, is what you
do to it? The Cambridge port of entry, if you ask me, is too wide.
The freshman arrives, dragging his civilization with him: an instinctive act, no doubt, but nevertheless encumbering. Not so with
a certain Oriental, as I have noticed him in the Square, his saffron
robe accented by a pair of Argyll socks. He walks like a rainbow,
but he is more than that: he is perceptively a student *of* Harvard.
He brought no baggage with him, and it is likely that he left no
noticeable possessions at the Potala of his particular Lhasa, and he
needs none here. He has known through centuries of prayerwheel
ritual that any Lhasa is what you do to it. His attitude is inherited.
Ours, alas, is not. He has never heard of instant culture.

Yet some of us not in saffron robes have vaguely, perhaps quite
perceptively, understood. The older we grow, the better we understand in retrospect. Thoreau lived to do more to Harvard — of

[1] James Marshall Plumer, Class of 1921.

which he feigned to disapprove — than Harvard did to him. His extension courses have included such differing pupils as E. B. White of Manhattan, H. M. Tomlinson of London River, and Mahatma Gandhi of the world — none of them familiar with the Yard except by inference. To Thoreau the place was still a clearing in the wilderness, and with that he could deal — as any *Walden* reader is aware. He would be pleased if we told him that in recent years a pair of raccoons had invaded the Yard (as they did) and that a shrike was once discovered in President Conant's hedge. There was, moreover, plenty of the Oriental in Henry's hardwood philosophy: "Give me the poverty that enjoys true wealth." These words are almost meaningless today. Yet who would say that Harvard does not remain a clearing in the wilderness — a wilderness far wilder than in Mather's time or in Henry's "restless, nervous, bustling, trivial Nineteenth Century," to which he alluded so specifically in 1854? Could I control the keeper of unwritten maxims, I would have it out in writing: Enter Harvard as Lois Crisler [2] entered northern Alaska under the Brooks Range "with your deep will, or [be indoors] in the nest of civilization even in wilderness." Does any one doubt on which side of the above comma there is an exit only?

Suspended somewhere between Carbon 14 and Strontium 90, we have now greater cause and less time to ponder the deep will. As I walk these familiar paths, diagonals most of them to sanctuaries beyond my layman's reach of understanding, the mind goes back to the fervent days of the Tercentenary, when all was clear anatomy, and the visual image of inexplicable Harvard loomed out of the fog as an etching of joy or deviltry emerges for one unstable instant while we turn the pages of *Finnegans Wake*. To be a student of Harvard requires almost an abnegation of the temporal, a long walk late at night with accredited ghosts of the place, the stab of loneliness right through a multitude of doors. Even so, the revelation may not come; there is just that whisk of the occult about it.

[2] *Arctic Wild* (New York: Harper, 1958).

IN SIGHT OF SEVER

My new-cut ashlar takes the light
Where crimson-blank the windows flare.

I wait for the flash. I watch for intimate signs of that older wilderness now vanished, as the quote from Kipling may suggest. "It is not down in any map, true places never are," said Melville. Yet once in a while it is. I think I became a lifelong student of Harvard that bright morning in my junior year when I stepped out of Jefferson and a class in advanced physics, looked up into the cloudless blue and saw — as not many have the luck to look and see by day — the sudden sulphurous flame-out of a meteor,

a star that spoke
In simple terms of fire and smoke,
But soundless with the stale report
Of ancient wars and dragon snort.

Not all the visiting professors in the world could relate my clearing in the wilderness to the clearing in my mind as did that moment, awesome and unexpected.

Life is the garment we continually alter but which never seems to fit, and we must make our adjustments as we go. I saw the white gulls gathered just this morning on a jigsaw floe downstream from the Anderson bridge, each one of them a weathercock as truly into the wind as the gilded vane on Memorial Church: a living sermon on whatever winds of doctrine youth (a symbol) might be testing in Sever or in Boylston as he boxed his classroom compass. And then I saw them rise in a cloud and beat their way by dozens into the updraft of a smokestack thermal, where they spread their wings and circled on long spirals of unending poise, as if some truth arrived at were sustained. Was there a memo of it? Perhaps the architects had this in mind when they built those enormous baskets — *In* and *Out* — on Leverett's twin towers, high above the neighbors' Georgian chimneys.

Some time ago a spate of unseasonable weather — all Cambridge weather is unseasonable — brought the welcome breath of spring into the Yard. The itinerant barred owl (*Strix varia,* presumably female) in the old pine tree east of University had weathered a bad gale and the cold spell, but now looked good for another semi-semester in an intellectual climate. For breakfast and dinner she had one native pigeon, chosen at random, but attested by the scatter of hodden feathers on the ground below. She dined early and late, when the Yard was clear of traffic: unaware, we may suppose, that pigeons are what wrong examination answers are turned into. She became an attraction. A number of students found her composure disquieting; and one undergraduate went out and shied a book at her — a French grammar — to which she paid small attention. A group of Lampooners in evening dress, dangerously equipped with bows and arrows, are said to have set upon this owl, though happily to no purpose. Once or twice I stood under the tree and clapped my hands in the manner of an angry *Strix* caught snapping her beak, and the late incumbent would raise a wise old head and look down balefully. It is somewhat uncomfortable looking at an angry (presumed) female owl. And this one, well we knew, might be Alma Mater herself.

> But language limits the sense it often mars —
> I still believe, for better or for worse,
> We look through one atom into all the stars,
> In the note of one insect hear the universe.

Thus, and all homage to him, John Hall Wheelock '08. So the clear injunction — for the mind, at any rate, if not for the stars and squirrels and birds and insects — is to keep the flyways and the runways open.

And the wallets and checkbooks, of course . . . of course.

15 February 1962